Excel
ANNOYANCES™

How to Fix the Most ANNOYING Things
About Your Favorite Spreadsheet

Curtis Frye

O'REILLY®

Beijing · Cambridge · Farnham · Köln · Paris · Sebastopol · Taipei · Tokyo

Excel Annoyances™
How to Fix the Most Annoying Things About Your Favorite Spreadsheet

by Curtis Frye

Copyright © 2005 O'Reilly Media, Inc. All rights reserved.
Printed in the United States of America.

Illustrations © 2004 Hal Mayforth c/o theispot.com.

Published by O'Reilly Media, Inc., 1005 Gravenstein Highway North, Sebastopol, CA 95472.

O'Reilly books may be purchased for educational, business, or sales promotional use. Online editions are also available for most titles (*safari.oreilly.com*). For more information, contact our corporate/institutional sales department: 800-998-9938 or *corporate@oreilly.com*.

Print History:		**Editors:**	Michael Oliver-Goodwin
			Robert Luhn
December 2004:	First Edition.		
		Production Editor:	Genevieve d'Entremont
		Art Director:	Michele Wetherbee
		Cover Design:	Volume Design, Inc.
		Interior Designer:	Patti Capaldi

RepKover™
This book uses RepKover™, a durable and flexible lay-flat binding.

0-596-00728-0
[C]

To Virginia, who has made me so happy.

To my family, who has supported me so well for so long.

To the memory of Albert and Helen Frye,
two grandparents I miss terribly.

Contents

Introduction

October 2003 was a good month for me. I was well into a relationship that eventually resulted in an accepted marriage proposal, I'd just finished the first draft of one long book, I had seen my *Excel Pocket Guide* (O'Reilly) hit the store shelves, and I was fresh and ready to tackle another project. That's when I got a call from Robert Luhn, who had recently come on board as an executive editor at O'Reilly. He asked if I'd like to put together a book proposal for O'Reilly's retooled Annoyances series. We kicked around a few ideas and eventually came up with *Excel Annoyances*, the book you now hold in your hands. I liked the road paved by Steve Bass in *PC Annoyances*, and I liked the notion of reinventing it for Excel—so I did the proposal dance, bade my legal representatives to work out a contract, and sat down for some serious writing.

WHY WRITE EXCEL ANNOYANCES?

Here's why: because practically *everyone* uses Excel. The installed base is huge, and it stretches across multiple versions of the program. In fact, many people *prefer* the earlier versions, or can't afford to upgrade to the latest and greatest. That's why we decided to cover *every* major version from Excel 97 to Excel 2003—which casts a pretty wide net.

Good thing, too, because the river of Excel annoyances runs deep and treacherous, populated by numerous species of sharp-toothed predators ready to chew up your data. How deep and treacherous? When we queried user groups across this fair land, we got 150 emails in a single week! Emails from newbies and Excel masters, homemakers and NASA engineers, all at their wits' end because of some Excel "feature," bug, quirk, flaw, or just-plain-dumb design decision. My job, in consonance with the fine folks at O'Reilly, was to figure out what bugged people the most, determine how to fix the problems, and also point out useful utilities, web sites, and other resources that might make their lives easier.

WHY THIS BOOK'S ESPECIALLY IMPORTANT RIGHT NOW

There's a lot of accumulated Excel angst out there, and with each new Excel version comes more *sturm* and more *drang*. But when it comes to managing your business (or your Little League team) with Excel, you don't have time for nail biting. You need solutions *now*. The faster you can navigate around the roadblocks, the faster you can make good decisions, earn that bonus, get promoted to partner, retire with full salary, and never use Excel again. To help you reach that pinnacle, dig into this tome—solutions to some of your most nettlesome Excel problems await within.

IS EXCEL ANNOYANCES RIGHT FOR YOU?

Has Excel refused to sort columns? Replaced a word without your permission? Changed a long column of dates into numbers like 000.2222335? Declined to modify a chart label? Laughed at your efforts to troubleshoot a troublesome macro? And are you just plain sick of seeing #### signs? If you answered yes to any of these questions, you need this book!

HAVE AN ANNOYANCE?

The hard part wasn't finding annoyances; the hard part was figuring which ones to cover and which ones to cut, for lack of space. Well, we obviously haven't covered every possible Excel annoyance, but take heart—future editions of this book will continue to explore the many twisted avenues of Excel. If you have a pet peeve not covered in *Excel Annoyances*, feel free to write us at *annoyances@oreilly.com* and tell us what's on your mind. We'll consider these annoyances for the next edition of this book.

HOW TO USE THIS BOOK

This book is divided into chapters, with each chapter covering a different aspect of Excel: data entry, formulas, formatting, exchanging data, printing, charts, macros/VBA, and the newest member of the Excel family, Excel 2003. You should probably skim through the book at least once, getting an overview of the available solutions, and then return to the pages with fixes that will help you right away.

Don't worry about typing in the long macro, VBA, and HTML code samples you'll find in this book. They're available for download at *http://www.oreilly.com/catalog/excelannoyances/downloads.csp*.

CONVENTIONS USED IN THIS BOOK

The following typographic conventions are used in this book:

Italic is used for filenames, URLs, email addresses, and emphasis.

Constant width is used for commands, keywords, and items that should be typed verbatim.

Constant width italic is used for text that should be replaced with user-supplied values.

Menu sequences are separated by arrows, such as Data → List → Create List. Tabs, radio buttons, checkboxes, and the like are identified by name, such as "click the Options tab and check the 'Always show full menus' box."

USING CODE EXAMPLES

This book is here to help you get your job done. In general, you may use the code in this book in your programs and documentation. You do not need to contact us for permission unless you're reporducing a significant portion of the code. For example, writing a program that uses several chunks of code from this book does not require permission. Selling or distributing a CD-ROM of examples from O'Reilly books *does* require permission. Answering a question by citing this book and quoting examples code does not require permission. Incorporating a significant amount of example code from this book into your product's documentation *does* require permission.

We appreciate, but do not require, attribution. An attribution usually includes the title, author, publisher, and ISBN, for example: "*Excel Annoyances* by Curtis Frye. Copyright 2005 O'Reilly Media, Inc., 0-596-00728-0."

If you feel your use of code examples falls outside fair use or the permission given here, feel free to contact us at *permissions@oreilly.com*.

ABOUT THE AUTHOR

Curtis Frye started messing around with a Texas Instruments computer way back when *floppy* disk drives cost hundreds of dollars. (Frugal lad that he was, he saved his programs on a cassette tape.) He went on to play with an Apple IIe in high school and helped users with Mac and DOS word processors at the Academic Computing Services center at Syracuse University. He didn't really start pounding on computers until he went to work for The MITRE Corporation in McLean, Virginia, and used Excel as

a project management tool. Part of the deal was simultaneously going to grad school at George Mason University *and* studying information systems, technology transfer strategies, operations research, export control regimes, C and Pascal programming, database design, and transborder data flows. After five academic departments and 13 classes, he didn't have an M.A., an M.S., or an M.F.A.— but he knew a bunch of neat stuff, and had a lot of fun in the process.

After five years of trying to make a go of working in an office, Curt left the Washington D.C. area in 1995 and ended up in Portland, Oregon, where he became a full-time writer. Of course, being an entry-level writer with exactly one magazine article under your belt means you had better have a day job. Curt worked as an actor, an improvisational comedian (and he still does, eight years and more than 800 shows later), theatrical carpenter, lighting technician, and lighting designer. After two years of writing articles for small publications that paid (sometimes), Curt got his big break when he answered an email on the Computer Book Publishing email list from a guy named Tim. Tim asked about books on genetic algorithms, an area Curt happened to know something about. Curt replied with a way-too-long email detailing the existing popular literature, what was covered, and what wasn't, and speculated on a few new angles to pursue. The Tim, of course, was Tim O'Reilly, who immediately signed up Curt to help write a market research report on web commerce.

Fourteen books later (plus a passel of online courses, and a few articles) Curt is an established author, with credits including such titles as *Microsoft Office Excel 2003 Step by Step*, *Excel Pocket Guide*, *Microsoft Office Excel 2003 Programming Inside Out* (as lead author), *Master Visually Microsoft Access 2000*, and *Privacy-Enhanced Business* (the master's thesis he never wrote). It's a good life, and he's glad there's room in the world for someone who works from dusk to dawn, not the other way around.

ABOUT THE CONTRIBUTORS

Ken Bluttman wrote the first draft of Chapter 6. He has been crafting custom Office solutions for more than a decade and, appropriately enough, is the author of *Developing Microsoft Office Solutions*. He has consulted for dozens of leading companies in finance, insurance, energy, and health care. He also develops Oracle and SQL Server database applications, XML applications, and a variety of web sites. Ken lives in New York with his wife, son, and dog.

Laurie Ulrich Fuller wrote Chapter 7. She has been working with computers since the early 1980s and has been teaching people how to use them since 1990. In the last decade, she's written hundreds of training manuals and taught thousands of students at classes conducted at client sites, at various corporate training centers, and at Temple University. In the early 1990s, she created her own firm, Limehat & Company, Inc., providing training, consulting, and technical documentation for growing businesses and nonprofit organizations. In the last 10 years, the company has moved into web design and hosting services. Laurie has also authored, co-authored, and contributed to more than 20 computer books for several major publishers, including *How to Do Everything with Office XP*, *Photoshop Elements 2 Bible*, and *Troubleshooting Microsoft Excel 2002*.

ABOUT THE TECHNICAL TEAM

Michael Oliver-Goodwin, the project editor, is a widely published writer and an experienced editor. He has helped edit magazines about computers (*PC World*, *MacWeek*, *InfoWorld*); written about computers and technology (for *Fortune*, *Good Housekeeping*, *Publish*, *Multimedia World*, *The Web*, and *The San Jose Mercury News*); authored books about computers; edited books about computers; and contributed to books about computers. Outside the technical field his book credits include *On the Edge* (an unauthorized biography of filmmaker Francis Coppola, published by William Morrow) and several cookbooks. He sold a screenplay to *Ghostbusters* director Ivan Reitman (which was never shot), his script for *Burden of Dreams* helped filmmaker Les Blank win a British Academy Award for Best Feature-Length Documentary, he's produced several calypso CDs for Rounder Records, and he's taught magazine feature writing at the Journalism department at San Francisco State University. Michael used every bit of his considerable skills to keep me on the straight and narrow path to good writing, which is more than a full-time job. I appreciate his patience, his good humor, and the many valuable contributions he's made to the book's content, tone, and overall flow.

Jeff Webb, the technical editor, has written about computers and technology for 20 years. His books include *Using Excel Visual Basic for Applications* and *Microsoft Visual Basic Developer's Workshop*. He also has written programming guides, articles, and sample applications for Microsoft and Digital Equipment Corporation, and he pitched in on some of the advanced material in this book on databases and VBA programming. Jeff is a terrific programmer, with an instinctive sense of what works and what doesn't in Excel. If you have to use VBA in Excel 2003, look for his *Excel 2003 Programming: A Developer's Notebook* from O'Reilly. Thanks, Jeff, for keeping me on my toes and suggesting such great fixes and improvements to my text and (especially) to my code.

Robert Luhn is the executive editor of O'Reilly's consumer group. He's been editing articles and books about spreadsheets since the days of VisiCalc, Microsoft Multiplan, VP-Planner, and 1-2-3. When he's not writing macros for fun in his editing retreat high atop Mt. Zugspitze, he raises "yeast cultures, crocuses, and small, unattractive animals." Robert arrived at O'Reilly in July 2003 and has been a joy to work with, first on the *Excel Pocket Guide*, and later, on this book. Some editors are like theatre directors, asking questions and inspiring the actor/writer to embark on a voyage of discovery. Robert can take that approach, but he's not afraid to give direct notes on what's working, what isn't, and how to fix what needs fixing.

Finally, please take the time to read the Colophon at the back of the book and tip your hat to the designers, copyeditors, layout artists, production editors, illustrators, and myriad other conscientious and hard-working professionals who made this paper-based block party we call *Excel Annoyances* happen. Publishing a book is about as difficult as launching a kindergarten into earth orbit, but these folks pulled it off brilliantly.

ACKNOWLEDGMENTS

It always comes back to family, doesn't it? I'm no exception. My parents, David Frye and Jane Fulgham, have always been there for me whether I needed a hand up or a good kick in the tail. My twin brother Doug and I have spent the last 10 years taking turns sending one another money when one of us had work and the other didn't. Doug just finished his doctorate in something really boring at George Mason University and got a job within a week, which means I can expect to be paid back within the year. Right, big guy?

My fiancée, Virginia Belt, is a retired ballerina and a working actor, director, choreographer, and university instructor. She is a *wonderful* addition to my life, has made me the happiest man in the world, and is looking over my left shoulder as I write this. Have I missed anything, honey? No? Good.

I'm represented in the computer book industry by Neil Salkind of Studio B. Neil has more jobs than my fiancée, and that's saying a lot. Even so, he still finds the time to get me work, negotiate my deals, develop business for Studio B, *and* teach psychology at the University of Kansas. He specializes in child psychology, which probably explains why he's so good with writers. David and Sherry Rogelberg run Studio B with a steady hand, and Stacey Barone and Jackie Coder help me out with my contracts and royalties. Studio B gave me a shot back in 1998 and I've never doubted my decision to go with them.

Finally, I'd like to thank Pat Short and Ruth Jenkins, the founders of ComedySportz Portland, for welcoming me into the group back in 1996 and giving me the chance (actually, several chances) to work through the baggage I brought with me from D.C. and to help people laugh in the process. Everyone in CSz is an important part of my family—you two most of all.

O'REILLY WOULD LIKE TO HEAR FROM YOU

Please address comments and questions concerning this book to the publisher:

O'Reilly Media, Inc.
1005 Gravenstein Highway North
Sebastopol, CA 95472
(800) 998-9938 (in the United States or Canada)
(707) 829-0515 (international or local)
(707) 829-0104 (fax)

There is a web page for this book, where you can download the utilities mentioned and some of the longer code samples, and find errata and additional information. You can access this page at:

http://www.oreilly.com/catalog/excelannoyances/

To comment or ask technical questions about this book, send email to:

bookquestions@oreilly.com

For more information about books, conferences, Resource Centers, and the O'Reilly Network, go to:

http://www.oreilly.com

Entering Data
ANNOYANCES

Data entry is the heart of Excel. If you can't get data into your worksheet quickly and accurately, you can't use the nifty tools at your disposal to analyze them. Excel does a lot of things right when it comes to data entry, but some things are downright peculiar. If you've ever had Excel correct your typing when you *know* what you entered was right, or turn a six-digit integer into a date, you know what I'm talking about.

The first part of this chapter shows you how to blow away Excel's everyday data annoyances, from it's habit of deleting leading zeros to correcting you obsessively. You'll also encounter (and solve) annoyances when creating forms, importing data, cutting and pasting, navigating in and among worksheets, and more. Finally, we'll focus on Excel's handy data validation feature. With validation rules, you can limit the kind of data users can enter in cells. The rules can require values to fall into a specific range, or force the user to pick values from a list. This is a boon to managing data entry, but it can be a major annoyance to set up.

GENERAL DATA ENTRY ANNOYANCES

KILL CLIPPY

The Annoyance: I can't tell you how many times I've been happily entering data, only to have that blasted paperclip "helper" thing elbow its way onto the screen. By the time I get rid of it, I've lost track of what I'm doing and it takes me forever to get back in the groove. If that Office Assistant really *were* a live office assistant, I'd have had fired him years ago! How do I make it go away?

The Fix: Clippy is one of the most-hated Office "innovations" in history. Microsoft had the good sense to turn off Clippy and his companion Office Assistant characters by default in Excel 2002 (the Office XP version) and in later versions.

In Excel 97, you can terminate Clippy permanently by opening the *\Program Files\Microsoft Office\Office* folder and renaming the *Actors* subfolder to something such as *Old_Actors* or *Ha_ha_ha*. Once Excel (and your other Office programs) can no longer find the *Actors* subfolder, Clippy will be unable to appear out of nowhere like a $1,000 bar tab.

If you're using Office 2000 or XP, you can turn off Clippy by going to the Control Panel and using either the Add/Remove Programs applet or (depending on your operating system) the Add or Remove Programs applet. In Windows Me, 2000, or XP, click Microsoft Office in the Currently Installed Programs list and then click Change. Click the Add or Remove button, click the Office Tools item, click Office Assistant, and then click Not Available. Confirm your choices and you're done. If you're running Windows 98, click the Microsoft Office entry in the Install/Uninstall tab, click Add/Remove Program, and step through the wizard until you can change the Office Assistant's setting to Not Available.

If you're using Office 2003, you can turn off Clippy by going through the Add or Remove Programs control panel. In the Currently Installed Programs list, click Microsoft Office 2003 and then click Change. Select the Add or Remove option button on the first page of the wizard and click Next. Check the "Choose advanced customization of applications" box and click Next. Expand the Shared Office Features item, click Office Assistant, click Not Available, and then click Update.

> Be forewarned that the Office Update wizard might ask for your Office installation CD to make these changes. You can avoid this request by installing every Office component to your hard disk.

There are several funny articles about giving Clippy the boot. You can find two of them at *http://www.techsoc.com/clippyfired.htm* and *http://www.techsoc.com/clippynow.htm*. For those with a darker sense of humor, you can find out how Clippy can help you to write one final letter at *http://www.techsoc.com/clippycide.htm*.

RETAIN LEADING ZEROS WHEN YOU ENTER DATA

The Annoyance: My company uses five-digit product codes, and some of them start with zero. My problem is that when I enter a product code with a leading zero, Excel deletes the zero. For example, Excel turns product 03182 into product 3182, which generates horrible errors in my macros, not to mention my inventory. How do I stop this behavior?

The Fix: Unless you tell it differently, Excel expects you to enter numbers without leading zeroes. This can also be a problem with scientific numbers (e.g., 0.16 microns), which likewise often have leading zeros. Fortunately there is a way to convince Excel to let you enter values with leading zeros, by treating those values as a bit of text and not a number. Here's how:

1. Select the cells that will contain numbers stored as text.

2. Right-click the cell and choose Format → Cells, then click the Number tab (as shown in Figure 1-1).

3. Click Text in the Category list and then click OK.

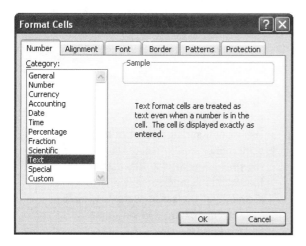

Figure 1-1. The Format Cells dialog box lets you tell Excel how to treat data entered or imported into your workbook.

You've changed the cells' format from General (which expects a number, or something readily identifiable as text) to Text, which treats everything (even numbers) as if it's the kind of alphanumeric text you'd find in a Word document.

You can use the same fix to prevent Excel from converting certain numbers (such as 100349 or 021264) into date/time format (a problem that's described in more detail in Chapter 3). For instance, in the medical field, where privacy is of paramount importance, you might use case numbers such as these to track your patients. If you don't want Excel to change these numbers to dates (Oct-3, 1949, in the first example), set the format of the cell to Text before you import or type in the case number.

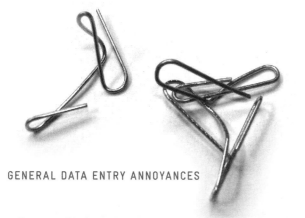

Genetic Information at Risk

If you use Excel as part of bioinformatics research, be especially watchful for errors when you import data from gene sequencing applications. For example, Excel might translate the gene code DEC1 and the RIKEN identifier 2310009E13 into the date 1-DEC and the scientific number 2.31E+13, respectively. You can find more information about these problems at *http://www.biomedcentral.com/1471-2105/5/80.*

EXTEND A NUMERIC SERIES AUTOMATICALLY

The Annoyance: I'm so tired of entering regular sequences of data into cells. I mean, typing 1 in cell A1, then 2 in cell A2, then 3 in cell A3, then 4 in cell A4...up to 100 or 200. This isn't a good use of my time! Isn't there some way to extend a data series automatically so that I don't get carpal tunnel typing row headings?

The Fix: You can enter a data series quickly and easily by typing the first two numbers in the series in adjacent cells. Then select those cells and drag the fill handle (that black square that appears at the bottom-right corner of the selected range, as shown in Figure 1-2) until the desired value appears in the tool tip that floats along next to your cursor.

The first two numbers in the series determine the relationship between successive cells for the rest of the series. For example, typing 1 in cell A1 and 3 in cell A2 would result in a series extended as 5 in A3, 7 in A4, and so on. Typing 5 in cell A1 and 10 in cell A2 would result in a series extended as 15 in A3, 20 in A4, and so on.

But what if you type in a series that doesn't have a regular progression? In that case, Excel will use linear regression to approximate future values in the series. This can be very cool. For instance, if you have 10 years of sales totals and want to see what the numbers will look like if sales continue on their current trend, you can select the cells and drag the fill handle to fill in projected future values.

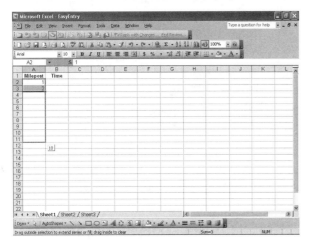

Figure 1-2. Dragging the fill handle enters subsequent values in your series quickly.

COPYING BEYOND A ROW OR COLUMN

You can copy a single cell's contents to other cells in the same row or column by clicking that cell and dragging the fill handle over the cells where you want to paste the value. To copy a cell over a rectangular range of rows or columns, select the cell you want to copy and drag the fill handle over the rows to which you want to copy the cell. Drop the fill handle. Then grab the fill handle again, which now should be highlighting the entire range of cells you just dragged over, and drag it over the columns where you want to paste the value.

There's actually a lot more to entering data series in Excel than simple linear projections. You can get at the more advanced series entry tools by right-dragging the fill

handle to display a shortcut menu where you can pick the type of growth you want the series data to exhibit. If you click Linear Trend, you get the same trends I described earlier. If you click Geometric Trend, however, you get a series in which each value increases exponentially (that is, the base value is squared). For example, in a linear series the series would begin 1, 2, 3, 4, while in a growth series it would begin 1, 2, 4, 8.

> The growth series discussed here represents powers of 2. Excel recognizes that the first element is 2^0, the second is 2^1, the third is 2^2, and so on. If the first four elements of the series were 1, 4, 9, 16, Excel would extend the series as 25 (5^2), 36 (6^2), and so forth.

The final item on the shortcut menu you see when you right-drag the fill handle is Series. The Series dialog box (shown in Figure 1-3) has controls that let you determine how you want to extend the data series you've defined. For example, you can select a linear or geometric expansion. Clicking the AutoFill option is the equivalent of dragging the fill handle to extend a series. Checking the Trend box tells Excel to calculate the average percentage change in the selected cells and to put that value in the "Step value" box.

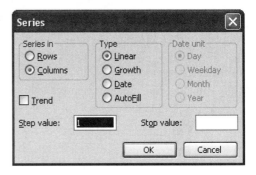

Figure 1-3. The Series dialog box gives you full control over the data you enter into your cells.

Formulas That Don't Change When Copied

Sometimes you *don't* want Excel to turn a simple drag-and-drop or copy-and-paste operation into a series. For more information on relative and absolute references, see the annoyance "Prevent Copied Formulas from Changing Cell References" in Chapter 3.

USE THE SERIES DIALOG BOX TO DEFINE A SERIES OF VALUES

The Annoyance: Can't I just define the beginning and end values of a data series and specify the increment? Dragging is nice, but my bosses tell me how to create a series based on the first value, the last value, and the difference between each value.

The Fix: At the bottom of the Series dialog box are the "Step value" and "Stop value" boxes, which let you create a data series beginning with a value defined in your worksheet. The step value is the difference between each item in the series, and the stop value is the last value in the series. For example, suppose you have the value 1 in cell A1. Select column A and choose Edit → Fill → Series. If you enter a step value of 2 and a stop value of 15, Excel will put values 1, 3, 5, 7, 9, 11, 13, and 15 in the range A1:A8. You need to select at least as many cells as you require for your series, though, or Excel will put values only in the cells you selected. For example, if you select cells A1:A3 and follow the procedure I just described, you'll get only the values 1, 3, and 5 in those cells.

CREATE DATA SERIES MINUS THE MOUSE

The Annoyance: I hate my mouse. I always end up dragging stuff I don't want to drag, or dropping it in the wrong cells, so even thinking about right-clicking this and right-dragging that fill handle thing gives me a panic attack. Isn't there some way to create a data series without typing, clicking, and dragging?

The Fix: Select options in the Series dialog box. You can create series based on dates and days without a bit of dragging. Excel knows about the following four sequences:

- Sunday, Monday, Tuesday, Wednesday, Thursday, Friday, Saturday
- Sun, Mon, Tue, Wed, Thu, Fri, Sat
- January, February, March, April, May, June, July, August, September, October, November, December
- Jan, Feb, Mar, Apr, May, Jun, Jul, Aug, Sep, Oct, Nov, Dec

Excel also will extend a time series for you. For example, extending a series that starts with 9:00 AM in cell A1 and 10:00 AM in cell A2 will place 11:00 AM in cell A3, 12:00 PM in cell A4, and so on. For information on creating your own series, see the next annoyance, "Create a Custom Fill Series."

If you want to create a time series, you must place a space between the final zero in the time and the AM or PM designator. If you leave out that space, Excel will treat the cell's contents as a General entry rather than a Time entry and won't extend the series for you. 12:00 AM works. 12:00AM doesn't.

Interesting things happen when you convert between a numeric series and a day or month series. For example, if you have the numbers 1 through 3 in cells A1:A3 and you right-drag the fill handle to cell A4 and click the Year option button, you'll get a series that progresses like so: 1, 367, 732, 1097. Those increments are 366 (the number of days in a leap year—in this case, 2004) and 365 (the number of days in the years 2005 and 2006).

CREATE A CUSTOM FILL SERIES

The Annoyance: The stupid built-in data lists in Excel don't have the values I want. Can I create my own fill series?

The Fix: Yes, you can easily define a custom repeating sequence. For example, if you're noting the amount of sodium chloride, carbon dioxide, and water produced by a chemical reaction, and you want to create a column with those labels repeating in the same order, you can type those values in cells A1:A3, select the cells, and drag the fill handle to repeat that sequence in every cell you drag the fill handle over. If you think you might use the sequence again for some reason, or if you want to use it for sorting your worksheet data, you can create a custom list. Here's how:

1. Type the values you want in your custom list in a group of contiguous cells in a single column or row.

2. Select the cells containing your list and then select Tools → Options, and click the Custom Lists tab (shown in Figure 1-4).

3. Verify that the cell range you selected appears in the "Import list from cells" box. If it doesn't, click the Collapse Dialog button (the tiny icon in the box at the far right), select the cells containing your list values, and then click the Expand Dialog button (in the box at the far right).

4. Click the Import button, and then click OK.

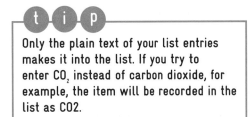

Only the plain text of your list entries makes it into the list. If you try to enter CO_2 instead of carbon dioxide, for example, the item will be recorded in the list as CO2.

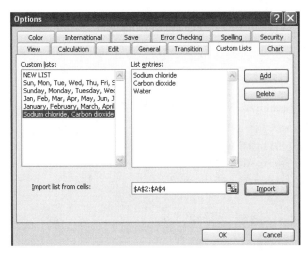

Figure 1-4. Create a custom list and you can use it to fill cells in a worksheet and to sort data.

ENTER DATA INTO MULTIPLE WORKSHEETS AT ONCE

The Annoyance: I'm adding data to a set of worksheets, and some of the matching cells on different sheets should contain the same data. For example, for the next three months I'm going to have five sales reps and a manager working from 9:00 a.m. until noon every day. I need to have a separate worksheet for each month (shown in Figure 1-5), and it's a pain to have to reenter the data; isn't there some way I can enter the data into cells in the range C2:C7 on all three sheets at the same time?

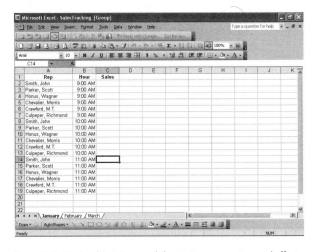

Figure 1-5. Typing data into several sheets at once saves time and effort.

The Fix: Entering data into the same cells on more than one worksheet at the same time sounds hard, but actually it's pretty straightforward. Simply select the sheet tabs (found at the bottom lefthand corner of the Excel window) of the multiple worksheets in question and start typing. To select more than one worksheet at a time, use the standard Windows technique: Ctrl-click individual sheets; click one sheet tab and then Shift-click another to select that range of sheets; or right-click any sheet tab and click Select All Sheets to grab 'em all.

When you select more than one worksheet, the term [Group] appears in the workbook's titlebar.

ALLOW MORE THAN ONE PERSON TO EDIT A FILE AT THE SAME TIME

The Annoyance: I hate letting anyone mess around with my workbooks, but I'm in a time crunch and I need to let a co-worker enter data into one of my workbooks at the same time I work on it. Obviously, we can't work on the same keyboard, but is there some way for both of us to edit the file at the same time?

The Fix: If you use Excel 2000 or later, you can allow more than one user to edit a workbook simultaneously. First, put the workbook in a folder that other users can access. Then select Tools → Share Workbook, and check the "Allow changes by more than one user at the same time" box.

If you want to restrict who can open your shared workbook, follow these steps instead:

1. Choose Tools → Protection → Protect and Share Workbook, and check the "Sharing with track changes" box.
2. Type a password in the "Password (optional)" box.
3. Click OK.

Now no one can open the workbook unless you tell him the password.

IMPORT PAPER FORMS

In May 2004 I was waiting at Portland International Airport for a flight to Frankfurt, Germany, when a worker handed me a survey asking my opinion on airport operations. I filled it out, handed it back, and asked who got stuck with tabulating the results. The worker assured me that no one had to spend time entering the bubble data; a computer handled it all. I doubt the airport used Excel to process its form data, but if you're on a budget and want to pull faxed or scanned form data into Excel, you can use FormIDEA from TechVision Software at *http://www.tkvision.com/*.

FormIDEA captures data from bar codes, paper forms with checkboxes, and bubbles, and even uses handwriting recognition algorithms to bring in handwritten text. A specialized educational edition of the program helps teachers to score, grade, and analyze tests. The full version of the program costs $499, but the educational version runs only $249 for a single teacher. The price for a school with approximately 600 students is listed at $1,950, but you should contact the company to verify pricing for anything more than a single-user license.

ADD A CARRIAGE RETURN TO A CELL'S CONTENTS

The Annoyance: I need to enter long paragraphs of text in some of the cells in my worksheet, and it would be great to start with a short headline on a separate line at the top. But every time I press Enter to separate the headline from the main text entry, Excel just takes me to a new cell. How in the world do I add a carriage return, line break, or whatever you call it? It's driving me crazy!

The Fix: Chill, baby. You can add a line break inside a cell by pressing Alt-Enter.

ADD SYMBOLS TO YOUR EXCEL WORKSHEET

The Annoyance: I work for a multinational manufacturing company, and although I work exclusively in English, I do occasionally have to type a name in a foreign alphabet. My boss insists that I use the characters from the original language (Danish, German, and French are common), but I don't know how to insert those letters, or other symbols, into my worksheet cells. Help!

The Fix: In Excel 2002 and later, you can choose Insert → Symbol to display the "Symbol dialog" box, which lets you pick the symbol you want to insert. Just click the Insert button after you select your symbol. In Excel 97 and 2000, you must use Windows' Character Map helper application to find the available symbols. To run Character Map in Windows XP, Me, or 98 select Start → Programs → Accessories → System Tools → Character Map. Once in Character Map, select the appropriate font, double-click the desired character (which copies it to the Clipboard), and then paste the character into your cell.

RESTRICT AUTOCORRECT INTERFERENCE

The Annoyance: Excel is unshakably convinced that I don't know how to spell. But Excel is wrong! I work for a company with an internal project code-named "ADN." Go ahead; try typing that name into a cell. I'll wait for you.

Excel changed it to "AND," didn't it? And you had to backspace over the code name and retype it, didn't you? Drives me nuts. How do I make that stop happening?

The Fix: You've got an overactive AutoCorrect feature. And although you should be grateful for all the times it's prevented you from typing "teh" instead of "the," it's still a pain when it changes something you know is perfectly fine the way you typed it.

If Excel changes a word you type, you can press Ctrl-Z to undo the change—but only as long as you pressed the spacebar after you typed the word Excel corrected. If you press either the Tab key or the Enter key, Excel makes the change and then shifts its focus to the next active cell. That means that when you press Ctrl-Z, Excel erases the last change you made in the cell you just edited.

You can turn off AutoCorrect entirely by selecting Tools → AutoCorrect Options and unchecking the "Replace text as you type" box on the AutoCorrect tab page of the dialog box (shown in Figure 1-6).

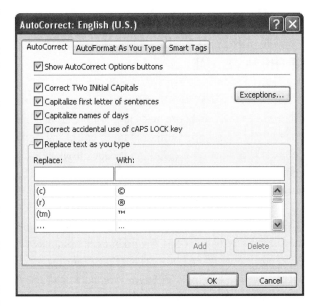

Figure 1-6. Stand up for what you know is right! Sometimes AutoCorrect requires a bit of manual correction.

If you want to modify only *some* of AutoCorrect's behavior, you can uncheck the various boxes on this tab so that Excel won't correct words starting with two or more capital letters, sentences (or what appear to be sentences) starting with a lowercase letter, lowercase day names, and the dreaded iNVERTED cAPS lOCK kEY. You even can define your own AutoCorrect entries by typing the term to be replaced in the Replace box, typing the term to replace it with in the With box, and clicking the Add button. By the same token, you can define exceptions to the initial-caps and first-letter rules by clicking the Exceptions button and filling in your exceptions in the dialog box that appears. Plus, you can delete individual AutoCorrect entries, such as the ADN/AND replacement you complained about, by selecting the entry from the list presented and clicking the Delete button.

USE AUTOCORRECT TO YOUR ADVANTAGE

You can use AutoCorrect to insert blocks of boilerplate text of up to 255 characters, such as category descriptions, accounting methods, or assumptions behind your numbers. After all, it's much easier to type *winter04bad* than to type *"The projections for the 2005 spring season might seem pessimistic, but we're anticipating a harsh winter that will delay the travel season for two or three more weeks than was the case in 2004."* The only downside is that Excel doesn't allow you to use more than one AutoCorrect entry in a cell. You can work around this by typing the second AutoCorrect term into an adjacent cell, and then cutting and pasting the second block of text to the target cell.

KEEP WEB AND FILE ADDRESSES AS PLAIN TEXT

The Annoyance: If you type a URL in a cell, it automatically becomes a hyperlink, which is usually exactly what I *don't* want to happen. How do I stop this?

The Fix: Excel 97 doesn't automatically format a URL as a hyperlink, so you're in luck. In Excel 2000, there's no way to keep Excel from formatting a URL as a hyperlink, but you can press Ctrl-Z right after it happens to remove the formatting. If you don't catch it then, you also can click the cell and choose Insert → Hyperlink → Remove Hyperlink. For Excel 2002 or later versions, which do default to hyperlink formatting, you can stop Excel from transforming a URL or file path into a clickable link by adjusting the AutoCorrect function. Choose Tools → AutoCorrect Options, click the AutoFormat As You Type tab, and uncheck the "Internet and network paths with hyperlinks" box.

IMPORTING DATA ANNOYANCES

COPYING A WORD TABLE INTO EXCEL 97 INTRODUCES BLANK ROWS

The Annoyance: When I copy a table from a Word document into an Excel 97 worksheet, Excel insists on assigning each cell in the Word table to two cells in the worksheet (shown in Figure 1-7). Worse yet, it merges some of the cells. Please tell me there's some way I can stop Excel from merging the cells! If not, can I at least undo the merges and delete the resulting blank rows after I paste my table?

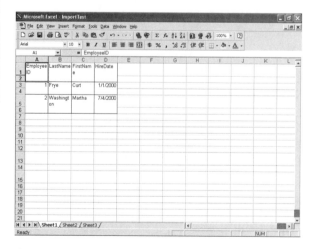

Figure 1-7. For some reason, you get two rows for one when you bring a Word table into Excel 97.

The Fix: David and Raina Hawley, the authors of *Excel Hacks: 100 Industrial-Strength Tips and Tools* (O'Reilly), wrote a great macro that removes blank rows from a selection. I added a section at the top of the procedure to remove text wrapping and cell merges from the imported list so that each row will be separate, allowing Excel to remove the blank rows. This macro assumes the data you imported is selected. If the list isn't selected, click any cell in the list, press Ctrl-* to select the list, and run this macro to clean up your data:

```
Sub FixWordTableInExcel97()
'Removes all cell merges and text wrapping from
'the pasted table and then deletes all blank
'rows added by the paste.

With Selection
.WrapText = False
.MergeCells = False
End With

Dim Rw As Range
With Application
.Calculation = xlCalculationManual
.ScreenUpdating = False

Selection.SpecialCells(xlCellTypeBlanks).Select

For Each Rw In Selection.Rows
If WorksheetFunction.CountA(Selection. _
EntireRow) = 0 Then
Selection.EntireRow.Delete
End If
Next Rw

.Calculation = xlCalculationAutomatic
.ScreenUpdating = True
End With
End Sub
```

David and Raina Hawley originally published the body of this macro (everything after `Dim Rw as Range`) at *http://www.ozgrid.com/VBA/VBACode.htm*. It is used here with permission.

DATA IN WORD FILES ISN'T AVAILABLE FOR IMPORT

The Annoyance: I saved a file with comma-separated values in a Microsoft Word (*.doc*) file that I'd like to import into Excel, but Word files don't show up when you select File → Open and open the "Files of type" list. Why don't they? And what can I do about it?

The Fix: The reason you can't import data from a Word file is because Word files contain a lot more data than what you see on the screen. If Excel actually imported a Word file, it would almost certainly stumble over formatting and other confusing data that only looks like a series of comma-separated values—and your worksheet would go haywire. The trick is to delete from your document anything that isn't a comma-separated value. So, instead of saving the file in Word's DOC format, choose File → Save As. In the "Save as type" drop-down menu, select Text Only or Plain Text (depending on your version of Word), and click Save. This saves the document as a text file, which Excel will happily import.

ASAP: HANDY UTILITY FOR IMPORTS

If you import a lot of data into Excel, whether it's text, database, or Excel files, you're probably tired of wrangling with the Text Import Wizard just to set a few options. Instead of running the wizard every time, or taking the time to create a macro for the most common tasks, download the free ASAP Utilities collection from eGate Internet Solutions at *http://www.asap-utilities.com/*. ASAP, written by Bastien Mensink, contains VBA routines that import data with the appropriate standard delimiting characters, import several space-delimited text files into a workbook, or combine space-delimited text files into a single text file. The package also contains a wide range of additional tools that can help you select cells that meet a given criterion, copy a worksheet's print settings, quickly export a selection to HTML, delete all the numbers in a set of cells (while leaving all alphabetical characters intact) or vice versa, and more.

CUT-AND-PASTE ANNOYANCES

PUT MORE THAN ONE ITEM ON THE CLIPBOARD

The Annoyance: I frequently want to copy items from one workbook into another—or even into another application—and it's tedious having to copy each cell, object, or image one by one, open the other document, paste what I copied, and then go back to my workbook and repeat. Can't I collect what I cut or copy into a single intermediate location and then paste whatever I like?

The Fix: It is possible to collect items you cut and copy in Excel into a single location, but how you do it changes drastically from version to version. In Excel 97, you'll have to create a separate workbook or worksheet, and paste your collection in there. It's a pain, but it works. Be sure to keep an eye on your workbook's size so that it doesn't slow down your system. I use 1MB as a guideline for when it's time to create a new "holding tank," but if you're running an older system with less memory, you might want to set this limit at 500KB.

Microsoft introduced the Office Clipboard in Office 2000, and it's been part of the suite ever since. The Office Clipboard keeps track of the last set of items you cut or copied (12 in Office 2000, 24 in XP and 2003) and makes them available to paste in any Office application, individually or all together. What's even more interesting is that any items you cut or copy in one version of Office are available in other versions of Office that are open. At one point I had Word 2003 and Excel 2000, 2002, and 2003 running at the same time—and each program had the same three cut-and-copied items available in its Office Clipboard.

To use the Clipboard in Excel 2000, follow these steps:

1. Choose View → Toolbars → Clipboard to display the Office 2000 Clipboard (shown in Figure 1-8).

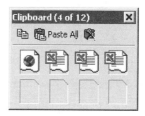

Figure 1-8. Paste-o-rama. With Office's enhanced clipboard, you can cut and paste multiple selections at once.

2. Follow any of these steps to use the Clipboard:

   • Click an item and click Paste to paste that item into your worksheet.

   • Click Paste All to paste every item in the Clipboard into your worksheet.

   • Click Clear All to empty the Clipboard.

In Excel 2002 and Excel 2003, follow these steps to use the Clipboard:

1. Choose View → Task Pane.

2. Click the Other Task Panes down arrow and click Clipboard to display the Clipboard task pane (the Excel 2003 version is shown in Figure 1-9).

Figure 1-9. The Office Clipboard is implemented as a task pane in Excel 2002 and 2003.

3. Follow any of these steps to use the Clipboard:

   - Click an item to paste it into your worksheet.
   - Click Paste All to paste every item in the Clipboard into your worksheet.
   - Click Clear All to empty every item in the Clipboard.
   - To delete individual items, hover the mouse pointer over an item, click the down arrow that appears next to it, and choose Delete to remove it.

PREVENT THE OFFICE CLIPBOARD FROM APPEARING

The Annoyance: I'm using Excel 2002, and whenever I cut or copy something, the Office Clipboard appears. It's driving me crazy. How can I send it away?

The Fix: The Clipboard toolbar won't appear by itself in Excel 2000. If you've enabled it and you want it to go away, just right-click an empty spot on any toolbar and uncheck Clipboard. However, the Clipboard task pane can (and often does) appear by itself in Excel 2002 and 2003 when you copy or cut something. To keep it from appearing, follow these steps:

1. Choose View → Task Pane.

2. Unless Clipboard is already there, click the Other Task Panes down arrow at the top of the task pane and click Clipboard.

3. Click the Options button at the bottom of the pane, and uncheck the Show Office Clipboard Automatically box.

CONTROL PASTED CELL FORMATS

The Annoyance: When I paste cells from one location to another, they keep their original formatting, which doesn't always fit in with the cells around their new location. Is there a quick way to change the pasted cells' format to that of their neighboring cells?

The Fix: In Excel 97 or 2000, you can use the Format Painter to copy an existing format from one group of cells to another. Just click the cell with the format you want to copy, click the Format Painter button on the Standard toolbar (look for the little paintbrush), select the cells where you want to apply the format, and release the mouse button, and the format is applied. In Excel 2002 or 2003, when you paste something into a cell, the Paste Options button appears at the bottom right corner of the cells you pasted. Click it and select the Match Destination Formatting radio button to make the pasted cells take on the formatting of their new neighbors.

INSERT OR DELETE SINGLE CELLS

The Annoyance: It's easy enough to insert a row or column into a worksheet by right-clicking the column or row header and choosing Insert, but sometimes I need to insert just a single cell. In one worksheet, I typed in the sales data correctly, except that I left out the data that was supposed to go into cell D4 (see Figure 1-10). I could just cut and paste the data, but isn't there a quick way to add a new cell at the D4 spot? And can I get rid of an extra cell?

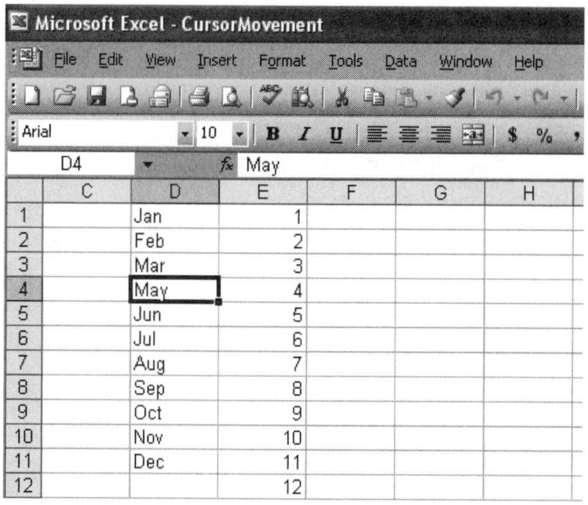

Figure 1-10. All this worksheet needs is a new cell at D4.

The Fix: Follow these steps to insert a cell into a worksheet:

1. Select a cell where you want a new, blank cell inserted.

2. Choose Insert → Cells, which displays the Insert dialog box.

3. Depending on what you want to do, click the "Shift cells right" or "Shift cells down" radio button and click the OK button. You can see the result of clicking "Shift cells down" in Figure 1-11. The existing cell (holding "May") is pushed down, and a new blank cell takes its place.

To insert multiple cells, simply select cells where you want new, blank cells inserted.

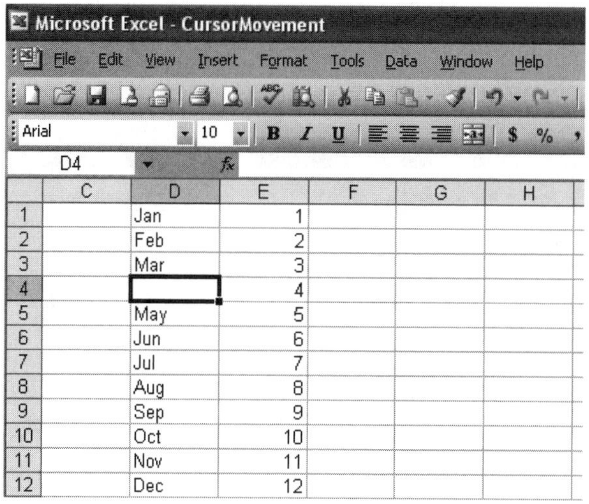

Figure 1-11. Make a new cell appear right where you need it.

To delete a cell or cells, follow these steps:

1. Select the cell or cells you want to delete.

2. Choose Edit → Delete.

3. Click the "Shift cells left" or "Shift cells up" radio button and click the OK button.

The cells don't have to be in the same row or column, or even next to each other. Hold down the Ctrl key, click the desired cells, and then select Edit → Delete.

TRANSPOSE ROWS AND COLUMNS

The Annoyance: My boss told me to enter the weekly sales totals for all the representatives in our dealership, but for some reason she wants the reps' names to appear as column headings and the week numbers as row headings. (A cut-down version of the worksheet appears in Figure 1-12.) Fine! Whatever she wants. But after the names started spilling off the right edge of the screen, she changed her mind and told me to make the rows into columns and the columns into rows. Is there any way to pull this off without cutting and pasting until my hand fall off?

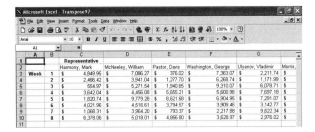

Figure 1-12. Enter data with the wrong row/column orientation? There's a way to flip 'em.

The Fix: Transposing rows and columns in a data selection isn't too crazy. Just follow these steps:

1. Select the data you want to transpose, including all of the heading rows and columns, and the data itself, and choose Edit → Copy.

2. Click a cell outside the range you copied and choose Edit → Paste Special.

3. In the Paste Special dialog box check the Transpose box at the lower right and then click OK.

4. Select the original, untransposed block of data, including all the heading rows and columns, as well as the data, and choose Edit → Clear → All.

5. Select the data you just pasted and choose Edit → Cut.

6. Click the cell at the top left corner of the range where you want the pasted data to appear and choose Edit → Paste. The result appears in Figure 1-13.

Formats don't transpose well. Remove borders, cell fill colors, and so on, from the cells you plan to transpose, and reapply them after the final paste.

Figure 1-13. Don't reenter the data—transpose it!

CHANGE THE DEFAULT SAVE LOCATION

The Annoyance: I hate the fact that when I try to save an Excel document, it always tries to save it first in the *My Documents* folder. I usually want to save it somewhere else. Any ideas?

The Fix: Instead of specifying the destination folder you want every time you save, just tell Excel what the default save folder should be. Choose Tools → Options and click the General tab shown in Figure 1-14. In the "Default file location" field, enter the path of your preferred save folder (such as *C:\Reports\2004*), click the OK button, and you're good to go.

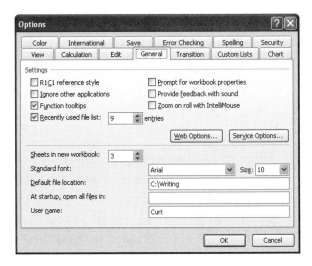

Figure 1-14. Use the controls on the General options page to change your default directory.

NAVIGATION AND DISPLAY ANNOYANCES

KEEP THE SAME ACTIVE CELL WHEN YOU MOVE TO A NEW WORKSHEET

The Annoyance: I switch around a lot between fairly similar worksheets, and it would save me hours of hassle if I could move from one worksheet to another and keep my cursor in the same position in the new sheet as the one I just left.

The Fix: Excel is designed to remember the last active cell on each worksheet, and to reactivate that cell when you open that sheet again. However, here's a macro you can use that will move you to the next worksheet in your workbook and place your cursor in the same active cell (it works in every version of Excel since Excel 97):

```
Sub NextSheetSameCell()

Dim rngCurrentCell As Range
Dim shtMySheet As Worksheet
Dim strCellAddress As String

'strCellAddress = ActiveCell.Address

'Comment out the line above to record the
'selected range's address, or comment out the
'line below to record the active cell's address.

strCellAddress = _
 ActiveWindow.RangeSelection.Address

Set shtMySheet = ActiveWindow.ActiveSheet

If Worksheets.Count > shtMySheet.Index Then

 shtMySheet.Next.Activate
 Range(strCellAddress).Activate

 Else

 Worksheets(1).Activate
 Range(strCellAddress).Activate

End If

Set shtMySheet = Nothing

End Sub
```

For good measure, I wrote the macro so that you can move to either the same active cell or the same *range* of selected cells as you move from worksheet to worksheet. In either case, the macro records the address of the selected cell or cells, activates the next worksheet in your workbook (or returns to the first worksheet if you're currently on the last one), and applies the recorded selection to the new worksheet. To edit the macro so that you transfer only to the active cell (even if more than one cell is selected), put an apostrophe in front of the line that reads `strCellAddress = ActiveCell.Address` and remove the apostrophe from in front of the line that reads `strCellAddress = ActiveWindow.RangeSelection.Address`.

If you find the macro useful, you can attach it to a custom button on the toolbar. To find out how, see "Run a Macro by Clicking a Toolbar Button or Menu Item" in Chapter 8.

EASY NAVIGATION

When you create workbooks with multiple worksheets and named ranges, you have to spend a lot of time scrolling through the Tab bar or trying to pick a named range from the list in the Name drop-down box. You can ease your navigation burden by downloading the shareware Navigator Utilities package from *http://www.robbo.com.au/download.htm*. Instead of digging through Excel's menus, Navigator makes it a breeze to view hidden worksheets and just as easily hide and protect them; quickly follow links across workbooks; work with named ranges; and call on a superior Find and Replace feature. The basic package is free, but for a $20 shareware registration fee you get a number of additional capabilities, such as password cracking.

SHRINK THE EXCEL WINDOW

The Annoyance: I have too much data in my worksheet to fit on a single screen. Can I shrink the contents of the window so that I can see everything at once?

The Fix: You can control the relative size of the contents of the Excel window using the Zoom field in Excel's standard toolbar. In the Zoom field on the toolbar (see Figure 1-15), click the down arrow and select a preset zoom value, or type a value directly into the field. The maximum zoom magnification is 400%; the minimum is 10%.

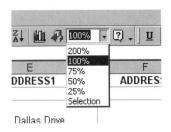

Figure 1-15. The Zoom field in the toolbar controls how large the body of your Excel worksheet appears in the Excel window. You can select prefab settings, or type in your own magnification.

Another way to shrink a worksheet that's too big to fit on one screen is to use a smaller font, and then resize the rows and columns to match:

1. Press Ctrl-A to select the entire worksheet, open the Font drop down on the toolbar, and select a smaller font.

2. While the entire sheet is still selected, choose Format → Column → AutoFit Selection.

3. While the entire sheet is still selected, choose Format → Row → AutoFit.

MAGNIFY A SELECTION

The Annoyance: I'm using a small range of cells in my worksheet, and I'd like to see just those cells, displayed as large as possible. I've been trying to use the Zoom field, but I can't get it right. Am I out of luck?

The Fix: Nope. Select the desired cells, and then follow these steps:

1. Choose View → Zoom to bring up the Zoom dialog box (as in Figure 1-16).

Figure 1-16. The Zoom dialog box gives you a list of zoom options to choose from.

2. Click Fit Selection.

3. Click OK.

MOVE TO THE LAST ROW IN A LIST

The Annoyance: I just imported a database table into my worksheet, but I don't remember how many rows were in the table. I hate scrolling through my worksheets without knowing how far I have to go. Isn't there a way that I can just go directly to the last row of the list?

The Fix: Press Ctrl-down arrow to go to the last cell used in the active column. You also can press Ctrl-up arrow to go to the first cell in the active column. Similarly, Ctrl-right arrow takes you to the last cell used in the active row, while Ctrl-left arrow selects the first cell used in the active row. Ctrl-End takes you to the bottom right corner of the worksheet; Ctrl-Home takes you to the very first cell (A1).

KEEP HEADERS CONSTANT AS YOU SCROLL

The Annoyance: I have a data list with nine columns that run down for several hundred rows. When I scroll down, the headers that tell me which columns contain which data scroll off the top of the screen, so I can't figure out which column is which. My friend, who used to work on the other side of my cube wall, knew how to keep all the top row headings visible on her worksheets no matter how far down she scrolled. But she got a better offer from another company and left last week without teaching me the trick. How did she do that?

The Fix: You can freeze one or more rows, columns, or both so that they remain visible when you scroll through a worksheet. To freeze one or more columns at the left edge of your worksheet, follow these steps:

1. Click the first cell in (or the column header of) the column to the right of the last column you want to freeze.

2. Choose Window → Freeze Panes.

To freeze one or more rows at the top edge of your worksheet, follow these steps:

1. Click the first cell in (or the row header of) the row below the last row you want to freeze.

2. Choose Window → Freeze Panes.

To freeze rows and columns along the top and left edges of your worksheet, follow these steps:

1. Click the cell below and to the right of the rows and columns you want to freeze (cell B3 in Figure 1-17).

2. Choose Window → Freeze Panes.

To unfreeze frozen rows and columns, choose Window → Unfreeze Panes.

Figure 1-17. It's easier to read worksheet data when the row and column headings stay visible as you scroll.

> You can't freeze columns and then freeze rows, or vice versa, using this technique. If you try, you'll see only the Unfreeze Panes item on the Window menu. To freeze columns and rows at the same time, you must click the cell below and to the right of the rows and columns you want to freeze.

You can create and manipulate these panes in freeform fashion using the mouse. Simply grab the small rectangular object just above the top arrow on the vertical scrollbar (the pointer changes to two lines with arrows on each side) and pull it down to just below the rows you want to freeze. Do the same with the small rectangular object just to the right of the right arrow on the horizontal scrollbar and drag it just to the left of the columns you want to freeze.

SEARCH A PORTION OF A WORKSHEET

The Annoyance: I'm the executive editor at a major computer book publisher, so I build and maintain some huge Excel workbooks. Some of the worksheets span 10 or 12 printed pages, with the columns tracking the date we offered a book contract, the date the signed contract was returned, the date we took delivery of the author's first-born, that sort of thing. My problem: when I want to find a date in a certain column, or even within a cell range, Excel insists on searching the entire worksheet. There's got to be a way to do pinpoint searching!

The Fix: I sympathize with your plight, since I suffer—er, benefit—at the hands of editors every day. Fortunately, you can limit your search to an area of a worksheet by selecting that area before you choose Edit → Find. If you want to search a column, for example, click the corresponding column header. To search a swath of the worksheet, just paint it out with your mouse, press Ctrl-F (the keyboard shortcut), and search away. Excel will highlight (or rather, "reverse" highlight) the found cell.

DIVIDE A WORKSHEET INTO MULTIPLE SCROLLABLE AREAS

The Annoyance: For some reason one of my co-workers put two different data sets on one worksheet. The first 50 rows hold data about our products, and rows 53–66 hold data about our suppliers. Moving either data set to another worksheet would mess up dozens of formulas in this and in other workbooks, but I'd love to be able to scroll around in the product rows, keep whichever row I want from that area on the screen, and still display the suppliers rows. Is there some way to make that happen?

The Fix: The trick is to divide your worksheet into two scrollable areas. Select the row below the last row you want in the top scrollable area, and choose Window → Split. The worksheet areas will have separate scrollbars, as shown in Figure 1-18, allowing you to view two entirely different areas of your worksheet at once.

You also can split the screen vertically using the same steps, except you select the column just to the right of the one you want in the left scrollable area.

To remove the split, choose Window → Remove Split.

While a workbook is split into panes, you can press F6 to move to the next pane in a clockwise direction, or press Shift-F6 to move to the next pane in a counter-clockwise direction.

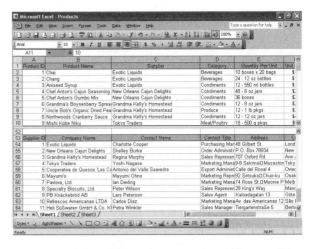

Figure 1-18. A split worksheet makes it easy to view widely separated data sets simultaneously.

DATA VALIDATION ANNOYANCES

RESTRICT DATA ENTRY WITH VALIDATION RULES

The Annoyance: I'm a manager at an engineering company, and I hired an out-of-work political science major to do data entry and other clerical stuff. We don't pay him a lot, but our deal is that he gets to learn about computers on our dime when he's doing data entry. There's only one problem: he types so badly that he makes a ton of mistakes—adding extra numbers, leaving some out, even hitting letters instead of numbers. Isn't there some way Excel can flag a mistake *before* he enters the data?

The Fix: The secret is using data validation. Click a cell (or a group of selected cells), and then turn on the validation feature by selecting Data → Validation and clicking the Settings tab. From the Allow drop-down menu, pick the type of validation criteria you want to use, and then specify its parameters from the drop-down menus that appear below. The type of validation you select in the Allow drop down determines what other options appear below. If you select Whole number, for example, you can specify whether the entered values should be *between* two other values, *not* between two other values, or *less than* or *greater than* a value. You can hard-code the value by picking "equal to" from the Data drop-down menu and typing the value into the Value field. Figure 1-19 shows the types of criteria you can create.

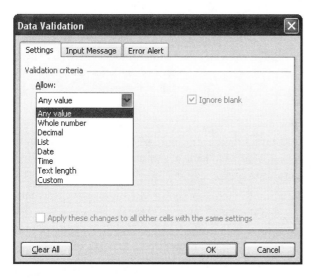

Figure 1-19. Limiting your colleague's actions was never so easy.

Some Special Data Formats

You can set four preset formats by choosing Format → Cells. Click the Number tab and select Special in the category list, and to the right you'll see Zip Code, Zip Code + 4, Phone Number, and Social Security Number. However, note that these special numbers change based on your computer's local language settings.

For instance, if he's supposed to be typing in Zip Codes, and you want to make sure he doesn't leave out digits or add extra ones, set the Text length validation rule to require a number between 5 and 5. If he's supposed to enter 94607 and he types 9460 by mistake, he'll receive an error message reading "The value you entered is not valid."

If you want to make sure he doesn't forget to enter data in a critical cell, uncheck the "Ignore blank" box in the Data Validation dialog. That forces him to enter *something* in the cell. (If you want, you can determine exactly what he needs to enter by selecting the appropriate entry in the Allow drop down.) If the "Ignore blank" box is grayed out, temporarily select anything except "Any value" in the Allow drop down; this makes the "Ignore blank" box accessible. After you uncheck it, you can return to "Any value" if you want, and the "Ignore blank" box, though grayed out, will remain unchecked so that he will have to enter something in the cell.

If you want to keep users from typing data into a cell, you can restrict them to selecting entries from a list. The trick: select List from the Allow drop-down menu. When you do, a field titled Source appears. You can define the list's values by either selecting a range of cells from the worksheet, or typing values into the Source field, with each one separated by a comma. Entries in the Source field can include spaces, semicolons, and almost any other character. The only character you *can't* use is the one that separates entries, i.e., the comma. For example, your list of categories might look like this: *Service Plans, Accessories, Sales, On-Site*.

CREATE A FORM TO EASE DATA ENTRY

The Annoyance: I'm a techie in training, but part of the deal I made with my employer is that I must perform a certain amount of data entry drudgery every day before I can learn anything interesting. The problem is that I *hate* entering data into a worksheet. I make mistakes. I lose my place. Can't I enter data into something that looks like the paper forms I have stacked right in front of me?

The Fix: Absolutely! All you need to do is select a data list in your worksheet, and Excel will use it to build a data entry form with an entry field for each item in your list. I guess your next question is probably going to be, "What's a data list?" I don't have a definitive answer for Excel 97, 2000, and 2002 (those versions of Excel don't recognize the concept officially), but I can show you something Excel *recognizes* as a list, and you can go from there. Figure 1-20 shows you a data list and the resulting data form.

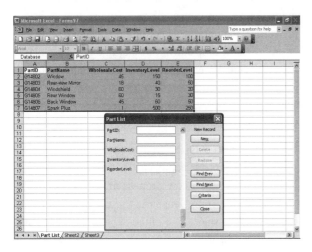

Figure 1-20. Data forms present a cleaner interface for entering data into your worksheets.

You should note several things about the data in the worksheet:

- As you can see in the figure, the headings in the first row of the list (PartID, PartName, and so on) turn into data entry fields.
- The columns in the data list either must butt up against the left edge of the worksheet, or there must be a blank column on each side of the data list.

> **t i p**
>
> You can test to see which cells Excel will include in your data list by clicking any cell in what you think is the list and pressing Ctrl-Shift-8. Basically, this tells you which group of cells meets the preceding criteria and which don't. For you VBA programmers out there, this is the equivalent of calling the `ActiveCell.CurrentRegion.Select` function when any cell in the list is the active cell.

To create a data entry form, select any cell or group of cells in your heading row and select Data → Form. Excel will create a form like the one in Figure 1-20. Type new data into the form and press Enter or click the New button, and the data is plugged into the worksheet. You can move from field to field in the form by pressing the Tab key, move to the previous field by pressing Shift-Tab, and move through existing data by clicking the Find Prev and Find Next buttons.

> **t i p**
>
> These instructions work if you want to create a data form in Excel 97, 2000, 2002, and 2003. Just remember that in Excel 2003, the term *list* refers to a data construct that takes advantage of that version's Extensible Markup Language (XML) capabilities. You'll learn more about how annoying Excel 2003 (in general) and XML (in particular) can be in Chapter 9.

BASE VALIDATION RULES ON FORMULA RESULTS

The Annoyance: I use a worksheet to track customer orders, and I'd love to add a validation rule to alert me when customers try to place orders that put them over their credit limit. I know I can create a formula in the cell next to the order total that would do this, but I'd rather use a validation rule so that I'm notified before I finish inputting the order. What's the secret?

The Fix:
You can use a formula as a validation rule. In this example, we'll assume the customer's outstanding balance is in cell C2, the credit limit is in cell C1, and the total price of the new purchase will be entered into cell C3. (You can adjust the formula to work with different layouts.)

1. Click C3, the cell where the price of the new purchase will be entered.

2. Select Data → Validation.

3. Click the Settings tab.

4. In the Allow drop-down menu, select Custom.

5. Type =SUM($C$2:$C$3)<=$C$1 into the Formula field, and click OK.

Now if the sum of the new purchase and the outstanding balance exceeds the customer's credit limit, Excel will display a data validation error message when you try to enter the new purchase.

The dollar signs in front of the column and row references ensure that those cell references won't change if you copy the formula. If the cell references were written as C2 and so on, the reference would change if you copied the rule to another cell. For more on relative and absolute references, see the annoyance named "Prevent Copied Formulas from Changing Cell References" in Chapter 3.

USE DATA IN ANOTHER WORKSHEET AS VALIDATION CRITERIA

The Annoyance:
I have the names of all 50 states in the U.S., plus the District of Columbia, in a list in one worksheet. What's killing me is that Excel won't let me use this list as the source for a "Pick from List" validation criterion in a cell on another worksheet! Isn't there some way to use a set of data from one worksheet as a source of validation criteria in another worksheet?

The Fix:
The trick is to define the list of states as a named range, which you then can refer to in the Data Validation dialog box's Source field. Here's how:

1. Select the cells that contain your valid entries.

2. Choose Insert → Name → Define to display the Define Name dialog box (shown in Figure 1-21).

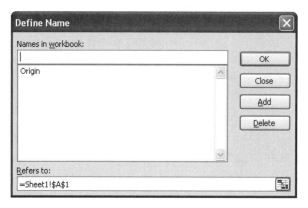

Figure 1-21. You can create references to groups of cells in the Define Name dialog box.

3. Type a name for the data range in the "Names in workbook" field, click the Add button, and then click OK.

4. Flip to the other worksheet, select the cells to which you're adding the validation criteria, and choose Data → Validation.

5. On the Settings tab, open the Allow drop-down menu and select List.

6. In the Source field, type an equals sign followed by the name of the named range (e.g., =States) and then click OK. Incidentally, range names are not case-sensitive, so =States and =states are considered the same thing by Excel.

AVOID DUPLICATE ENTRIES IN A COLUMN

The Annoyance:
I take inbound calls at a tech-support center, and we track the various callers by recording their phone number in a spreadsheet. The number of *different* callers is supposedly vital information, and

my boss is seriously annoyed if I accidentally enter a caller twice. How can I make sure I avoid duplicate entries in the list?

The Fix: You can create a data validation criterion that uses a formula to check for previous entries of the same value in the column—but you must prepare the worksheet before you enter any actual data. Here's how:

1. In whichever column you want to add the validation criterion (in this example it's column C) click the second cell (C2 in this case). This example assumes you're using row 1 for headings; if not, feel free to customize the formula in step 4 to start in a different cell.

2. Select Data → Validation.

3. In the Allow drop down, select Custom.

4. Type `=COUNTIF($C$2:$C$65536, C2)=1` in the Formula field, and click OK.

5. Grab the fill handle, and drag from cell C2 down as far as you want your no-duplicates validation rule to apply.

This formula starts by noting the value in cell C2 and counts the number of times the value occurs in the range $C$2:$C$65536. Because the formula checks the value in the active cell, there will always be at least one occurrence. However, if Excel finds two occurrences the program recognizes the value is a duplicate and rejects it.

Because of the way the cell designations are written, as you drag the formula down from cell C2, the range $C$2:$C$65536 remains constant from cell to cell because of the dollar signs in front of the column and row references. (For more information on relative and absolute references, see the annoyance named "Prevent Copied Formulas from Changing Cell References" in Chapter 3.) But C2 changes to C3 in cell C3, to C4 in cell C4, and so on. I chose the range $C$2:$C$65536 because an Excel worksheet can have up to 65,536 rows, so that range covers 'em all.

EXPLAIN DATA VALIDATION RULES

The Annoyance: I give each of my data entry staffers a printout listing the validation criteria for each cell in my workbook. But I'm still getting complaints because after a week or two they misplace the printout, and then when they enter the wrong data all the Excel error message says is: "The value you entered is not valid. A user has restricted values that can be entered into this cell." This is stupid! Isn't there some way I can get Excel to provide more specific error messages?

The Fix: Sure thing. You can create custom messages when you create your validation rules. The Data Validation dialog box has three tabs: Settings (which you use to create the validation rule), Input Message (which lets you display a dialog box when a user clicks a cell with the validation rule), and Error Alert (which displays various different alert boxes when the user attempts to enter an invalid value into the cell). So, there are actually two ways to skin your cat: using an input message or using an error alert.

You can use an input message to remind your data entry people what's supposed to go in a given cell. Here's how:

1. Click the cell you want to modify.

2. Choose Data → Validation, and click the Input Message tab.

3. Check the "Show input message when cell is selected" box.

4. Type a title and an input message in the fields provided. For instance, your message could say "Zip Codes only."

The only trouble with input messages is that they pop up every time a user enters a cell, even if they already remember what kind of data goes there. This can be, um, annoying.

If you prefer to correct users after they actually make a mistake, use the error alert box. There are three types of error alert boxes: Information, Warning, and Stop. (Figure 1-22 shows the three different styles of error alert boxes.) Here's how each one operates:

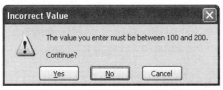

Figure 1-22. The type of error alert box you create determines whether a user can ignore your criteria.

Information

This box offers the user two choices: OK, which closes the dialog box, *enters* the invalid data, and moves the cell pointer to the next cell; and Cancel, which *deletes* the entry and keeps the pointer in the same cell. Unless you make the Title and Error Message text very specific, an information box can simply confuse the user more. For instance, it will help if the title reads something like "You were supposed to enter five numbers!" and the error message reads along the lines of "Clicking OK will enter the invalid data. Clicking Cancel will delete the entry and let you try again."

Warning

This error alert box, by contrast, indicates that the user has entered invalid data and asks if he wants to continue. The box has three buttons: Yes, which closes the dialog box, *enters* the invalid data, and moves the cell pointer to the next cell; No, which returns the user to the cell with the cell's contents highlighted; and Cancel, which *deletes* the entry and keeps the pointer on the same cell. As with the Information box, providing a helpful text message is a must.

Stop

This type of error alert box makes it impossible for the user to leave the cell while it contains invalid data (see Figure 1-23). The Stop box has two buttons: Retry, which returns the user to the cell with the cell's contents highlighted; and Cancel, which *deletes* the entry and keeps the pointer on the same cell. As in the two preceding examples, providing a helpful text message is a must.

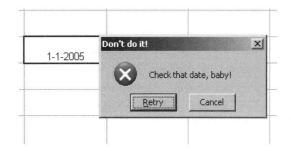

Figure 1-23. Error alert boxes appear only after someone enters invalid data.

The Other Rules

The Rules: Time-Tested Secrets for Capturing the Heart of Mr. Right, **is alternately praised as a key to successful dating for women and maligned as a manual for manipulating men. In either case, Amazon.com notes that many customers who bought this book also bought...*Comedy Writing Secrets* by Mel Helitzer.**

To create an error alert box, follow these steps:

1. Click the cell you want to modify.

2. Choose Data → Validation, and click the Error Alert tab.

3. Make sure the "Show error alert after invalid data is entered" box is checked.

4. From the Style drop down, select the type of alert you want to create, enter text for the title and error message in the fields provided, and click OK.

HIGHLIGHT INVALID WORKSHEET DATA

The Annoyance: I provide IT support for a building supply company, and one of my prime responsibilities is maintaining a spreadsheet with lots of customer information, including credit limits. Over the last six months I've entered several hundred records, but I just found out the minimum credit limit is supposed to be $1,000—and I *know* some of the customer records I entered listed credit limits lower than that. I added a validation rule to every cell in the column, requiring a number 1,000 or higher, hoping Excel would display all the cells with invalid data, but nothing happened. Do I have to go through the worksheet row by row to find values lower than $1,000? There's gotta be a faster way to find invalid data!

The Fix: In Excel 97 and 2000, you can tell Excel to circle any cells with invalid data by choosing Tools → Auditing → Show Auditing Toolbar. On the Auditing toolbar, click the Circle Invalid Data button to draw a red circle around any cell that contains invalid data (as shown in Figure 1-24).

In Excel 2002 and 2003 the menu items have changed a bit, but the process is basically the same: choose Tools → Formula Auditing → Show Formula Auditing Toolbar. On the Formula Auditing toolbar, click the Circle Invalid Data button to draw a red circle around any cells that contain invalid data.

To remove the circles, click the Clear Validation Circles button on the Formula Auditing toolbar.

COPY A VALIDATION RULE TO ANOTHER CELL

The Annoyance: I use Excel to track the hours volunteers work at a hospital. I created a named range that contains all their names, and I use that range as the source for my List validation rule. The problem is that I want to copy the validation rule, and just the validation rule, to another cell in my worksheet instead of having to re-create it. Please tell me there's a way to do that!

The Fix: To copy the validation rule from one cell to another, follow these steps:

1. Select the cell containing the validation rule, and choose Edit → Copy.

2. Select the target cells and choose Edit → Paste Special to display the Paste Special dialog box (shown in Figure 1-25).

3. Select Validation and click OK.

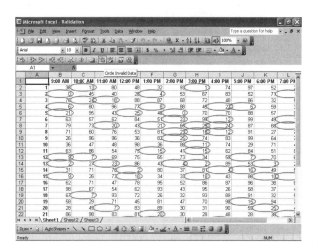

Figure 1-24. Excel identifies cells with data that violates the cells' validation rule.

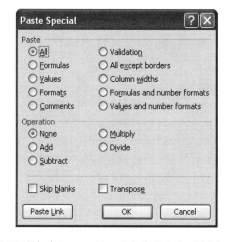

Figure 1-25. Pick what you want to paste in the Paste Special dialog box.

PREVENT EXCEL FROM SCROLLING TOO QUICKLY

The Annoyance: In every Windows version of Excel I've ever used, when I'm scrolling down through a workbook the scroll starts nice and slow for a second or two...before kicking into warp speed and leaving me thousands of rows further down than I wanted to be. How do I keep Excel from going turbo?

The Fix: This is a known bug in Excel 2002 and earlier versions. Microsoft *finally* fixed it in Excel 2003, but that doesn't help anyone with an earlier edition. If you have a wheel mouse, no problem: just use the wheel to scroll down at a perfectly controllable speed. If you *don't* have a wheel mouse, this is a perfect excuse to buy one! Come on, they're cheap!

If you insist on working with an older mouse, and still want to limit Excel's scrolling speed, I recommend clicking the scrollbar just above or below the slider to move up or down one screen at a time (the equivalent keyboard commands are Page Up and Page Down). Pressing Alt-Page Up moves you one screen to the left, while pressing Alt-Page Down moves you one screen to the right.

EXCEL FOR GOLFERS

One of my goals in writing *Excel Annoyances* was to give you more time for leisure pursuits—such as golf. DJI Computer Solutions released the first version of Handicap Manager for Excel in May 1997, and has been adding on to it ever since. The program can track scores and handicaps for multiple users and leagues, generate reports (including in HTML format), combine nine-hole scores for 18-hole handicapping, and more.

Three versions of the program currently are available:

- ☒ **Personal Version (up to 10 golfers), $19**
- ☒ **League Version (up to 100 golfers), $39**
- ☒ **Golf Club Version (unlimited golfers), $79**

You can download a fully working 30-day trial version from *http://www.djicomputer.com/ HandicapManager.htm*; after that, you'll need to buy a registration code to activate the program. DJI offers free or discounted upgrades between versions, depending on the age of your last registered version of the program.

Format
ANNOYANCES

2

When all is said and done, formatting objects in Excel is reasonably straightforward. The Formatting toolbar and the Format Cells dialog box make most common tasks pretty easy. But if you try to push Excel past the formatting basics, things can go wrong in a hurry. For example, for the longest time I didn't know how to work with Excel's color palette, that collection of mysterious and mysteriously repeating colors that appear in charts, graphs, and cell backgrounds.

Another aspect of Excel that took me a while to get a handle on was custom formats. No, not *conditional formats*, which change the appearance of a cell and its contents based on the value in the cell, but *custom formats* that control how Excel displays dates, times, and special information such as Social Security numbers and Zip Codes. You can use custom formats to establish some rules on how a cell's contents will be displayed, but you don't have nearly the variety of formatting options that are available to you through the Conditional Formatting dialog box.

This chapter includes more than 30 annoyance-fixes you can use to control the appearance of your workbooks, from a one-click method of wrapping text within a cell, to a macro that can find out exactly which colors are available in your workbook.

CELL FORMATTING ANNOYANCES

FORMAT PART OF A CELL'S CONTENTS

The Annoyance: OK, I'll come clean: I've been using Excel for only a couple of days, and I'm not that great with computers anyway. But I did finally figure out how to format a cell: I click it and do whatever I want with the buttons on the Formatting toolbar, or sometimes I choose Format → Cells and work with the Format Cells dialog box. But how do I format *part* of a cell's contents? There has to be a way to make a single word bold!

The Fix: This is so easy you'll kick yourself when I tell you. To format part of a cell's contents, click the cell to display its contents in the Formula Bar just above the worksheet and below Excel's toolbar. Select the characters you want to format *in the Formula Bar*, and use the buttons on the Formatting toolbar to change the characters' appearance. This might seem basic, but you'd be surprised how many folks miss this.

WRAP TEXT IN A CELL WITH JUST ONE MOUSE CLICK

The Annoyance: I create a lot of worksheets with longish text labels and explanations about the assumptions behind the data, so to wrap the text I end up choosing Format → Cells, clicking the Alignment tab, and then checking the "Wrap text" box...again and again and again. Isn't there some way to put the "Wrap text" checkbox on the toolbar? Four mouse clicks seems like a lot of work for such a frequent task.

The Fix: There really ought to be a "Wrap text" button in the Excel command bar system, but Microsoft hasn't provided one. In the meantime, you can attach the following macro to a custom toolbar button:

```
Sub WrapTextMacro()
 Selection.WrapText = True
End Sub
```

And, of course, to unwrap text, use this matching macro:

```
Sub UnWrapTextMacro()
 Selection.WrapText = False
End Sub
```

To find out how to attach the macro to a custom toolbar button, see "Run a Macro by Clicking a Toolbar Button or Menu Item" in Chapter 8.

CHANGE WORKSHEET TAB COLORS

The Annoyance: I work for a manufacturing company, and one aspect of my job is figuring out how much a new machine will cost to build. I keep each product on a separate worksheet in an Excel 2000 workbook. But because I get new (or updated) prices for many of the parts almost every day, it's a pain to remember which worksheets I've updated and which ones I haven't since the last time my project leader reviewed our progress. Is there any way I can change the color of a worksheet tab to flag which ones have been changed and which ones need updating?

The Fix: In Excel 2002 and 2003 you can change the color of a worksheet tab by right-clicking it, choosing Tab Color, and picking the color you want. (If you prefer to write a VBA procedure, you can use the Worksheet object's Tab property.) In Excel 97 and 2000, the worksheet tabs aren't exposed in the object model, so there's no way to change the tab's color. You can change a worksheet's name, though, simply by double-clicking the worksheet's tab and typing the new worksheet name. So, the best workaround for these earlier versions is to add an asterisk or some other character to the worksheet's name to flag its condition.

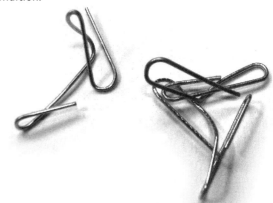

CONDITIONAL FORMATTING ANNOYANCES

CHANGE CELL FORMATTING BASED ON THE CELL'S VALUE

The Annoyance: I'm a commercial gardener and I use Excel to track the temperature in my greenhouses. I want to automatically flag any hours during which the temperature is less than 75 degrees by displaying that cell's value in red text. How do I do it?

The Fix: Conditional formatting is one of Excel's handiest features. To change a cell's formatting based on its contents, follow these steps:

1. Select the cells you want to format and choose Format → Conditional Formatting to display the Conditional Formatting dialog box, shown in Figure 2-1.

Figure 2-1. Use the Conditional Formatting dialog box to change how your data looks based on its value.

2. Open the second drop-down menu and choose the comparison operator (between, less than, greater than, or equal to) you want to use to evaluate your data. Then type the associated values (the values the data is between, less than, greater than, or equal to) in the third and fourth boxes. (The fourth box doesn't always appear; it depends on the Boolean operator you pick.) For this example, select "Less than" from the second drop-down menu, and in the box to the right, type in the value 75.

3. Click the Format button to tell Excel how it should format cells with values of less than 75. You can specify color, font style, underline, and strikethrough. Click OK when you're done.

4. Click OK to apply the format, or click the Add button to create up to two more rules for the cell. (You could, for instance, apply another Boolean operator, such as greater than, to flag numbers less than 75 but greater than, say, 25.)

EXCEL APPLIES THE WRONG CONDITIONAL FORMAT

The Annoyance: I'm a casino host with thousands of players who want to pit their rabbits' feet against my employer's statistical advantage. I like to display my customers' credit limits in different colors, based on how much they're good for, but the conditional format I created (shown in Figure 2-2) doesn't get the colors right. My formula checks whether the player's credit limit fits the three listed criteria and should display the limit amount in gold for players with limits of at least $1 million, blue for players with limits of at least $500,000, and green for players with limits of at least $100,000. What am I doing wrong?

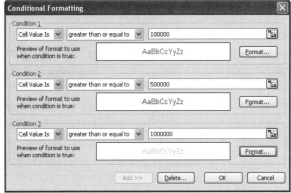

Figure 2-2. This badly constructed conditional formula incorrectly formats the cells of players with limits of more than $500,000.

The Fix: Excel applies the conditions from first to third, and the conditional formats shown in Figure 2-2 are in the wrong order. Put the most restrictive condition at the top of the list (players with limits of $1 million), then the second ($500,000), and then the third ($100,000). The correct way to structure this conditional format is shown in Figure 2-3.

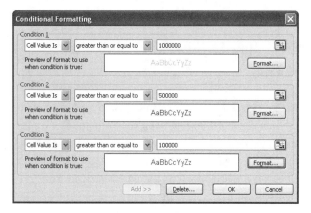

Figure 2-3. This version of the same conditional format works correctly. The criteria should progress from most restrictive to least restrictive.

LOCATE CELLS WITH CONDITIONAL FORMATS

The Annoyance: I work for a firm that specializes in data mining and natural-language processing. My expertise is in topic identification, which basically means I write code that scans newspaper and magazine articles and makes intelligent guesses about the articles' subject area based on the words used. One worksheet I created for my presentation to our review board uses hundreds of conditional formats to highlight how improved accuracy in one area cascades to other areas. It took me hours to set them up, and now that my presentation is over I need to find the cells with the conditional formats and return them to their original formats—but I'm slammed and don't have hours to spend. How do I find those cells?

The Fix: To find cells with conditional formatting, choose Edit → Go To, click the Special button, select Conditional Formats, and click OK. All cells with conditional formatting will be highlighted.

TEMPLATE ANNOYANCES

CREATE A WORKBOOK TEMPLATE

The Annoyance: I create worksheets for many different projects, but they all have the same basic layout (shown in Figure 2-4) and formulas. I'd like to save the general layout of the workbook (one worksheet for each month, the color scheme, the formulas, etc.) so that I don't have to go through the rigmarole of saving the base workbook under a new name. It gets even worse when I press Ctrl-S as a reflex after I delete the data but before I save the workbook under its new name. Isn't there some way to create a template I can call up like the ones that come with Excel?

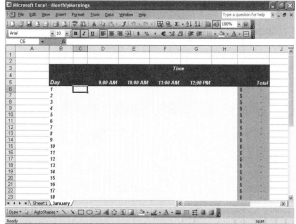

Figure 2-4. This could be a template—but how do you call it up when you need it?

The Fix: To create a workbook template, follow these steps:

1. Create the workbook with all headings, labels, and such, but without data.

2. Choose File → Save As, and in the "Save as type" box, select Template (*.xlt).

3. Verify at the top of the dialog box that in the "Save in" dropdown, the Templates folder is selected. Type a name for the template in the "File name" box below and click the Save button.

After you save a workbook template, you can create a new workbook based on that template. The precise steps you follow depend on the version of Excel you're using:

- In Excel 97 or 2000, choose File → New and in the General tab, double-click the desired template.

- In Excel 2002, choose File → New to display the New Workbook task pane, shown in Figure 2-5. Click General Templates and then double-click the template you want to use.

Figure 2-5. In Excel 2002, you go through the New Workbook task pane to get to the list of available templates.

- In Excel 2003, choose File → New to display the New Workbook task pane and then click On My Computer to open the Templates dialog box.

CREATE A WORKSHEET TEMPLATE

The Annoyance: I created a workbook with 12 formatted worksheets and saved it as a workbook template. Works great! But occasionally I need to add worksheets with a similar format to other workbooks. Why can't I create a work*sheet* template instead of a work*book* template?

The Fix: To create a worksheet template, build the worksheet, delete all other worksheets in the workbook (just right-click the worksheet's tab and select Delete), and choose File → Save As. In the "Save as type" box, select Template (*.xlt). To add a worksheet based on that template to a workbook, right-click any sheet tab, choose Insert, and double-click the template you want from the General pane.

COLOR MANAGEMENT ANNOYANCES

REPLACE REPEATED COLORS IN THE EXCEL COLOR PALETTE

The Annoyance: I'm the vice president of sales and marketing of a 5,000-person corporation, and I want my assistant to create a pie chart that shows the relative sales percentages of our 70 products. I've finally gotten over the fact that Excel can display only 56 colors at a time. Really, I have. But what I *truly* hate is that the color palette has some repeat colors in it. I need every color I can get! Can I replace those repeat colors in the Excel color palette with new ones?

The Fix: You can, indeed. The repeat colors in the Excel palette, listed by `ColorIndex` value, are:

- Color 32 (repeats Color 5, Blue)
- Color 27 (repeats Color 6, Yellow)
- Color 26 (repeats Color 7, Magenta)
- Color 28 (repeats Color 8, Cyan/Aqua)
- Color 30 (repeats Color 9, Dark Red)
- Color 29 (repeats Color 13, Violet)
- Color 31 (repeats Color 14, Teal)
- Color 54 (repeats Color 18, Plum)
- Color 34 (repeats Color 20, Light Turquoise)

To change colors in the Excel color palette, follow these steps:

1. Choose Tools → Options and click the Color tab to see the current workbook's color palette. Figure 2-6 shows the positions of the repeat colors in the default Excel palette (the repeats are crossed out).

2. Click the color you want to replace and click the Modify button.

3. In the Colors dialog box, click the desired replacement color. If you don't see the color you want or if you want to enter a precise RGB value, click the Custom tab (see Figure 2-7). (RGB is an abbreviation for "Red, Green, Blue," which are the three primary colors of light.)

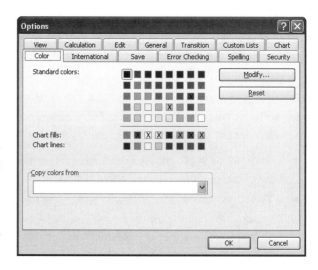

Figure 2-6. "X" marks the spot of a repeat color in Excel's palette.

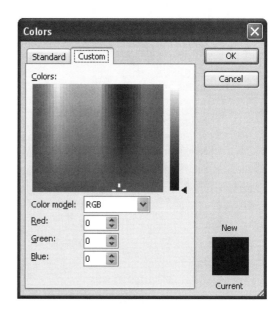

Figure 2-7. When you know the exact color you want, use the Custom tab to define it.

4. To define your color, go to the Custom tab and click near the color you want in the Colors box. Then go to the vertical color bar to the right and pick the exact color you want. Another approach: type the values for the red, green, and blue components of the color in the appropriate boxes at the bottom of the Custom tab.

TRANSLATE BETWEEN COLOR PALETTE POSITION, COLOR NAME, AND COLORINDEX VALUE

The Annoyance: I'm an Excel VBA programmer, and I just found out the colors in the default Excel color palette are *not* arranged by the value of their ColorIndex property. Instead, the darker colors are arranged at the top of the palette and the lighter colors are at the bottom. That means I can't just look at the palette and count the colors to know which value I should set as the ColorIndex property. Is there any way to find out the ColorIndex property value for each color in the default palette?

The Fix: Excel keeps an internal list of the colors in a workbook's color palette; that list is called the *Color Index*. Black is color 1, white is color 2, red is color 3, and so on. When you program in VBA, you change an object's color by assigning a new value to its ColorIndex property. Table 2-1 shows the ColorIndex value and name (where available) of each position in Excel's default color palette.

Excel doesn't re-sort the colors in the palette if you make a change, so the mapping of palette position to ColorIndex value stays constant.

COPY ANOTHER WORKBOOK'S COLOR PALETTE

The Annoyance: I've finally created an Excel color palette with 56 colors I like—but I can't figure out how to copy that palette to another workbook!

The Fix: To copy a color palette from one workbook to another, follow these steps:

1. Open the workbook with the color palette you want to copy.

2. Open the workbook with the color palette you want to change.

3. In the workbook whose color palette you want to change, choose Tools → Options, click the Color tab, and open the Copy Colors From drop-down menu to display a list of open workbooks. Choose the workbook with the color palette you want to copy from, and click OK.

Table 2-1. Mystery solved: which ColorIndex value and name go with which spot on the Excel color palette?

1 Black	53 Brown	52 Olive Green	51 Dark Green	49 Dark Teal	11 Dark Blue	55 Indigo	56 Gray 80%
9 Dark Red	46 Orange	12 Dark Yellow	10 Green	14 Teal	5 Blue	47 Blue-Gray	16 Gray 50%
3 Red	45 Light Orange	43 Lime	50 Sea Green	42 Aqua	41 Light Blue	13 Violet	48 Gray 40%
7 Pink	44 Gold	6 Yellow	4 Bright Green	8 Turquoise (Cyan)	33 Sky Blue	54 Plum	15 Gray 20%
38 Rose	40 Tan	36 Light Yellow	35 Light Green	34 Light Turquoise	37 Pale Blue	39 Lavender	2 White
17	18 Plum	19	20 Light Turquoise	21	22	23	24
25	26 Pink	27 Yellow	28 Turquoise (Cyan)	29 Violet	30 Dark Red	31 Teal	32 Blue

DISPLAY THE RGB VALUES OF COLORS IN A WORKBOOK'S COLOR PALETTE

The Annoyance: I'm a run-of-the-mill spreadsheet guy, but my client has me working with a high-end graphic designer, and *she* asked me to give her a list of the RGB values of each color in my workbook's color palette so that she can use those colors in her work. Sheesh! How in the world can I do that without spending an hour with a pencil and a yellow pad?

The Fix: This macro writes to the active worksheet the RGB values of each color in your workbook's color palette:

```
Sub PrintRGBValues()

Dim intNumColor As Integer
Dim strHexVal, strRGBVal As String

    'Create the column headers.
    Range("A1").Select
    ActiveCell.Formula = "Color"
    ActiveCell.Offset(0, 1).Formula = "Index"
    ActiveCell.Offset(0, 3).Formula = "Red"
    ActiveCell.Offset(0, 4).Formula = "Green"
    ActiveCell.Offset(0, 5).Formula = "Blue"

    ActiveCell.Offset(1, 0).Activate

    For intNumColor = 1 To 56

    ActiveCell.Offset(0, 1).Formula = _
    Str(ActiveCell.Interior.ColorIndex)
    ActiveCell.Offset(0, 3).Value = rgbVal And &HFF
    ActiveCell.Offset(0, 4).Value = rgbVal \ &H100 _
    And &HFF
    ActiveCell.Offset(0, 5).Value = rgbVal \ _
    &H10000 And &HFF
    ActiveCell.Offset(1, 0).Activate
    Next intNumColor
    End Sub

    ActiveCell.Offset(1, 0).Activate

    Next intNumColor
    End Sub
```

Alert! This macro will overwrite all existing data in your worksheet! To avoid this, create a new worksheet, copy the color palette from the original sheet as noted earlier in this chapter, and then run the PrintRGBValues macro on the new sheet. The result is shown in Figure 2-8.

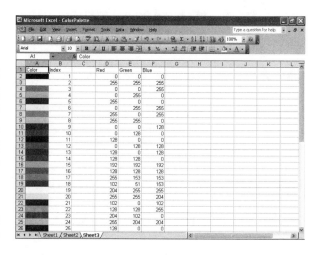

Figure 2-8. No more guessing about RGB values with this accurate report.

MANAGE COLORS AND FORMATS WITH A CUSTOM ADD-IN

The Annoyance: I'm a visual person, so formatting a cell by writing code or clicking checkboxes in the Format Cells dialog box really annoys me. Is there some way for me to see the colors and font settings I'm creating as I create them—and then apply them quickly? Plus, can I save these formats to a toolbar button?

The Fix: The good folks at OzGrid Business Applications have, in fact, created just such a tool—one that works with every version of Excel from 97 to 2003. The Cell Color Assistant adds a new toolbar that holds color and formatting combinations (font color, background color, bold, italic, underline, and default text) you've created. Figure 2-9 shows a version of the Cell Color Assistant toolbar with six (of a maximum 50) formats added. (The Cell Color Assistant costs $19.95, but you can buy it as part of larger add-in collections to save lots of money.)

Figure 2-9. The Cell Color Assistant puts formats at your fingertips.

To install the Cell Color Assistant toolbar, follow these steps:

1. Get OzGrid's Cell Color Assistant by visiting *http://www.ozgrid.com/Services/excel-cell-color.htm*.

2. To install the Cell Color Assistant, double-click the installation file and follow the directions in the installation wizard.

3. In Excel, choose Tools → Add-Ins, check the Cell Color Assistant box, and click OK.

After you install the Cell Color Assistant, you can create a format, assign it to a button on the toolbar, and apply the format by clicking the button. Simply follow these steps:

1. If necessary, choose View → Cell Color Assistant to display the Cell Color Assistant toolbar.

2. Click the Create Color Buttons button (it looks like a color wheel), select "Add or change a button" on the Cell Color Assistant toolbar, and click OK.

3. Click the button you want to change and click OK to display the Cell Color Assistant dialog box (shown in Figure 2-10).

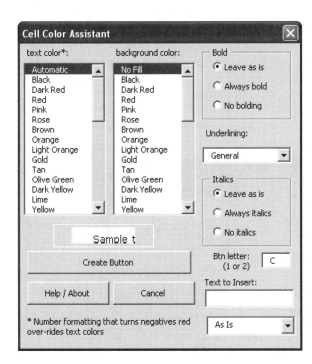

Cell Color Assistant

Figure 2-10. The Cell Color Assistant dialog box enables you to pick the color, other formatting, and background color of a cell's contents.

4. Make your choices and click OK to add the button to the toolbar.

To apply a format to selected cells, click the Cell Color Assistant toolbar button that represents the desired format.

The Cell Color Assistant dialog box lets you search for cells with the same format as a selected cell. To perform a search:

1. Select the cells you want to search for a given format.

2. Click the Create Color Buttons button on the Cell Color Assistant toolbar, choose the "Select fonts based on color" option, and click OK to display the Format Select Options dialog box (shown in Figure 2-11).

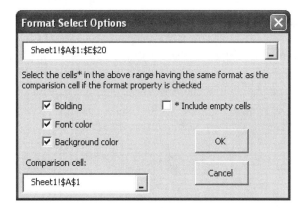

Figure 2-11. Define the options for your format search in the Format Select Options dialog box.

3. Check the boxes representing the attributes you want to match.

4. Click the Comparison Cell box, click a cell with the desired format, and click OK to have the add-in select each cell that shares the format characteristics you chose.

WORKBOOK FORMATTING ANNOYANCES

CHANGE EXCEL'S DEFAULT FONT

The Annoyance: Arial, the font Excel uses by default, is great for reading on my computer screen, but it doesn't look that good on paper when I print budget reports. How do I change the default font?

The Fix: Microsoft apps generally default to Arial because the text is easy to read onscreen—there's lots of space in the font's characters and the lines are thin. To change Excel's default font, choose Tools → Options, click the General tab, and in the "Standard font" drop down pick a new font from the list (see Figure 2-12). If you're dreaming about characters that look good in print, try Times New Roman or Courier. Other fonts that look good on screen and on paper include Verdana and Tahoma. Unfortunately, there's no way to set one font as your on-screen default and another font as your printout default.

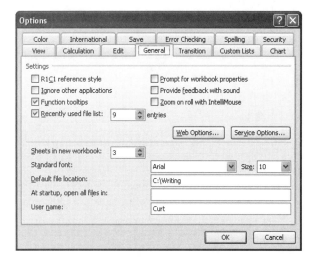

Figure 2-12. You can change the standard font when you print a workbook, and change back when you're ready to continue working on your computer.

If you send a workbook to other users who don't have your new font installed on their computers, Excel displays the name of your font in the Font drop-down menu on the toolbar, but displays the workbook using the user's standard font.

HOW TO TELL A STYLE FROM A FORMAT

The Annoyance: I use the currency format for cross-tabular worksheets because I like to have the dollar sign right next to the numbers. Then, for lists, I use the accounting format, which puts the dollar sign at the left edge of the cell, out of the way of the numbers. However, when I click the Currency Style button on the Formatting toolbar, Excel applies the accounting format. Is this a bug? How do I get Excel to apply the currency format like it promised?

The Fix: It's easy to be confused by the Currency Style button and how it operates, but in fact, the button acts correctly. The problem is that Excel uses the very similar terms *style* and *format* to mean different things. Clicking the Currency Style button doesn't actually apply the Currency format you find in the Format Cells dialog box: it applies the Currency style. Excel has a limited range of built-in styles, which you can see by choosing Format → Style and opening the "Style name" drop down (shown in Figure 2-13).

To format a cell in the Currency format, press Ctrl-Shift-4.

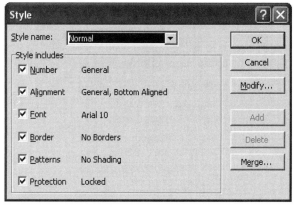

Figure 2-13. The Style dialog box contains Excel's built-in styles.

SIMPLIFY EXCEL FORMATTING WITH STYLES

The Annoyance: I'm a project manager at a consulting firm that requires us to format our data, data labels, and headings using the same style, whether we create a table in Word or a worksheet in Excel. I've got a good handle on creating styles in Word, but how do I do it in Excel?

The Fix: To create a style in Excel, follow these steps:

1. Choose Format → Style to display the Style dialog box.

2. Type a unique name in the "Style name" drop down and click the Modify button.

3. Use the controls in the Format Cells dialog box to define your style, click the OK button, and then click the Add button.

To apply the style, select the cells you want to format, choose Format → Style, pick the style from the "Style name" drop-down list, and click OK.

PICK AND CHOOSE WHICH STYLE ELEMENTS TO APPLY

Excel actually gives you a unique style option that you don't get in Word or PowerPoint: you can select which elements of a style to apply to a cell and save that unique combination of formatting as a new style. The Style dialog box, shown in Figure 2-13, has checkboxes that correspond to each tab in the Format Cells dialog box (Number, Alignment, Font, Border, Patterns, and Protection). Unchecking a box means the settings on that tab page—as defined by the style you've created—won't be applied the next time you use it.

SEARCH FOR CELLS WITH SPECIFIC FORMATTING

The Annoyance: I'm a new hire at an engineering firm, and I'm supposed to revise my predecessor's files for the final project report. My problem is that he formatted certain cells in boldface using the Times New Roman font, which looks an awful lot like another format used throughout the worksheet (boldface in the Tahoma font). Finding all the Times New Roman cells and changing them is making me insane. Help!

The Fix: If you're using Excel 2002 or 2003, you're in luck! To replace the formatting in worksheet cells, just follow these steps:

1. Choose Edit → Replace, and click the Options button to display the expanded Find and Replace dialog box. If you can identify a cell with the exact format you're looking for, click the down arrow at the right edge of the Format button next to the Find What box, select Choose Format from Cell, and click the cell with the target format.

2. If you can't immediately identify a cell with the exact format you're looking for, use the controls in the Find Format dialog box to set the format you want to find, and click OK.

3. Click the Format button to the right of the Replace With box and set the replacement format.

4. Click the Find All button to list the address of every cell with the format you want to replace (shown in Figure 2-14). Then click the Replace All button to replace every instance of the format or the Find Next button to select the next cell in the worksheet with the format, and click Replace.

There's no easy way to search for cells by format in Excel 97 and 2000, but you can use the fact that most formatting in Excel involves the appearance of data in a cell. In Excel VBA, the Font object records a cell's text formatting. The most useful properties of the Font object for our purposes are:

- Bold, which you can set to either True or False

- Italic, which you can set to either True or False

- `Name`, which is the name of the font (e.g., Arial or Times New Roman)

- `Size`, which is the text size in points

- `ColorIndex`, which reflects the color of the text

You also can test a cell's fill color using the `InteriorColor.ColorIndex` property.

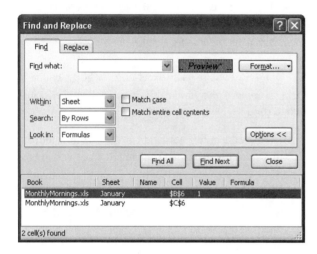

Figure 2-14. When you click Find All, the addresses of cells that meet the search criteria appear at the bottom of the Find and Replace dialog box.

To find and select all cells on the active worksheet with the same font characteristics and cell fill color, click a cell with the appropriate formatting and run the following `FindFormatting` macro. Once you do this, you can use the controls on the Formatting toolbar, or in the Format Cells dialog box (choose Format → Cells), to reformat the selected cells.

```
Sub FindFormatting()
Dim MyCell As Range
Dim strCellList, strFontName, strLastCell _
As String
Dim strUsedRange, strCellStyle As String
Dim intSize, intColorIndex, intFillColor _
As Integer
Dim blnTest, blnBold, blnItalic As Boolean

With ActiveCell.Font

  strFontName = .Name
  intSize = .Size
  intColorIndex = .ColorIndex
  blnBold = .Bold
```

```
  blnItalic = .Italic
End With

intFillColor = ActiveCell.Interior.ColorIndex

  With ActiveSheet.Cells
    strLastCell = _
    .SpecialCells(xlCellTypeLastCell).Address
  End With

  strCellList = ActiveCell.Address
  strUsedRange = "$A$1:" & strLastCell

For Each MyCell In Range(strUsedRange).Cells
blnTest = False
 If MyCell.Font.Name = strFontName Then
  If MyCell.Font.Bold = blnBold Then
   If MyCell.Font.Italic = blnItalic Then
    If MyCell.Font.ColorIndex = intColorIndex
Then
     If MyCell.Font.Size = intSize Then
      If MyCell.Interior.ColorIndex =
intFillColor _
       Then blnTest = True
      End If
     End If
    End If
   End If
  End If
 End If

If blnTest = True Then _
  strCellList = strCellList & ", " & _
  MyCell.Address
End If

Next MyCell

On Error Resume Next
Range(strCellList).Select

If Err Then MsgBox ("Couldn't select cells. " &
_
  "There may be too many " _
  & "cells with this format.")
End Sub
```

THE CASE OF THE VANISHING GRIDLINES

The Annoyance: I inherited a workbook from a co-worker who, for some reason, hid all the gridlines in every worksheet in the workbook. It's almost impossible to make sense out of the worksheet's data without the gridlines! How can I bring them back?

The Fix: To display a worksheet's gridlines, choose Tools → Options, click the View tab and make sure the Gridlines box is checked, and click OK. Gridlines still hiding? Take a look at the Color drop-down menu at the bottom of that View pane. If your gridlines are defined as the same color as the background (usually white), choose Automatic (the default) or another contrasting color from the palette to make them visible.

Fingerprinting Cells

The FindFormatting **macro doesn't check every formatting element of a cell to see if it fits the pattern. It checks only the five most common attributes. It's the same with fingerprinting. When comparing two fingerprints, investigators don't look for a complete match—they look for 10 unique points in each fingerprint that match.**

HIDE AND UNHIDE ROWS AND COLUMNS

The Annoyance: I use several columns of formulas in my worksheet, and although they need to be there for the sheet to work, I don't want them to actually *appear* in the worksheet. Is there some way I can hide those rows or columns so that no one can see them?

The Fix: No problem. To hide a row or column, right-click its header column and choose Hide. When you want to redisplay the row or column, select the headers of the rows above and below the hidden row (or the columns to the left and right of the hidden column), right-click, and choose Unhide. If you hide Column A, you must press Ctrl-A to select the entire worksheet before you right-click Column B's heading and choose Unhide.

If you want to make sure prying eyes are kept away from those hidden rows or columns, you can require users to enter a password. To set a password to unhide hidden rows or columns, display the worksheet with the hidden rows or columns, choose Tools → Protection → Protect Sheet, type a password into the "Password (optional)" box, and click OK. Anyone who wants to reveal those hidden rows or columns will find the Unhide command grayed out. To get to it, first they'll have to select Tools → Protection → Unprotect Sheet, and supply a valid password.

If you try to hide a row and a column at the same time, you'll hide every cell in the worksheet. To bring the worksheet back, click Format → Column → Unhide.

HIDE AND UNHIDE SHEETS

The Annoyance: I like to use a named range as the source for validation rules that require my users to enter data by picking entries from a list. What I *don't* like is having to put those lists in the body of the workbook for everyone to see. I'm not worried about my colleagues editing the lists; I just think the extra worksheet where I keep the lists shouldn't clutter up the long series of worksheet tabs. Is there any way to keep the worksheet in the workbook, but keep it out of view?

The Fix: To hide one or more worksheets, select the sheets' tabs (using either Ctrl-Click or Shift-Click), and choose Format → Sheet → Hide. To unhide the sheets, choose Format → Sheet → Unhide, select the sheets to unhide, and click OK. If you want to keep the hidden sheet away from prying eyes, you can require users to enter a password to change the worksheet's structure. To set a password to unhide hidden sheets, choose Tools → Protection → Protect Workbook, type a password in the "Password (optional)" box, and click OK. To remove the protection, choose Tools → Protection → Unprotect Workbook and type the password in the dialog box that appears.

CUSTOM FORMAT ANNOYANCES

CREATE CUSTOM NUMBER DISPLAY FORMATS

The Annoyance: I keep the statistics for my rec-league hockey team. One of the statistics I'm always asked about is "plus/minus," which is the number of times you're on the ice when your team scores a goal (a plus) minus the number of times you're on the ice when the other team scores (a minus). I want to display the negative numbers in red, as usual, but our team color is green and I'd like to display the positive numbers in green. Oh, and I'd like to display text values, such as a note that someone hasn't played yet, in blue. How do I do it?

The Fix: To define a custom format, choose Format → Cells, select Custom in the Category list, and enter your custom codes in the Type box. You can specify up to four format codes in a custom format. The codes apply (in order) to positive numbers, negative numbers, zero values, and text. In your case, the format to display positive numbers in green, negative numbers in red, and text in blue is `[Green](###);[Red](###);;[Blue]"Has not played"`.

As you can see, a semicolon separates each format. Because you don't require special handling for zero values, I left that element empty (that's why there's nothing between the second and third semicolons). If you specify only two codes, Excel assumes the first is for values of zero or greater and the second is for negative numbers. If you specify only one code, Excel uses it for any value in the cell.

The available number codes are:

- #, which tells Excel to display only significant digits and not to display insignificant zeros (e.g., a cell with the code ### would display 035 as 35).
- 0 (zero), which tells Excel to display insignificant zeros if a number has fewer digits than there are zeros in the format (e.g., a cell with the code 000 would display 035 as 035).

- ?, which adds spaces for insignificant zeros on either side of the decimal point (such as 0.035) so that decimal points align when formatted with a fixed-width font, such as Courier New.

You can use the following eight colors in a custom format: white, black, red, blue, yellow, green, cyan, and magenta. But don't try to specify more than three sets of custom formats for a given cell; Excel simply won't accept them. For that you'll have to use VBA.

Formats Don't Change the Underlying Data

It's important to remember the distinction Excel makes between a cell's contents and how those contents are displayed. For example, if you type the value .3 in a cell, Excel can display the value as 0.3 (the General format), 30% (the Percent format), $0.30 (the Accounting format), or 0.300 (if you require three digits to the right of the decimal point, including insignificant zeros). None of the formats changes the underlying value of .3; it's all in how you want to present that value to the user.

ADD TEXT TO A DISPLAYED NUMERICAL VALUE

The Annoyance: I track my bakery's ingredients inventory, which includes bags of flour, cans of almonds, and pounds of butter. I can enter each description into the cell (e.g., "120 bags"), but Excel then treats the entry as text, not a number. I know how to count each item in my inventory (by can, by bag, by pound, etc.), so what I'd like to do is add a word such as *units*, *bags*, or *cans* after the value in the cell. Is there some way to add text to the contents of a cell and still have Excel treat the value as a number?

The Fix: You can add text to the value of a cell by following these steps:

1. Choose Format → Cells and select Custom in the Category list.

2. In the Type box, you'll see General, which is the default value. Immediately after it, type `" units"` (including the quotes and the space after the first quote). The entry should read `General" units"`.

3. Click OK.

The format you just created will put the word *units* behind any value you enter into the cell—but Excel still will treat the value you entered as a number, not text. Of course, you can substitute any word you want for *units*, such as *bags*, *cans*, or *pounds*.

You also can create a format that changes depending on the value typed into the cell. To create such a format, you add conditions enclosed in square brackets in front of each partial format, and separate the segments with a semicolon. For example, the format `[<>1]General" units";[=1]General" unit"` will cause Excel to follow the value 1 with the word *unit* and values other than 1 with the word *units*.

What's interesting about this type of custom format is that Excel adds the text (in this case, *units*) to the result of any formula that uses the value, as shown in Figure 2-15. In the first column, both cells (B2 and B3) have the `[<>1]General" units";[=1]General" unit"` format applied, so the result (in B4) has that format as well. In the second column, only the top cell (D2) has the custom format, but the formula result cell still takes on the custom format. In the third column, however, the Accounting format was applied to the result cell (F4), which overrides the custom format. In fact, any built-in format will take precedence over a custom format.

Figure 2-15. You can easily create a custom format that mixes numbers and text—yet the numbers still are treated as numbers.

ROUND VALUES WITHOUT USING THE ROUND( ) FUNCTION

The Annoyance: I'm a currency broker, and I often perform calculations using currency values that have three or more digits after the decimal point. I've been trying to create a custom format to round up the result of my calculations to hundredths of a dollar, but so far nothing I've tried works. My time is too valuable to waste on hacking my worksheet. Can you help?

The Fix: To format a cell so that it rounds up calculations to hundredths of a dollar, choose Format → Cells, select Custom in the Category list, and type `#.##` in the Type box. In a custom format, the # symbol displays only significant digits, does not display insignificant zeros, and rounds up the value if the number of digits after the decimal point exceeds the number of # signs. For example, the format #.## will display 12.1 as 12.1, 12.12 as 12.12, 12.123 as 12.12, and 12.126 as 12.13.

If you want to display a set number of digits after the decimal point, you can use the 0 (zero) character, which displays insignificant zeros if a number has fewer digits than there are zeros in the format. For example, the format #.00 will display 12.5 as 12.50, and the format 00000 will display 15 as 00015. The format #.00 also rounds up values, so 12.565 is displayed as 12.57.

ROUND VALUES TO THE MILLIONS AND DISPLAY "MILLIONS" AFTER THE VALUE

The Annoyance: I prepare the annual report for a multinational corporation, and all the dollar values on the summary sheets are in millions, even when they're less than $1 million. Can I create a custom format to display in millions up to the first two decimal places after the values are rounded? In other words, I'd like to display the value $12,256,119 as $12.26 million and the value $12,201,000 as $12.2 million.

The Fix: You can create a custom format using the thousands separator (the comma, when the local language is set to U.S. English) in combination with other codes. The thousands separator hacks off three zeros each time it occurs in the code, so the code `#,` will display 3100 as 3. To fix this specific annoyance, the code to display up to the first two digits after the decimal with a dollar sign in front and the word *million* after the rounded value is `$#.##,," million"`.

ALIGN NUMBERS IN A COLUMN BY DECIMAL POINT

The Annoyance: I work in a chemistry lab and I use an Excel spreadsheet to track the results of precipitation experiments (chemical precip, not rain measurement; rain is meteorology). My supervisor requires three things:

- The data must be accurate to three digits after the decimal point.
- The decimal points in the numbers must align regardless of the number of digits before or after the decimal point.
- The data must display only significant digits (no trailing zeros).

I was good until that last requirement, but now I can't figure out how to make the alignment happen. Is it possible?

The Fix: It's possible. You can format a cell so that it adds spaces to your values instead of zeros by creating a custom format that includes question marks and displays the contents of the cell in a fixed-width font such as Courier New. For example, the format #.??? will display the values 12.123, 12.12, and 12.1, all lined up by decimal point, as shown in Figure 2-16. As with other custom number formats, the ? symbol causes Excel to display a value rounded to the same number of decimal places as there are question marks. In this case, 12.1235 will be displayed as 12.124.

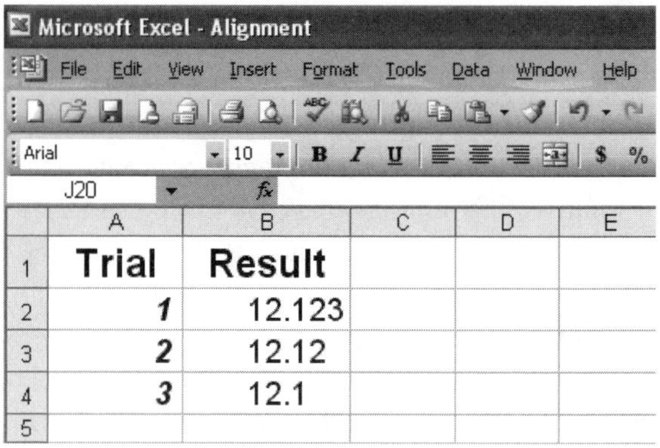

Figure 2-16. Use the question mark character to align cell values around the decimal point, without worrying about trailing zeros.

CREATE A CUSTOM DATE FORMAT

The Annoyance: I need to enter a date in my Excel 2000 spreadsheet and keep it in a particular format: 2003-12-01. Excel insists on changing it to a format that it prefers (12/1/2003). I tried changing the cell format to General, and it looked like it accepted the new format I specified. But the next time I tried to put in the value, the software changed the format *back* to 12/1/2003! This is maddening! How do I tell Excel that dates are supposed to look like 2003-12-01?

The Fix: You can create custom formats so that Excel knows how to format data in the pattern you define.

To create a custom format that requires dates to follow the 2003-12-01 style, follow these steps:

1. Choose Format → Cells, click the Number tab , and click Custom from the Category list to display the list of custom formats shown in Figure 2-17.

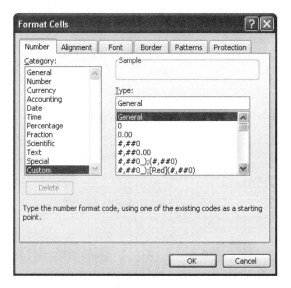

Figure 2-17. Create custom formats using the tools in the Format Cells dialog box.

2. Type yyyy-mm-dd in the Type box, and click OK.

Table 2-2 lists the codes used to create date-related special formats.

Table 2-2. Excel's custom-format elements for dates.

Display	Code
Months as 1–12	M
Months as 01–12	mm
Months as Jan–Dec	mmm
Months as January–December	mmmm
Show only first letter of month	mmmmm
Days as 1–31	D
Days as 01–31	Dd
Days as Sun–Sat	ddd
Days as Sunday–Saturday	dddd
Years as 00–99	Yy
Years as 1900–9999	yyyy

CREATE CUSTOM TIME FORMATS

The Annoyance: I track web site usage for a small company that gets about 15,000 hits per day. My manager is very interested in the amount of time each visitor spends on the site. I've figured out how to more or less differentiate one visitor from another, but my boss wants me to display each visitor's total time on the site in minutes, even if the number of minutes goes more than an hour. I formatted the column with the format code mm:ss, but when I tested it by typing 00:72:00 (no hours, 72 minutes, and no seconds) into a cell in the column, Excel disregarded the hour component and displayed the time as 12:00, not 72:00. How do I make Excel display the elapsed time as 72:00?

The Fix: To format a cell to display a time in minutes, even if that time exceeds an hour, use the custom code [mm]:ss. Table 2-3 lists the codes you can use to create custom time formats. Use the procedure listed in the previous annoyance-fix to create your custom time format.

Table 2-3. Use these format codes to create a custom time format.

Display	Code
Hours as one or two digits (9, 10)	H
Hours as two digits (09, 10)	Hh
Minutes as one or two digits (9, 10)	M
Minutes as two digits (09, 10)	Mm
Seconds as one or two digits (9, 10)	S
Seconds as two digits (09, 10)	Ss
Hours as one digit followed by AM or PM	h AM/PM
Time as 4:36 PM	h:mm AM/PM
Time as 4:36:03 P	h:mm:ss A/P
Elapsed time in hours (36.14)	[h]:mm
Elapsed time in minutes (78.45)	[mm]:ss
Elapsed time in seconds (14892)	[ss]
Fractions of a second (maximum three digits after the decimal)	h:mm:ss.000

Chapter 3 solves additional problems encountered when using dates and times in Excel.

SETTING DATE AND TIME USING OTHER LOCAL RULES

The Annoyance: My manager asked me to create workbooks in which some of the worksheets use the U.S. date system of month/day/year as the default, and other worksheets use the German (and European) default of day/month/year. I'm using Excel 2002. Can I change the local language for individual cells, or do I have to do it for an entire workbook?

The Fix: You're in luck. Excel 2002 and 2003 allow you to format just a group of selected cells to use a time, date, or special format that's particular to another region. (Unfortunately, Excel 97 and 2000 lack this talent.) Here's how:

1. Select the cells you want to format.

2. Choose Format → Cells, and in the Number tab, select Date, Time, or Special in the Category list.

3. Open the "Locale (location)" drop-down menu and select a country to see the available formats in the Type list (Figure 2-18 shows the result for dates in France).

4. Click the desired format and then click OK.

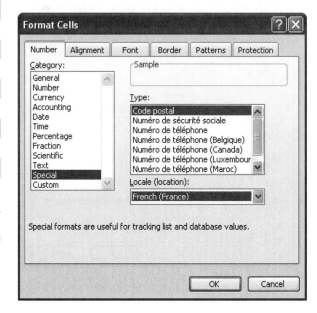

Figure 2-18. The time, date, and special formats you see depend on which locale you pick.

APPLY SPECIAL FORMATS FOR ZIP CODES

The Annoyance: Is there a special format I can use to let Excel know the data I'm about to enter is a five-digit or nine-digit Zip Code? I enter a lot of customer contact information for our mailing list. Our private customers usually know only their five-digit Zip Code, but the corporate customers usually know their nine-digit Zip Code.

The Fix: To format a cell to expect Zip Codes, choose Format → Cells, and in the Number tab, select Special from the Category list. Then you can select Zip Code (for five-digit Zip Codes) or Zip Code + 4 (for nine-digit Zip Codes). Excel expects values of either five or nine digits, so it adds leading zeros if you don't enter them—or if Excel removed them when you entered the data. Special formats for Social Security numbers and phone numbers also are available.

LEVERAGE ZIP CODE INFORMATION

Marketing is all about knowing who your customer is, and increasingly, knowing *where* that customer is. That's why more and more stores ask for your Zip Code when you're at the checkout counter. With that information in hand, a company can figure out how many customers are from the same area and what their shared interests might be. For companies that deliver products, use direct mail, or have a squadron of traveling salespeople, calculating distances between Zip Codes is especially useful. If your company fits that profile, you might want to turn to Zip Code Tools at *http://www.spheresoft.com/zipcodetools*. This $49 add-in from Spheresoft not only calculates distances between Zip Codes, but also can provide a list of Zip Codes within a certain radius. Another related tool worth considering is Spheresoft's $25 Zip Code Demographics add-in. Based on the 2000 census, this database of basic demographic information is aimed squarely at direct marketers who need to hone their mailing lists. The program can generate an array of information based on Zip Code data, such as population, average household income, housing units, total land area, and more. Because Zip Code Demographics works as an add-in, you call on its features as you would any other built-in Excel function (such as =SUM). For more information, go to *http://www.spheresoft.com/zipcodedemographics/*.

ADDING CUSTOM FOREIGN CURRENCY SYMBOLS

The Annoyance: I support an auto-racing team, so I work with a lot of international suppliers who list their product prices in euros, yen, and British pounds. I know I can use Insert → Symbol in Excel 2002 and later (or the Character Map helper application in Excel 97 and 2002) and pick the symbol I want to use when I'm entering data into a worksheet. But I can't figure out how to add the symbols to a custom format. How do I do it?

The Fix: If the symbol you want to use is sitting in a worksheet cell already, you can copy the symbol and paste it into the Type box. If it isn't, take the following steps (while in the Type box) to add a currency symbol to a custom format using the keyboard:

1. Make sure your keyboard's Number Lock key is turned on.

2. Hold down the Alt key and type one of the following codes *using the numeric keypad* (this won't work if you type the numbers using regular keyboard keys):

   - 0128 for the € (euro) symbol
   - 0163 for the £ (pound) symbol
   - 0165 for the ¥ (yen) symbol

3. Type the number code to represent the amount, such as #.00 to represent a currency amount with two decimal places (the # symbol displays significant digits only, while the 0 character displays insignificant zeros, displaying 14 as €14.00).

For more information on how to enter symbols into a cell, see the annoyance "Add Symbols to Your Excel Worksheet" in Chapter 1.

You can find the current exchange rate for a wide range of currencies at *http://www.xe.com/*.

GET AROUND IN OFFICE

You many have noticed that in Office 2002, Microsoft introduced the Task pane, which appears at the right edge of Office documents and lets you perform common tasks such as creating new documents and opening recently viewed files. That's handy, but you can do better if you use Office 2000, XP/2002, or 2003. The Office Navigator add-in (*http://www.sharewareorder.com/Office-Navigator-download-download-19980.htm*) is a file, folder, and template manager that puts a ton of options at your fingertips. For example, Office Navigator can list the last 200 files and the last 20 folders you opened. You can add new file types, control shortcuts, load templates with a click, customize file views by folder, and more. Office Navigator is available as a free download, but the $24.95 registration fee buys you future upgrades and eliminates nag screens.

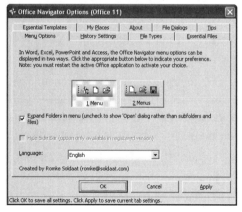

Get maximum control of Office's files, folders, and templates with Office Navigator.

PLAY PAC-MAN IN EXCEL

If you are a child of the 1980s like I am, you probably spent half of your teen years playing *Pac-Man*, maneuvering that friendly yellow character through a maze and eating power pellets so that you could gain enough strength to gobble up four monsters (Inky, Pinky, Blinky, and Clyde) and win the game. I was delighted to find an Excel version of *Pac-Man* at *http://www.xl-logic.com/pages/games.html* (scroll down to the *paccyman_v1.zip* item and download it; it's a separate workbook complete with instructions). The game runs a little slowly on PCs with anything less than a 1GHz P4 chip, but the playing field in this version looks exactly like the original game. Very cool.

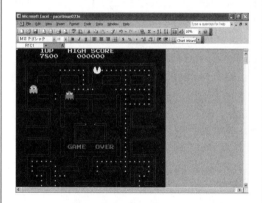

Pac-Man in Excel? You bet. Just download a free workbook and you're back in 1980. All hail Namco for keeping me off the streets as a middle-schooler!

Formula
ANNOYANCES

Transforming the data in your worksheets using formulas is what Excel does best. What could be annoying about that? Lots! Take one horrible example: consider what happens when you create a formula in one cell and copy it to another cell. If you don't build the formula just right, the cell references in the formula might change based on where you pasted the copied formula! I'll show you how to prevent this and other annoyances from happening.

Dates and times can present significant challenges in formulas. The arithmetic isn't particularly hard—it just doesn't always work the way you'd expect it to. Excel uses an exotic numerical system to refer to dates that seems totally arbitrary. But don't worry: you'll learn how to deal with this and other Excel quirks by the time you finish this chapter.

Finally, you'll learn how to wrestle array formulas to the ground. This is one of Excel's most powerful tools and one of the most annoying, because array formulas can be way confusing at first. But once you understand them, they end up saving you a lot of time.

FORMULA ENTRY AND EDITING ANNOYANCES

PREVENT COPIED FORMULAS FROM CHANGING CELL REFERENCES

The Annoyance: I track sales for a department store using the worksheet shown in Figure 3-1. My boss asked me to highlight sales for the jewelry department, so I copied the formula from cell F15 to cell F18—but the formula changed from `=SUM(F3:F14)` to `=SUM(F6:F17)`. I'm screwed! How do I keep that formula from changing?

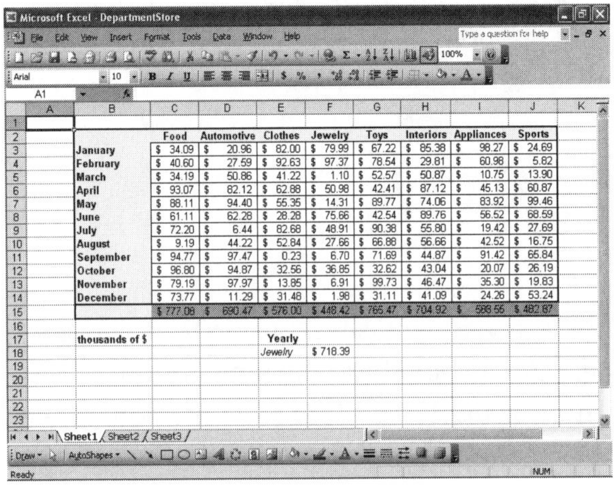

	Food	Automotive	Clothes	Jewelry	Toys	Interiors	Appliances	Sports
January	$ 34.09	$ 20.96	$ 82.00	$ 79.99	$ 67.22	$ 85.38	$ 98.27	$ 24.69
February	$ 40.60	$ 27.59	$ 92.63	$ 97.37	$ 78.54	$ 29.81	$ 60.98	$ 5.82
March	$ 34.19	$ 50.86	$ 41.22	$ 1.10	$ 52.57	$ 50.87	$ 10.75	$ 13.90
April	$ 93.07	$ 82.12	$ 62.88	$ 50.98	$ 42.41	$ 87.12	$ 45.13	$ 60.87
May	$ 88.11	$ 94.40	$ 55.35	$ 14.31	$ 89.77	$ 74.06	$ 83.92	$ 99.46
June	$ 61.11	$ 62.28	$ 28.28	$ 75.66	$ 42.54	$ 89.76	$ 56.52	$ 68.59
July	$ 72.20	$ 6.44	$ 82.68	$ 48.91	$ 90.38	$ 55.80	$ 19.42	$ 27.69
August	$ 9.19	$ 44.22	$ 52.84	$ 27.66	$ 66.88	$ 56.66	$ 42.52	$ 16.75
September	$ 94.77	$ 97.47	$ 0.23	$ 6.70	$ 71.69	$ 44.87	$ 91.42	$ 65.84
October	$ 96.80	$ 94.87	$ 32.56	$ 36.85	$ 32.62	$ 43.04	$ 20.07	$ 26.19
November	$ 79.19	$ 97.97	$ 13.85	$ 6.91	$ 99.73	$ 46.47	$ 35.30	$ 19.83
December	$ 73.77	$ 11.29	$ 31.48	$ 1.98	$ 31.11	$ 41.09	$ 24.26	$ 53.24
	$ 777.08	$ 690.47	$ 576.00	$ 448.42	$ 765.47	$ 704.92	$ 586.56	$ 482.87

thousands of $		Yearly	
		Jewelry	$ 718.39

Figure 3-1. When you copy this formula from cell F15 to cell F18, it changes to include the wrong cells.

The Fix: The formula changed when you copied it because you used *relative references* in the original formula instead of *absolute references*. In the worksheet shown in Figure 3-1, if you copied the formula from cell F15 to E15, Excel would change it to `=SUM(E3:E14)`, which is correct. If, however, you wrote the formula as `=SUM($F$3:$F$14)`, Excel would copy the formula as `=SUM($F$3:$F$14)` no matter where you moved it. The dollar sign in front of a row or column designator indicates the reference is an *absolute reference*, which should not change when the formula is copied. Thus, to ensure the formula in cell F15 copies correctly, you should write it as `=SUM($F$3:$F$14)`.

You can mix absolute and relative references in a cell designation, so (for example) the rows referenced could change but the columns couldn't. Some of the possibilities:

- `$A$1` keeps both the row and column constant.
- `$A1` keeps the column constant but allows the row to vary.
- `A$1` keeps the row constant but allows the column to vary.
- `A1` allows both the row and column to vary.

TOGGLE BETWEEN RELATIVE AND ABSOLUTE REFERENCES

The Annoyance: A friend just taught me about using absolute references so that cell designations won't change when I copy the formula somewhere. The only trouble is that last week I created a worksheet including several dozen complicated formulas using relative references because I didn't know any better. Is there any way to change relative references to absolute references without typing a dollar sign in front of each column and row designator?

The Fix: To change formula references from relative to absolute, click the cell that contains the formula, select the entire formula on the Formula Bar, and press F4. This even works if you want to change a range's reference type. Just highlight the range on the Formula Bar and press F4. Keep pressing it to see different variations.

Pressing F4 when a formula is highlighted changes the references in this order:

- Absolute rows and columns (`$A$1`)
- Absolute rows and relative columns (`A$1`)
- Absolute columns and relative rows (`$A1`)
- Relative rows and columns (`A1`)

REFER TO CELLS ON ANOTHER WORKSHEET

The Annoyance: I pride myself on my self-control, *BUT I WILL TOTALLY BLOW A GASKET* (ahem!) if I can't figure out how to reference a cell from another worksheet or workbook in a formula.

The Fix: To use cells from another worksheet or workbook in a formula, follow these steps:

1. Begin entering the formula in the active cell (e.g., =SUM($C$14+)).

2. Navigate to the other workbook or worksheet that contains the cell or range you want to reference. The formula you started entering should remain on the Formula Bar (as shown in Figure 3-2).

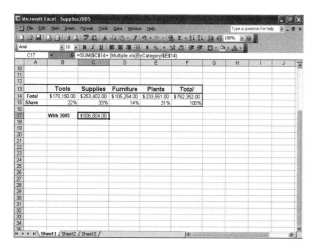

Figure 3-2. Excel adds the complete cell reference (including workbook and worksheet name) when you reference a cell in another workbook.

3. While you're in the other workbook or worksheet, select the cells you want to reference in the formula and press Enter. Excel will complete the formula in the first worksheet and even close any open parentheses.

The reference you create when you click a cell in another worksheet in the same workbook follows the pattern "SheetName!Cell" (e.g., AllData!F25). If you click a cell in another workbook, the reference follows the pattern "[WorkbookName]SheetName!Cell" (e.g., [FormulaTest2. xls]Sheet1!$A$3).

There are a couple of important details to note about the cell references you create. The first is that Excel's default behavior is to create an external link to a cell in the same workbook with a relative reference, but with links to cells in other workbooks it uses an absolute reference. The second detail worth noting is that the full name of the external workbook, including the file extension, is in the reference—you just can't see it at first. Until you save and close the workbook, the full path of the file—even if the workbook is in another folder—doesn't appear in the reference. Once you save, close, and reopen the workbook, the full path of the external file appears in the formula. In either case, if you move or rename the external workbook, the link will fail.

LEARN R1C1 NOTATION

The Annoyance: I inherited a workbook from a former co-worker, including a monthly sales worksheet for three departments at our auto dealership, shown in Figure 3-3.

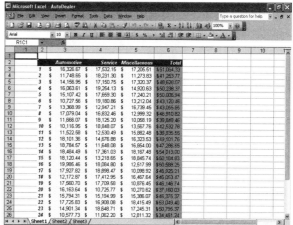

Figure 3-3. What evil lurks in the heart of this worksheet?

The worksheet works fine, but the formulas are weird. For example, the formula in cell C34, which I think is supposed to calculate the sum of cells in the range C3:C33, is =SUM(R[-31]C:R[-1]C). How do I read this formula, and should I change it back to =SUM(C3:C33), which I do know how to read?

The Fix: Excel has two systems for defining cell references: *A1 notation* and *R1C1 notation*. A1 notation, the default system, identifies cells by noting the intersection of a lettered column and a numbered row. R1C1 notation, in which both rows and columns are numbered, is a holdover from older spreadsheet programs. The systems get their names from the address of the cell at the top lefthand corner of the worksheet—A1 in standard notation, R1C1 (Row 1, Column 1) in R1C1 notation. When a workbook uses R1C1 notation, the column headers have numbers instead of letters. (See Figure 3-3.)

Although it's fairly easy to read cell references in R1C1, that system handles relative references differently than A1. In R1C1, you use numbers in brackets after the row or column marker (R or C) to indicate which direction and how far to go to find the referenced cell. Negative numbers tell you to move up or to the left, while positive numbers tell you to move down or to the right. For example, `=SUM(R[-31]C:R[-1]C)` in cell R34C3 starts the range 31 rows up and in the same column (at cell R3C3), and ends at cell R33C3.

To use R1C1 notation, choose Tools → Options, click the General tab, and check the "R1C1 reference style" box. To return to A1 notation, uncheck the checkbox.

CREATE A REFERENCE TO A PIVOTTABLE CELL

The Annoyance: I like to use PivotTables in my presentations because they let me rearrange the worksheet data dynamically as I speak. Unfortunately, I can't figure out how to link to a cell in a PivotTable in Excel 2000.

The Fix: It's easy to create links to PivotTable cells in Excel 2002 and 2003, but in Excel 97 and 2000 it's a lot harder. You can't exactly create a link to a cell, but there is a way to find the value you want. One way is to pivot the PivotTable so that it appears exactly the same as the source data list, as shown in Figure 3-4. Then find the cell with the value you want to use in the formula, and link it to the cell in the source data list instead of the cell in the PivotTable.

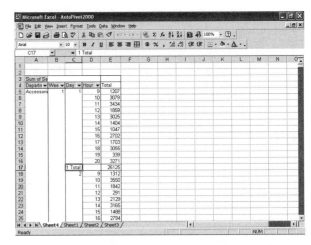

Figure 3-4. When you make your PivotTable look like the original source data, you can cut and paste the values for use in a formula.

Another tack: create a new worksheet named PivotCopy to hold a copy of your PivotTable data. Then select the entire PivotTable, press Ctrl-C, choose Edit → Paste Special, and then click the Values radio button. This pastes the values from the PivotTable into your new PivotCopy worksheet. When you need to create a formula, instead of linking to the PivotTable, link to the appropriate cell in the PivotCopy worksheet.

For more PivotTable annoyances, see Chapter 4.

DEFINE THE INTERSECTION OF TWO RANGES IN A FORMULA

The Annoyance: I need to track how frequently different groups of workstations are used during different times of day at my Internet café. I use the worksheet shown in Figure 3-5. My problem is that I need to find the average usage for certain workstations at certain times of the day as efficiently as possible. For example, I might want to know the average usage for Workstations 14 and 15 (rows 19 and 20) between the hours of 1:00 PM and 3:00 PM (columns G and H). To do that now I use a formula such as `=AVERAGE(G19:H20)`, and it's a pain to have to run my index finger along the rows and the columns to find different intersections of rows and columns—and to remember those cell addresses long enough to type them into every formula that's like this. The formulas are hard to parse, too! All this would be much easier if I could have the formula find the cells at the intersection of the ranges by itself. Is there any way to tell Excel to operate on the cells at an intersection of two ranges in my worksheet? Or (better yet) at the intersection of two named ranges?

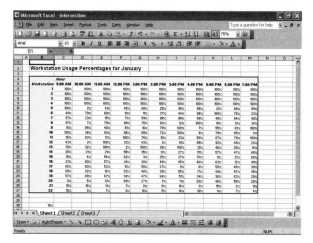

Figure 3-5. It's useful to be able to refer to cells that mark the intersection of two ranges.

The Fix: You can have Excel use the intersection of two ranges in a formula. Just separate the ranges with a space. When a space is used in a formula argument where Excel expects a range of cells, the program treats the space as an intersection operator. To find the average usage of Workstations 14 and 15 (rows 19 and 20) during the 1:00 PM and 2:00 PM hours (columns G and H), create the formula =AVERAGE(C19:M20 G6:H27).

You also can use the intersection operator to have Excel find the intersection of two named ranges. If the ranges in the previous formula were named WKST14, WKST15, PM1, and PM2, you would create the formula =AVERAGE(WKST14: WKST15 PM1:PM2).

I explain how to write a macro that creates named ranges from your worksheet labels and data in the "Named Range Annoyances" section later in this chapter.

NEST FUNCTIONS WITHIN FUNCTIONS

The Annoyance: Excel has a nice little dialog box that appears when you choose Insert → Function (shown in Figure 3-6). This makes it really easy to write functions because once you select the function you want a box pops up that lets you enter the function's parameters. However, if the parameter you want to enter is the result of another function—in short, if you want to nest a function inside another function—you have a problem. The dialog box doesn't let you select a function as a parameter to another function. Basically you have to remember the syntax of the function you want to nest and type it in—and usually, by the time I'm halfway into writing the second function I forget how I want the first one to go.

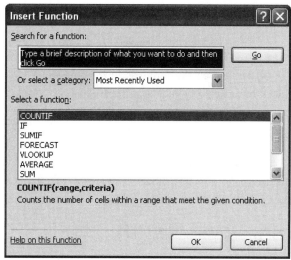

Figure 3-6. The Insert Function dialog box works wonderfully, but only for one formula at a time.

The Fix: It would be great if you could open a second instance of the Insert Function dialog box—but you can't. The best workaround is to create the nested function first, put it in a cell, and copy it to the Clipboard before you begin creating the main function with the Insert Function dialog box. Then you can simply paste it in. Another technique, if you've got plenty of memory, is to start two instances of Excel and switch between the two dialog boxes.

DELETE A FORMULA AND KEEP THE RESULT

The Annoyance: I created a worksheet with lots of random data to demonstrate a point to a colleague. As it happens, the demo is quite useful, and I'd like to keep it as is, but the `RAND()` functions I put into the worksheet keep generating new values every time I change something in the worksheet—and sometimes they aren't as good as the values I have now. How do I freeze the values I have in the worksheet now?

The Fix: To replace a formula with its result, click the cell with the formula, choose Edit → Copy and then Edit → Paste Special, and select the Values radio button to paste the value in the cell where the formula was. This procedure works for multiple cells, too.

MARK CELLS THAT CONTAIN A FORMULA

The Annoyance: I used the Paste Special feature to replace all the formulas in my worksheet with values, but I suspect I might have missed a few formulas. Is there a way I can get my worksheet to highlight all the cells that still contain a formula?

The Fix: To show every cell in the active worksheet that contains formulas, choose Edit → Go To, click the Special button, and select Formulas.

DISPLAY FORMULAS IN CELLS

The Annoyance: Sometimes, when I show my workbooks to my colleagues, I want to display the formulas, but I hate having to click each "formula" cell one by one. My solution is to type the formula (but without the equals sign at the front) in a cell just below, or next to, the cell with the actual formula. This is totally tedious, and it doesn't look that great either. Isn't there some way I can get Excel to toggle between its normal mode and one in which it displays the actual formulas in all the cells?

The Fix: To display the formulas in a workbook instead of the formulas' results, choose Tools → Options, select the View tab, and in the "Window options" section

check the Formulas box. This procedure also removes all number formatting from the worksheet. A sample of what a worksheet in this view would look like is shown in Figure 3-7.

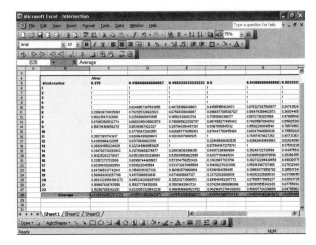

Figure 3-7. You can display the formulas in your worksheet without taking up additional cells.

DROP YOUR OWN PROCEDURE INTO A FORMULA

The Annoyance: I use a VBA procedure to calculate employees' commissions, but when I try to drop that procedure into an Excel formula it doesn't work. Before I spend another afternoon staring at Excel error messages and contemplating mayhem, can you tell me what I'm doing wrong?

The Fix: Make sure you're doing a couple of things right. First, you need to create a code module to store your VBA function. Press Alt-F11 to run the Visual Basic Editor. In the Visual Basic Editor, choose Insert → Module, and type or paste your code into the module. Press Ctrl-S to save your work, and then choose File → Close to return to Microsoft Excel.

Next, be sure you created or pasted a *function procedure* and not a *sub procedure*. A sub procedure doesn't return a value that can be used in a formula. A function procedure, by contrast, is designed to return a result that can be used by another function in a formula. For example, you could create the formula =AVERAGE(SUM(A1:A3)+SUM(B1:B3)+SUM(C1:C3)), which uses three instances of the SUM function to create values that the AVERAGE function uses to calculate its result. An example of a function procedure is:

```
Function Divide(Value1, Value2) As Single

Divide = Value1 / Value2

End Function
```

It's important to note that you must assign the result of the function's calculations to a variable with the same name as the function (in this case, Divide). If you assign the result to another variable, such as sngResult, the function always will return 0.

This function accepts two inputs, which it recognizes as Value1 and Value2. In most cases, those inputs will be cell references. The Divide function returns its value as a single-precision decimal number, which it calculates using the formula in the body of the function. If your procedure is indeed a function, and the function is in one of the active workbook's VBA code modules, you can insert the function into a cell by typing the function as part of a formula (e.g., =DIVIDE(A1,A2)) or by selecting it in the Insert Function dialog box and filling in the arguments, as shown in Figure 3-8.

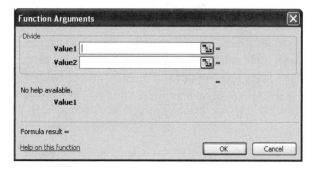

Figure 3-8. When you define your own functions, Excel creates an interface you can use to fill in its arguments.

Finally, make sure your function procedure isn't restricted from view. When you put the Private keyword in front of

a function procedure's opening line, such as Private Function Divide(Value1, Value2) As Single, you can't use the function in a worksheet formula.

For more information on the Private keyword, see the "Prevent a Procedure from Being Called from Another Workbook" annoyance in Chapter 8.

PERFORM THE SAME OPERATION ON A GROUP OF CELLS

The Annoyance: I own one-third of an Internet café. Tomorrow night I need to present a workstation-by-workstation profit summary to my two partners, and I thought it would be neat to divide all the values in the worksheet by 3 to illustrate how much each of us made from each computer. Is there a way to divide each "profit total" cell in my worksheet by 3 without creating a series of formulas in another part of the workbook?

The Fix: The Paste Special dialog box contains option buttons you can use to add, subtract, multiply, or divide the contents of the cells that are highlighted. To divide those cells by 3, for instance, follow these steps:

1. Type the value 3 in a cell outside the range you want to affect. Then, click that cell and select Edit → Copy.

2. Select the cells with the values you want to divide.

3. Choose Edit → Paste Special and click the Divide radio button (it's in the Operation section).

If you use the Paste Special dialog box operation on a cell that contains a formula, Excel adds the operation to the formula. For example, if the formula in a cell is =AVERAGE(C3:C26), performing the operation described in this fix makes the formula =(AVERAGE(C3:C26)/3).

MONITOR WATCH VALUES

The Annoyance: I'm a stock market day trader, so I created an Excel web query that draws data from a stock quote site to update my portfolio values worksheet.

I'd like to keep some of the values in that worksheet visible whenever I'm in Excel, even if I'm working on another workbook with the stock values worksheet minimized or hidden behind another window. Is there a way to watch just those values without creating a VBA procedure?

The Fix: In Excel 2002 and later, you can use the Watch Window to view the values in selected workbook cells. Here's how:

1. Choose Tools → Formula Auditing → Show Watch Window and click Add Watch.

2. Type the address of the cell (or cells) you want to watch into the "Select the cells that you would like to watch the value of" field, or click the Collapse Dialog button and select the cells you want to watch.

3. Click Add to have Excel create a watch for each cell selected. One possible result is shown in Figure 3-9.

Figure 3-9. You can watch cells from several workbooks in the same Watch Window.

To delete a watch, click the watch and then click the Delete Watch button in the Watch Window.

If you're using Excel 97 or 2000, the easiest way to set up your own Watch Window is to create a separate workbook with links to the cells you want to monitor, and then resize the workbooks so that your tracking workbook appears next to any other workbooks you have open. Figure 3-10 shows what that arrangement might look like. If you run your monitor at very high resolution, you might be able to find an even better arrangement.

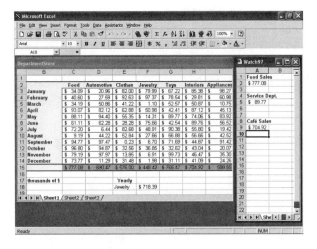

Figure 3-10. A separate workbook serves quite well as a Watch Window in Excel 97 and 2000.

ADD COMMENTS TO A FORMULA

The Annoyance: I'm a firm believer in documenting everything I do in a workbook, whether that means adding text boxes with directions on how to fill out a form, or adding comments to a VBA procedure so that my colleagues can understand what I've done (or where I messed up). But I can't seem to add comments to complex Excel formulas. There's gotta be a way.

The Fix: Unless you're satisfied with adding a comment to the cell *containing* the formula, there's no elegant way to add a comment *within* most Excel functions. There is one way that you can add a comment to some formulas: the N function, which is designed to return a value converted to a number. When you put text enclosed in double quotes inside the N function's parentheses, Excel returns an empty (null) string. If the value 100 was in cell A1 and the value 200 was in A2, the formula =A1+A2+N("These are the busiest hours of the day.") would return 300. Because the N() function always returns zero when a quote-enclosed string is in the parentheses, you can add the +N(string) function to any formula without affecting the result.

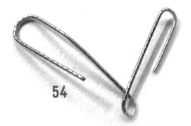

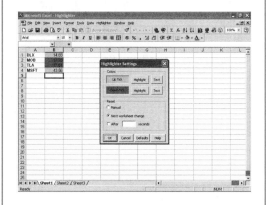
IMPROVE EXCEL'S STATISTICAL ACCURACY

The Annoyance: I am by no means a professional statistician, but I do a lot of statistics. I read an article that said Excel's statistics functions are woefully inadequate, particularly when computing standard deviations, which is one of the basic statistical calculations. Is there any way around this problem?

The Fix: B. D. McCullough and Berry Wilson discussed Excel's statistics problems at length in "On the Accuracy of Statistical Procedures in Microsoft Excel 97" (*Computational Statistics & Data Analysis*, 31:27-37, 1999). The problems they identified persisted through Excel 2002, but the new statistics package in Excel 2003 performs much more accurate calculations than were possible in previous versions of Excel. You can read all about it in Microsoft Knowledge Base article #828888 (*http://support.microsoft.com/default.aspx?kbid=828888 &product=xl2003*). However, the KB article indicates problems still exist when you're working with values at the extremes of distributions. If you need higher precision than Excel can provide, you should consider buying a third-party statistics add-in. Some notable choices:

- *XL*Stat (*http://www.xlstat.com/*)
- Analyse-it (*http://www.analyse-it.com/*)
- StatTools (*http://www.palisade.com/html/stattools.asp*)
- WinSTAT (*http://www.winstat.com/*)

FORMULA ERROR AND AUDITING ANNOYANCES

TELL EXCEL WHAT IS AN ERROR AND WHAT ISN'T

The Annoyance: I've figured out how to convince Excel to treat numbers I type into cells as text so that it doesn't delete leading zeros. But since I started using Excel 2002, when I copy those cells to another set of text-formatted cells the program marks the cells with an annoying green flag telling me there's some sort of nonfatal error or inconsistency. This problem never came up in Excel 97 or 2000, so I assume this is some new method Excel's programmers came up with to torture me. Help!

The Fix: To prevent Excel 2002 or 2003 from marking cells that store numbers as text with an error flag, select Tools → Options, select the Error Checking tab (shown in Figure 3-11), and uncheck the "Number stored as text" box.

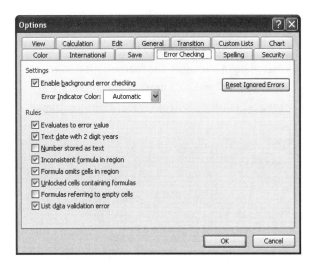

Figure 3-11. Use the Error Checking tab's controls to avoid distracting cell markers in cells that don't really contain errors.

The Error Checking tab contains other checkboxes that prevent Excel from marking cells that exhibit other characteristics. The two you should consider unchecking immediately are "Inconsistent formula in region" and "Formula

omits cells in region." These types of error flags are helpful for worksheets that summarize lists of data (e.g., sales by hour), but they aren't very helpful on summary worksheets that use data from all over a workbook.

FIND FORMULA PRECEDENTS

The Annoyance: I've got financial data flying at me from all sides, and I have to work fast to keep up. As a result, I've built formulas with so many inputs I can't always remember which part of a formula refers to which cells. When things get crazy, any number of cells start trying to divide by zero because I'm off by one column or row in a cell name. Please tell me there is an easy way to see which cells and ranges are referenced in a given formula without going through it element by element!

The Fix: In Excel 2002 or 2003, to view the cells that contribute values to the formula in the selected cell, choose Tools → Formula Auditing → Trace Precedents. Excel will draw pointers from the selected cell to the cells used in the formula, as shown in Figure 3-12. The formula in cell C5 uses values from cells A1, A2, and A3 in the current worksheet, plus a value from a cell outside of the worksheet. To show pointers in Excel 97 or 2000, choose Tools → Auditing → Trace Precedents.

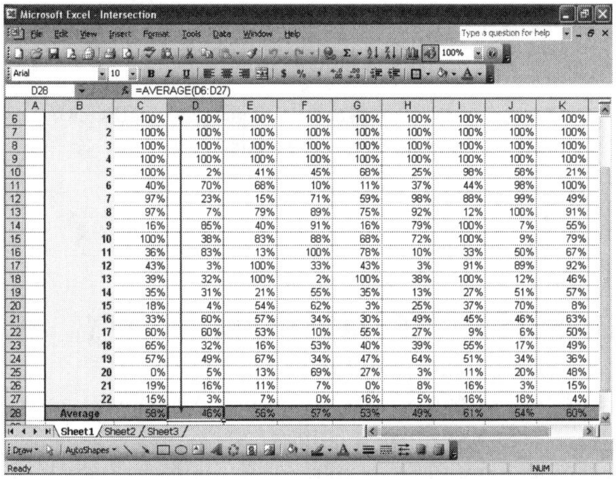

Figure 3-12. When formulas get complicated, use Trace Precedents as a visual aid to make sure everything works as planned.

To remove the precedent arrows, choose Tools → Formula Auditing (or Auditing) → Remove All Arrows.

The worksheet icon at the end of a black dotted line indicates that the formula uses at least one cell from outside the workbook. Excel displays only one black dotted line regardless of how many external cells you use in the formula, but you can display a full list of those cells by double-clicking the dotted line. The special Go To box you'll see appears in Figure 3-13. To move to a cell, click the reference and click OK.

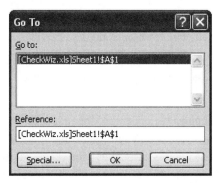

Figure 3-13. The Go To box lets you view cells in other workbooks that are used in the active cell's formula.

HIGHLIGHTING AS YOU GO

In version 2002 and later, Excel highlights the cells and ranges used in a formula with a light, colored border. The same color is used on the Formula Bar to highlight each argument in a formula as you create it. The borders disappear after you leave the cell, but clicking the cell and then clicking anywhere on the Formula Bar or pressing F2 will bring the highlights back. Excel 97 and 2000 don't highlight the cells and ranges as you type in a formula, but will highlight the cells and color the cell and range references when you press F2.

DISPLAY ALL DEPENDENT CELLS

The Annoyance: I wanted to add some new columns to a worksheet I use to track my departmental expenses (food, lodging, transportation, and so on), but my boss told me I couldn't move any existing columns to make room for the new categories because other secretaries have built formulas that pull values from my workbook. How can I get a list of which cells in my worksheet are being used by others?

The Fix: To view the cells (whether in your worksheet or on someone else's computer) that are using values from your Excel 2002 or 2003 worksheet, start by opening all the dependent workbooks; in your case you'll need to get those other secretaries to open their worksheets. Then, in Excel 2002 or 2003, open your own worksheet, select the cell you want to audit, and choose Tools → Formula Auditing → Trace Dependents. In Excel 97 or 2000, follow the same procedure, except choose Tools → Auditing → Trace Dependents.

Formula Elements That Can't Be Traced

The following worksheet items can be referenced by formulas, but cannot be traced by using auditing tools:

- References to text boxes, embedded charts, or pictures on worksheets
- Cells in PivotTables
- References to named constants
- Cells in closed workbooks

Excel draws pointers from the active cell to any cells containing formulas that use the value in the active cell. Excel indicates any cells outside the current worksheet with a black dotted line terminated by a worksheet icon. Double-clicking the dotted line displays a Go To box with a list of the cells that use the selected cell's value.

To remove the precedent arrows, choose Tools → Formula Auditing (or Auditing) → Remove All Arrows.

MASK ERROR MESSAGES IN A WORKSHEET

The Annoyance: I don't mind having friends come over to my house when I'm in the middle of a redecorating spree; I can always regale them with tales of how great the room is *going* to look after the paint dries. I'm less sanguine about sharing my workbooks when they're full of error messages such as DIV/0! and NAME. The thing is, I often create sheets with formulas that are designed to work on data that will be entered later. Once that data is entered, the formulas work fine and display proper values—but until the data is entered those cells display those annoying error messages, which make it look like I don't know how to build a worksheet. Is there any way to turn off error messages such as DIV/0! and NAME while leaving the formulas active so that they will process and display the proper values once the data in entered?

The Fix: There's no way to turn off error messages completely, but you can use a conditional format to change the font color to white (or another color that matches the cell background) to hide those errors.

This works only with Excel-generated messages. If you use this trick with existing entries in a cell, they'll still show up.

Just follow these steps:

1. Select the cells that contain the error messages. (To apply the conditional format to every cell in a worksheet, select cell A1 and press Ctrl-A.)

2. Choose Format → Conditional Formatting.

3. Open the first Condition 1 drop down and select Formula Is.

4. In the second field, type:

    =ISERROR(*ActiveCellAddress*)

    where *ActiveCellAddress* is the address of the first cell you selected. If you selected cell A1 and then dragged to select other cells (or pressed Ctrl-A to select every cell in the worksheet), you would type =ISERROR(A1).

5. Click the Format button and select the Font tab. In the Color drop down, select the white color box (or the color box corresponding to your cells' background color).

6. Click OK twice to clear the dialog boxes and to apply your conditional format.

When you enter the address of the first active cell in the ISERROR formula, Excel understands that it is supposed to extend that address throughout the range you selected, and will change each cell's conditional format to reflect that first active cell's contents.

ARRAY FORMULA ANNOYANCES

DEPLOY ARRAY FORMULAS

The Annoyance: I inherited an inventory-tracking workbook (shown in Figure 3-14) from an engineer in my custom computer-building company. Somehow, she created what appears to be a formula that calculates the total value of our inventory by multiplying the number of each part on hand by that part's price, and then adding the individual results. The formula, which is stored in cell D7, is {=SUM(B2:B6*C2:C6)}. Why are there curly braces around the formula, and why do I get a VALUE! error when I try to edit the formula?

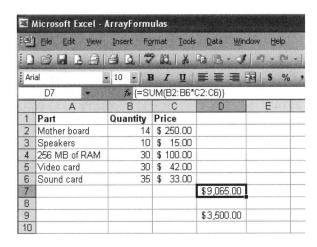

Figure 3-14. The formula in cell D7 lets you skip a lot of partial calculations in cells D2:D6.

The Fix:

The formula in question is an *array formula*, which means it operates on ranges of cells instead of on individual cells. To see how an array formula works, break the formula {=SUM(B2:B6*C2:C6)} into its component parts. The innermost operation, B2:B6*C2:C6, multiplies the range B2:B6 by the range C2:C6, which means cell B2 is multiplied by cell C2, B3 by C3, and so on. Instead of writing the individual results to cells in the worksheet, Excel maintains the results in an array in program memory. The second operation, SUM, tells Excel to add the values in the results in memory and display the result in the cell that contains the formula (D7 in this case).

To turn a formula into an array formula, type it as a normal formula, such as =SUM(B2:B6*C2:C6), and then press Ctrl-Shift-Enter. Excel will recognize the formula as an array formula and add the curly braces for you. Don't try to type in the curly braces by hand! If you do, Excel will think the formula is text and will just display {=SUM(B2: B6*C2:C6)} instead of performing the calculation. Also, if you don't press Ctrl-Shift-Enter, the formula will generate a #VALUE! error because you can only multiply one range by another in an array formula.

SCIENTIFIC EQUATION EDITOR

Back in the day, a slide rule was a badge of honor for every engineer, but these days rocket scientists can't get by without a really good scientific calculator. Making the transition to Excel can be tough after you've spent the majority of your adult life using a calculator to create your equations and formulas, but there's an add-in application called Abacus that lets you enter your Excel formulas through a scientific calculator interface. Best of all, Abacus lets you change the button layout. The program fills in parentheses automatically, supports keyboard shortcuts, and lets you type directly into the formula if you want. You can download a 30-day trial version of Abacus from *http://www.numericalmethods.com/ abacus.shtml*. If you want to buy the program, it will set you back $19.95. Note that Abacus works with Excel 97, 2000, and XP/2002, but has not been tested with Excel 2003.

Even rocket scientists feel good to be back on familiar ground.

RECALCULATION ANNOYANCES

RECALCULATE NOW!

The Annoyance: The formulas in my workbooks use many values from other sources—and because the source data changes frequently, Excel has to recalculate the formulas constantly. This takes up so much of my computer's processing power that much of the time it's impossible to get anything done. Can I control when and how Excel recalculates my formulas?

The Fix: To control when Excel recalculates the formulas in your workbook, select Tools → Options, and click the Calculation tab (shown in Figure 3-15).

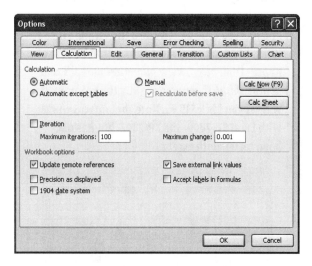

Figure 3-15. Prevent unnecessary recalculations using the Calculation tab of the Options dialog box.

The default is Automatic, which means Excel will recalculate your workbook whenever the value in a cell used in any of the workbook's formulas changes. If you click the "Automatic except tables" radio button, Excel only recalculates formulas that aren't part of a data table (a *data table* is a range of cells that shows how changing certain values in your formulas affects the results of the formulas).

If you select the Manual radio button, Excel will recalculate your formulas only when you press F9, or click the Recalculate Now button on the Calculation tab. Furthermore, unchecking the "Recalculate before save" box means Excel won't update the formula results every time you save the workbook—it will do so only when you press F9, or click the Recalculate Now button on the Calculation tab. To recalculate just those formulas on the active worksheet, click the Calc Sheet button on the Calculation tab.

Table 3-1 describes the keyboard shortcuts that relate to recalculations.

Table 3-1. Choose which formulas to recalculate, even if the formulas are in other open workbooks.

Key(s)	Result
F9	Calculates all formulas that have changed since the last calculation, and formulas that are dependent on them, in all open workbooks.
Shift-F9	Calculates formulas that have changed since the last calculation, and formulas that are dependent on them, in the active worksheet.
Ctrl-Alt-F9	Calculates all formulas in all open workbooks, even if there were no changes.
Ctrl-Shift-Alt-F9	Rechecks dependent formulas, and then calculates all formulas in all open workbooks, even if there were no changes.

SPEED UP RECALCULATIONS

The Annoyance: My sales tracking and summary workbook is, admittedly, a spaghetti bowl of array formulas, formulas that use values from other workbooks, and several thousand rows of sales data. When I open this workbook, it can take up to 15 minutes to finish recalculating all its formulas. Can I speed up the recalculation process?

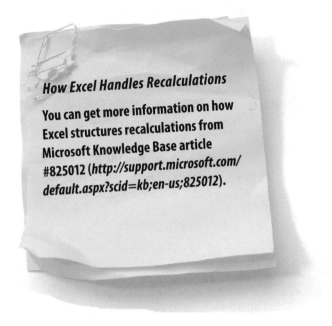

The Fix: There are a number of ways to speed up workbook calculations:

- Where possible, create links only to workbooks that are on your computer, thus reducing the possibility that network slowdowns will affect your recalculations.

- If you use a web query or database query to bring external data into your workbook, Excel attempts to update the query results every time you recalculate the worksheet that contains the query. If you don't need to update the query's results, highlight the cells that contain the results, choose Edit → Copy, and then, with the same cells still selected, choose Edit → Paste Special → Values to break the link to the query.

- Reduce your use of array formulas. Array formulas use RAM, so if you're running a lot of applications at once, your system resources might be so low that Windows is using your hard disk as extra memory—which is much slower than RAM access. (Or try adding more RAM. It couldn't hurt.)

- If you're using Excel 2000 or later, save the workbook as an HTML web page file, and then resave it as an Excel workbook. When you save a workbook as a web

page, Excel cleans up internal and external pointers that can become garbled as workbooks get more complex.

- Optimize your database queries so that they return the minimum data set you need for your answer. In other words, don't download a huge table if you need only a few rows. If possible, have your database administrator write a query that creates a table with exactly the data you need.

DATE AND TIME ANNOYANCES

DISPLAY PARTIAL HOURS AS DECIMAL NUMBERS

The Annoyance: I'm a private consultant, and I would like to create a time sheet for myself using Excel. But I'm having a devil of a time getting Excel to subtract time and output total hours to one decimal place. For instance, I formatted all the cells used in the calculation with the hh:mm:ss time format, which means that when it subtracts 7:00:00 from 12:00:00, it shows I worked 5:00:00 hours in the morning (see Figure 3-16) instead of 5.0. When I put in the afternoon time (start 12:30:00, stop 17:00:00, or 4.5 hours worth) it shows the total time I worked as 9:30:00. How do I make Excel display the time worked as decimal values—in this case, 5.0, 4.5, and 9.5 hours?

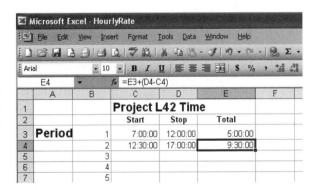

Figure 3-16. You shortchange yourself when you multiply a time serial number by an hourly rate.

The Fix: To display a time as a decimal value, such as 9.5 hours, follow these steps:

1. Click the cell where the result is to appear and select Format → Cells, click the Number tab, and select Number from the Category pull-down list.

2. Type this formula in the cell: `=HOUR(value)+(MINUTE(value)/60)`, replacing *value* with the address of the cell that contains the time or the formula that generates the time you want to convert into a decimal value. In the worksheet shown in Figure 3-16, you would use the formula `=HOUR(E4)+(MINUTE(E4)/60)`.

ROUND HOURS TO THE NEXT TENTH OF AN HOUR

The Annoyance: I bill my clients by the tenth of an hour, rounding up (of course). How can I get my worksheet to round up the time I spend on a project (recorded in hundredths of an hour) to the next tenth of an hour?

The Fix: To round a time value to the next tenth of an hour, first make sure the cell is formatted as General by selecting Format → Cells, clicking the Number tab, and

---

MANAGE FORMULAS EFFECTIVELY

Workbooks can take on a life of their own, expanding to the point where you're tempted to throw up your hands in frustration, start over from scratch, change jobs, or just hide under your desk. If you decide to overhaul your workbook, or start over, you'll need a good handle on the formulas in your workbook, particularly if it's been a while since you or someone else built the sucker. The Formula Manager add-in from OzGrid is a terrific tool you can use to identify and summarize the formulas in your workbooks.

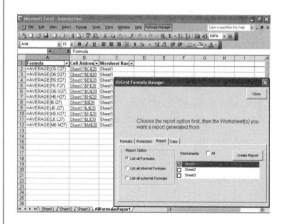

It's often easier to edit your workbook when you know what's where.

For example, you can change the background color of every cell that contains a formula that meets your criteria (such as using the value in a particular cell, or using a cell value from a particular outside workbook). You also can protect, or even hide, cells that contain formulas that meet your criteria so that your colleagues can't change them by mistake. Another handy feature allows you to use the report generator to list the formulas on one or more worksheets, or in the entire workbook. The result of one such report appears in the figure. Note that the list has AutoFilter arrows at the top. If you want to find the addresses of the cells that contain a specific formula, you can use the AutoFilter arrows to do just that. Finally, you can use the Formula Copy feature to copy a formula to another cell without any references changing, even if you used relative references in the original formula. You can buy Formula Manager at *http://www.ozgrid.com/Services/Excel_Formula_Add-in.htm* for $29.95. To make the add-in available in Excel, choose Tools → Add-Ins → Browse, navigate to the folder where you unzipped the add-in, and click OK.

---

selecting General from the Category list. Then type a formula such as `=ROUNDUP(C13,1)` into the cell where you want the rounded value to appear. This formula will take its raw data from cell C13, but you can use any cell reference you want. The `ROUNDUP` function, which rounds any value up to the specified number of decimal places, expects a cell reference or range as its first argument and a number of digits as its second argument. The number of digits indicates how many decimal places should be displayed in the formula's result. For example, if cell C13 contained the value 4.335, the formula `=ROUNDUP(C13,2)` would generate the result `4.34` (displaying two decimal places), while the formula `=ROUNDUP(C13,1)` would generate the result `4.4` (displaying one decimal place).

ROUND HOURS TO THE NEXT QUARTER OF AN HOUR

The Annoyance: I'm an accountant, and one of my clients insists that I bill her by the quarter hour because that's the only way she can enter my invoices into her system. How do I round up my elapsed times to the next quarter of an hour?

The Fix: I'll provide two versions of this formula. Both formulas use a series of nested `IF` statements to determine to which quarter the time should be rounded. The first version works if you converted the number of hours you're rounding to a decimal value such as 2.4. In this example, the formula assumes the value is in cell A15:

```
=IF(A15-INT(A15)>0.75,ROUNDUP(A15,0),IF(A15-INT
    (A15)>0.5,INT(A15)+0.75,IF(A15-INT(A15)>0.25,
    INT(A15)+0.5,IF(A15-INT(A15)>0,INT(A15)+0.25,
    A15))))
```

The second version of the formula works if you use a standard time format such as 2:25; it assumes the time is in cell D16:

```
=IF(MINUTE(D16)>45,HOUR(D16)+1,IF(MINUTE(D16)>30,
    HOUR(D16)+0.75,IF(MINUTE(D16)>15,HOUR(D16)+
    0.5,IF(MINUTE(D16)>0,HOUR(D16)+0.25,HOUR
    (D16)))))
```

If you prefer to create a user-defined function to make this formula available throughout your workbook, you

can use the following VBA code to do so. This function emulates the second of the two preceding formulas, as it expects a standard time value (e.g., 4:45). After you add the function as a VBA code module, you can call it as if it were any other Excel function. If the time value you wanted to convert to a decimal number were in cell C2, for example, you would write the formula as `=QuarterRound(C2)`.

```
Function QuarterRound(timValue) As Single

    intHour = Hour(timValue)
    sngMinute = Minute(timValue) / 60

    If sngMinute > 0.75 Then
    QuarterRound = intHour + 1
    Exit Function
    End If

    If sngMinute > 0.5 Then
    QuarterRound = intHour + 0.75
    Exit Function
    End If

    If sngMinute > 0.25 Then
    QuarterRound = intHour + 0.5
    Exit Function
    End If

    If sngMinute > 0 Then
    QuarterRound = intHour + 0.25
    Else: QuarterRound = intHour
    End If

End Function
```

To get more information on how to add this function to your workbook, see the "Create a New Code Module" annoyance in Chapter 8.

SAVE A DATE OR TIME AS TEXT

The Annoyance: When I create a chart, I'd like to add the date and time to its title (e.g., Portfolio Value as of June 3, 2005, 3:00 PM), but I have had zero luck getting Excel to create the title automatically! I've managed to create a value in cell A1 that's generated by the formula `=NOW()`, which produces the current date and time. So far, so good. But then when I try to use the `CONCATENATE` function on the value in cell A1, as in the formula `=CONCATENATE("Portfolio Value as of ", A1)`, Excel produces the comically unhelpful *Portfolio Value as of 38026.3457975694*, or something similar. No amount of fussing with cell formats has helped. How the heck do I make Excel do the grunt work for me?

The Fix: The trick is saving the date and time as a text value using the `TEXT()` function and using the appropriate date or time custom formatting codes to feed a value to the `CONCATENATE` function that it understands. For example, if you wanted to use the current date as part of a cell value, you would create the formula `=CONCATENATE("Right now it is ",TEXT(NOW(),"mmmm d, yyyy"))` to produce the value *Right now it is September 20, 2004.*

The `TEXT()` function creates a text string from the displayed value of a date or time. It expects two inputs: a source for the value and the format in which the value is to be displayed.

You will find a complete list of available time and date custom formatting codes in Tables 2-2 and 2-3 in Chapter 2.

FIND THE NUMBER OF WORKDAYS BETWEEN TWO DATES

The Annoyance: I'm a project leader at a computer-game studio, and I spend a lot of time creating schedules for graphic design, building the game engine, and play-testing. We have found that output actually goes up if we don't drive our employees until they drop, so I base my schedules on a five-day workweek. Can Excel help me figure out the number of workdays between two given dates?

The Fix: To find the total number of workdays between two days, use the `NETWORKDAYS()` function. The `NETWORKDAYS()` function has the following syntax:

    NETWORKDAYS(Start_Date, End_Date, Holidays)

`Start_Date` is the address of the cell that contains the earlier of the two dates, `End_Date` is the address of the cell that contains the later of the two dates, and `Holidays` is an optional cell range with dates of holidays that aren't part of the usual holiday calendar (for example, Patriot's Day, which Massachusetts and Maine—but no other states—celebrate on the third Monday in April).

If a project's start date (1/2/2005) is in cell A4, the end date (8/3/2005) is in cell B4, and there are no holidays that aren't on the federal holiday calendar, you can enter the formula `=NETWORKDAYS(A4,B4)` into a blank cell to compute the number of workdays (153) between the start date and the end date.

The `NETWORKDAYS()` function is part of the Analysis Tool-Pak, an Excel add-in that comes with the program but isn't installed by default. If you get a `#NAME?` error when you enter the `NETWORKDAYS()` formula, choose Tools → Add-Ins, and check the Analysis ToolPak box to install the add-in.

ADD HOURS, MINUTES, OR SECONDS TO A TIME

The Annoyance: I schedule trucks for a regional courier service, so I spend a lot of my day figuring out how long it will take a driver to get from one location to another. I track those intervals in Excel and, over time, I've managed to come to grips with the fact that Excel represents times and dates as numeric values based on counting the number of days, and *parts* of days, that have elapsed since January 1, 1900. I've formatted my results cells so that they display combined dates and times using the format 3/14/01 1:30 PM. Unfortunately, the custom-built Excel add-in I use to compute driving time between two locations outputs a whole number (representing the total number of hours) in one cell, a whole number (representing the number of minutes) in another cell, and a whole number (representing the number of seconds) in a third cell. My problem is that when I try to combine these values to produce a recognizable number of hours, minutes, and seconds, and to add them to other hours, minutes, and seconds, Excel produces perfectly useless random numbers. How do I add hours, minutes, and seconds to times reliably in Excel?

The Fix: As you noted in your question, when you work with time and day serial numbers, you're actually working with decimal values. For example, 12 hours would be entered as .5, while 18 hours would be entered as .75. The trick to adding decimal numbers representing hours, minutes, and seconds to an existing Excel time or date is to divide the time you want to add by the portion of the day it takes up. That means:

- To add hours, divide the number by 24; that is, to add five hours, add 5/24. For example, if cell A2 contains a date or time, and cell A3 contains a decimal number representing hours, you could create the formula =A2+(A3/24) in cell A4 to add the hours in cell A3 to the date or time in cell A2.

- To add minutes, divide the number by 1440; that is, to add five minutes, add 5/1440. For example, if cell A2 contains a date or time, and cell A3 contains a decimal number representing minutes, the formula =A2+(A3/1440) would add the minutes in cell A3 to the date or time in cell A2.

- To add seconds, divide the number by 86,400; that is, to add five seconds, add 5/86400. For example, if cell A2 contains a date or time and cell A3 contains a decimal number representing seconds, the formula =A2+(A3/86400) would add the seconds in cell A3 to the date or time in cell A2.

Be sure to format the cell where you create your formula so that it displays your date and time values correctly. For example, if you want to display a time in hours, even if that value is more than 24 hours, you should format the cell with the code [h]:mm:ss.

You can find out more about date and time formats from the "Create a Custom Date Format" and "Create Custom Time Formats" annoyances in Chapter 2.

IMPRESS HISTORIANS WITH ROMAN NUMERALS

The Annoyance: I work for a movie producer who likes to display the copyright dates of his films in Roman numerals. Is there some way that Excel can help me to convert a year to Roman numerals?

The Fix: To convert a value to Roman numerals, use the ROMAN() workbook function. If the year 2005 were in cell A1, for example, the formula =ROMAN(A1) would return MMV.

FIND THE NUMBER OF A WEEK

The Annoyance: I track sales at my fashion boutique by the week, which helps me compare my weekly performance from year to year. Does Excel know how to find the number of the week in which a given day falls?

The Fix: The function to derive the week in which a particular day occurs is WEEKNUM, but the function isn't available in Excel until you activate the Analysis ToolPak add-in. To install the Analysis ToolPak, choose Tools → Add-Ins, check the Analysis ToolPak box, and click OK. Once the Analysis ToolPak is installed, type the formula =WEEKNUM(*cell*) into a cell. Then replace *cell* with the actual cell address where you've stored the date for which you want the week number.

NAMED RANGE ANNOYANCES

CREATE NAMED RANGES

The Annoyance: I'm a volunteer track coach at the local high school, and I record my runners' times, by event, in an Excel worksheet (shown in Figure 3-17). I can create formulas that use the cell addresses for each runner's times, but I'd have to look in the worksheet to see which runner's times I was working with in a particular formula. I'd rather create a shortcut reference I can use to refer to each runner's times, especially if I could use those labels as names in my formulas. Is this what people mean when they talk about "named ranges?" If so, how can I create named ranges from the existing worksheet?

The Fix: To create named ranges from existing data labels, first select the entire range of cells, including the labels you want to use as the names of your ranges, which is the range A3:G22 in the worksheet shown in

Figure 3-17. (In this case, the ranges represent each runner's times, so you wouldn't select the race distances in row 2.) After you select the data range, choose Insert → Name → Create to display the Create Names dialog box shown in Figure 3-18. Check the box that identifies the location of the rows or columns to which you want to give names ("Left column" in the current example) and click OK to create the names. From now on, instead of referring to row numbers or column letters in formulas and cell references, you can use the label names.

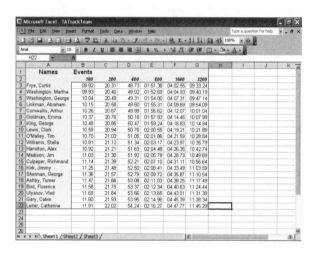

Figure 3-17. Existing data labels are sufficient to create named ranges.

Figure 3-18. The Create Names dialog box lets you pick where the names should come from.

If you want to create two sets of names from the same worksheet, such as the Internet café usage tracking worksheet in Figure 3-5, select the "Top row" and "Left column"

boxes. What you need to watch out for, though, are instances in which you have a label in the cell at the top left corner of your worksheet, such as cell B5 in Figure 3-5. In that case, Excel can't determine where one set of labels ends and the other begins. It's better to put labels that aren't used for a row or column a few cells away from your data.

UPDATE EXISTING FORMULAS TO USE NEWLY DEFINED NAMED RANGES

The Annoyance: When I created my worksheet to track computer usage in my Internet café, I used cell references in all my formulas. Since then I have created named ranges for each workstation (WKST01, WKST02, etc.) and for each hour of the day when I'm open (AM09, AM10, PM03, etc.). Can I automatically update my formulas to use the named ranges I created, or do I have to perform the updates by hand?

The Fix: To update cell references to names, select Insert → Name → Apply. In the Apply Names dialog box (shown in Figure 3-19), select the names you want to apply, and click OK.

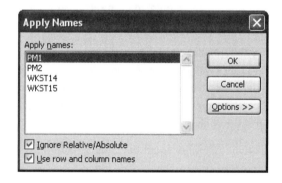

Figure 3-19. You can choose which names you want to apply to your formulas.

CREATE NAMED CONSTANTS

The Annoyance: I manage the web site for a major retail chain. We have stores in every state in the U.S., so our lawyers advised us to collect sales tax for each online purchaser based on his or her state. Is there a way to assign a constant value to a name so that I can use that name in my sales tax calculations? It would be much easier to use a name incorporating a state's two-letter abbreviation in my formula instead of the cell reference or (shudder) the actual sales tax percentage.

The Fix: To create a constant, choose Insert → Name → Define, click the "Names in workbook" field, and type the name to which you want to assign the constant value. Then in the "Refers to" field, type an equals sign followed by the value you want to assign to the name. For example, if the sales tax rate in Virginia were 5%, you could create the name TaxRateVA and type =.05 in the "Refers to" field. Click the Add button, then the OK button. Now, if the amount of the sale were in cell C4, you could create a formula such as =C4*TaxRateVA to calculate the sales tax for a customer's purchase.

CREATE A SELF-EXTENDING NAMED RANGE

The Annoyance: I hire bands to play in a blues club. We use a number of bands regularly, but every so often I hear a band that's so good I want to add it to our list. I'm an experienced Excel user, but my assistant isn't, so I created a Pick from List validation rule to make data entry easier for both of us (no more misspellings, etc.). The list uses a named range called Bands. The problem is that every time we add a new band I need to redefine the range of the data called by Bands. Is there a way to extend a named range dynamically so that it automatically will expand to add any new values I add to the list?

The Fix: For this example, let's assume the band names are in sheet 1, column A, and that the first band's name is in cell A2. To create a named range that updates its reference, choose Insert → Name → Define, type a name into the "Names in workbook" field, and then type the following formula into the "Refers to" field:

    =OFFSET(Sheet1!$A$2,0,0,COUNTA(Sheet1!$A:$A))

The OFFSET function takes the following five arguments: Reference, Rows, Columns, Height, and Width. The Reference argument requires the absolute reference of the first cell in the range (in this case, cell A2 in sheet 1). The Rows and Columns arguments tell the function how far to move from the reference cell to begin its selection. In this formula, Excel doesn't move from the reference cell (both arguments have the value 0). The Height argument, the last in the preceding formula, uses the COUNTA function to count the number of cells below cell A2 in column A that contain a value, and to extend the range to the last cell with a value, as shown in Figure 3-20. Now, whenever you add a new band name to the list, Excel will include it in the named range, which means the band would be included in the list called by the validation rule.

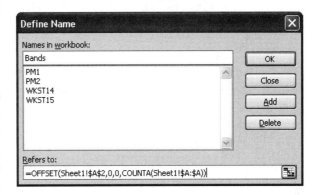

Figure 3-20. The OFFSET formula lets Excel extend the range to the end of the data, not just to a specific cell.

What's interesting about the OFFSET function in this case is that if you have a series of six cells with band names, a blank cell, and then a seventh cell with a band name, Excel will extend the range all the way to the last cell with a name instead of stopping after the seventh cell. You will, however, find a blank entry in the Pick from List validation rule. This behavior occurs only if exactly one blank cell is between the two values. If there are two or more blank cells, the OFFSET function stops at the last cell before the blanks.

CREATE A NAMED RANGE FROM MULTIPLE SHEETS

The Annoyance: I created a workbook to track sales for my computer-building company, with a different worksheet for each month in the year. I plan my tax payments based, in part, on my quarterly revenue, so I'd like to create a named range that includes the total "summary" cells for each monthly sheet (e.g., summaries for January, February, and March). Is there a way to create a named range made up of cells on more than one worksheet?

The Fix: Creating a named range is all about selecting the cells you want to include in the range *at the right time*. That time is after you select Insert → Name → Define, when the Define Name dialog box is open and the "Refers to" field is empty. Type a name in the "Names in workbook" field, and then click the "Refers to" field. First, select the sheet tab of the first worksheet that contains cells to be included in the range, select the cells on the active sheet you want to use, and then type a comma at the end of the code that appears in the "Refers to" field.

To add cells from another sheet, click the sheet tab of the next worksheet with cells to include, and select the cells. If you want to add cells from more sheets, type another comma and repeat the selection process. Otherwise, remove the final comma (if there is one), click the Add button, and then click the OK button.

PASTE A LIST OF NAMES

The Annoyance: I can't figure out how to print out a list of the named ranges (and the cells the ranges refer to) in my workbook. What do I do?

The Fix: To paste a list of the active workbook's named ranges into a worksheet, click an empty, out-of-the-way cell, press F3 to display the Paste Name dialog box (shown in Figure 3-21), and click the Paste List button.

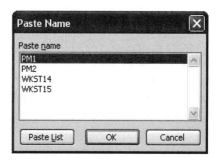

Figure 3-21. The Paste Name dialog box does more than add named ranges to formulas.

You also can use the Paste Name dialog box to include a named range in a formula. When you reach the point in the formula where you want to enter the named range, press F3, select the named range to add, and click OK.

SELECT AN ENTIRE NAMED RANGE

The Annoyance: I want the contents of every cell in a named range to appear in boldface. Can't I do this without formatting the individual cells?

The Fix: You can select every cell in a named range by clicking the down arrow to the right of the Name box (found just above cell A1), clicking the named range you want to select, and just clicking the bold button on Excel's toolbar.

AVOID RENAMING CELLS IN A NAMED RANGE

The Annoyance: I found out by accident that selecting an entire named range, choosing Edit → Cut, and pasting the cells into another location changes the named range's references. I keep my employees' names in cells A1:A40 on my People worksheet, so the named range's definition is People!$A$1:$A$40. Cutting the values from the cells and pasting the cells into my January worksheet changed the named range's reference to January!$A$1:$A$40. Is this normal behavior, and if so, why? Isn't there some way I can prevent Excel from changing my named range references?

The Fix: One of Excel's quirks is that when you cut and paste all the cells that make up a named range (no more and no less), Excel updates the named range's "refers to" property to the cells' new location. I guess the logic is that if you cut an entire named range and paste it somewhere else, Excel assumes you want to move it. You can prevent Excel from updating the range reference by *copying* the selection instead of cutting it.

TEXT FORMULA ANNOYANCES

PARSE FIXED-LENGTH SUBSTRINGS

The Annoyance: I work for a car dealership, so I work with a lot of Vehicle Identification Numbers (VINs). A VIN is 17 characters long and contains information about the car maker, the car model, the year it was made, and so on. The dealership's VIN tracking software writes the VIN of every car we have on the lot to a text file. What I want to do is break down each car's VIN (a representative sample is shown in Figure 3-22) into meaningful chunks. Can Excel do that?

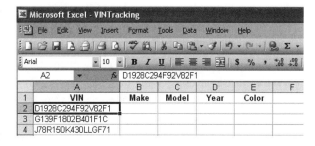

Figure 3-22. You can use this data's pattern to separate it into its component parts.

The Fix: The trick is to import the data and use an Excel wizard to parse the string. The following works when each field in the string is of a known length:

1. Choose File → Open, click the down arrow at the right of the "Files of type" drop down, and select All Files (*.*). Select the file you want to import, and click the Open button. This starts the Text Import Wizard.

2. Select the Fixed Width option and click the Next button.

3. On the second page of the wizard, click the ruler above the data preview area to set where each break line goes. Figure 3-23 shows an import with four break lines—the string will be broken into five chunks.

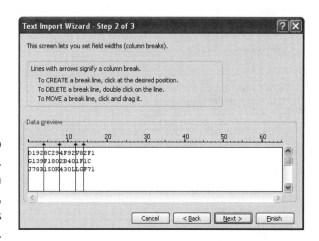

Figure 3-23. The lines mark the breaks between substrings in data that isn't delimited by spaces or other characters.

4. To move a break line, drag it to the desired location. To delete a break line, double-click it. Click Next when you're done.

5. If you want to define a format for any of the fields you've just defined, click the field and use the Column data format controls at the top right of the wizard page to define the format. When you're done, click the Finish button. The string of VIN data—now neatly sliced up—is popped into separate cells in your worksheet.

PARSE DATA OF INCONSISTENT LENGTHS

The Annoyance: The manufacturing firm I work for labels the storage location of its parts using a system that generates part codes of anywhere from 10 to 12 characters. Each element of the part code starts with a known letter (T for type, S for section of the shop, and B for bin). If I have a list of product codes such as T301S40B280 and T20S497B123, can I use Excel to separate the type, section, and bin numbers of the parts and store them in separate cells?

The Fix: The easiest way to parse data of an inconsistent length from a range of cells is to use a VBA procedure that examines the data to find where the key points occur, and brings the data between the points into the target cells beside the cell that contains the original product code. The following procedure does just that:

```
Sub TranslateCode()

Dim c As Range
Dim intT, intS, intB As Integer
Dim strCurrentRange As String

strCurrentRange = _
Selection.CurrentRegion.Address

For Each c In Selection.CurrentRegion

'Find the string position where each substring
'begins.
intT = InStr(c.Value, "T")
intS = InStr(c.Value, "S")
intB = InStr(c.Value, "B")

'Write the substrings to cells 1, 2, and 3 to
'the right.
```

```
'This routine leaves out the code letter at the
'start of the substrings.
'Put a single quote in front of the following
'three lines to disable them.
c.Offset(0, 1).Value = Mid(c.Value, 2, intS - 2)
c.Offset(0, 2).Value = Mid(c.Value, _
 intS + 1, intB - intS - 1)
c.Offset(0, 3).Value = Mid(c.Value, intB + 1)

'These code lines include the code letter at
'the start of the substrings.
'Remove the single quote from in front of these
'lines to use them.
'c.Offset(0, 1).Value = Mid(c.Value, 1, intS - 2)
'c.Offset(0, 2).Value = Mid(c.Value, intS, intB _
'- intS - 1)
'c.Offset(0, 3).Value = Mid(c.Value, intB)
Next c

End Sub
```

This procedure selects the current region of cells, finds the position where each key character occurs, and then uses the `Mid` function along with those positions to pull the information elements from the code. The `c.Offset` method assigns the value of each substring to cells 1, 2, and 3 columns to the right. If you wanted to include the code letter at the start of each substring, which this procedure leaves out, you would add a single quote in front of the three active lines beginning with `c.Offset` and remove the single quote in front of these three lines of code:

```
c.Offset(0, 1).Value = Mid(c.Value, 1, intS - 2)
c.Offset(0, 2).Value = Mid(c.Value, intS, intB _
- intS - 1)
c.Offset(0, 3).Value = Mid(c.Value, intB)
```

To edit the code, follow the steps in the "Edit a Macro" annoyance in Chapter 8.

DIVIDE TEXT INTO MULTIPLE COLUMNS

The Annoyance: When I imported a table of contact information from a database, I discovered that the database stored each customer's first and last name, separated by a space, in the same cell. I want to place the first and last names into separate cells, so I can perform a mail merge in Word with salutations such as "Dear Mr.

Frye" instead of "Dear Mr. Curtis Frye." But I surely don't want to do this by hand, cell by cell! Tell me how I get Excel to do this for me!

The Fix: To separate two words separated by a space into two columns, follow these steps:

1. Click anywhere in the column to the right of the data you want to separate and choose Insert → Column.

2. Select the column with the text you want to separate and choose Data → Text to Columns.

3. In the Convert Text to Columns Wizard, select the Delimited option and click Next.

4. Put a check in the Space box in the Delimiters section of the dialog, and uncheck all other boxes in that section. A preview of how your data will be separated appears in the data preview area (shown in Figure 3-24). Click Next.

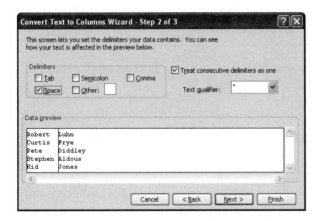

Figure 3-24. Excel shows you how it will separate your data when you click OK.

5. If you want to define a format for any of the fields you defined, click the field and use the column data format controls to define the format. Click Finish.

GET RID OF SPACES AND INVISIBLE CHARACTERS

The Annoyance: I receive weekly updates from the Parts Department's database, but when I import those files into Excel they seem to contain all kinds of extra spaces and invisible characters that my database administrator calls "control characters." Whatever they're called, those characters mess up my searches. Is there a way I can get rid of the extra spaces and nonprinting characters?

The Fix: To remove extra whitespace from a cell's contents, leaving one space (and one space only) between words and after punctuation marks, use the TRIM() function. If a cell contained the text *Excel annoys   me.* (with two spaces after *Excel* and five after *annoys*), the function would return the string Excel annoys me. The TRIM() function is handy for cleaning up comments from web sites or customer comment forms. If the data from which you wanted to remove excess whitespace were in cell G3, you would create the formula =TRIM(G3) in whatever cell you wanted the trimmed data to appear.

To remove nonprinting characters from a string, use the CLEAN() function. The CLEAN() function doesn't get rid of whitespace, so you can combine both functions by creating the formula =TRIM(CLEAN(*cell*)). If the data from which you wanted to remove excess whitespace and nonprinting characters were in cell G3, you would create the formula =TRIM(CLEAN((G3))) in whatever cell you wanted the trimmed and cleaned data to appear.

COUNTING AND CONDITIONAL SUM ANNOYANCES

SUM VALUES THAT MEET A CRITERION

The Annoyance: I own a computer-building company, and although most of my orders are less than $5,000, I do get a few that total more than $10,000. I'd like to know how much of my revenue comes from the big orders—which I guess means figuring out what percentage of my orders are for $10,000 or more. Is there some way to find the sum of all my orders for amounts of $10,000 or more, and then use that sum to determine the percentage they contribute to my revenue?

The Fix: You can find the sum of cells that meet any given criterion by using a SUMIF formula. To create a SUMIF formula, choose Insert → Function, type SUMIF in the "Search for a function" pull down, and click OK to display the Function Arguments dialog box for the SUMIF function (shown in Figure 3-25). With Excel 2000 and 97, select All in the "Function category" list and then SUMIF in the "Function name" list, and click OK to get the Function Arguments dialog box.

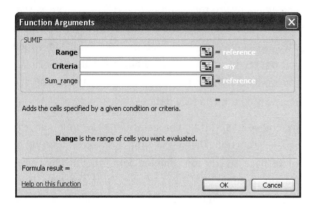

Figure 3-25. The SUMIF Function Arguments dialog box lets you define the rules that your data must meet to be considered in the sum.

In the Range field, type the name of the range you want to evaluate in the formula, type the range's cell addresses, or click the Collapse Dialog button at the far right in the field and select the cells. Then, in the Criteria field, type in the evaluation rule Excel should use to determine whether the cell it's looking at should be included in the conditional sum. For example, you could create a rule such as >10000, or <500. Finally, in the Sum_range field, type the address of the cell that will hold the result, and click the OK button.

COUNT VALUES THAT MEET A CRITERION

The Annoyance: Thanks a lot, but I think I'd be just as happy if I knew the *number* of orders in my worksheet for amounts of $10,000 or more. How do I count the number of orders that meet a criterion without creating a VBA procedure to do it?

The Fix: You can use the COUNTIF function to count the number of cells in a range that contain a value that meets a criterion. The COUNTIF function expects two arguments: the range being examined and the criterion a cell must meet to be counted (the Function Arguments dialog box for the COUNTIF function appears in Figure 3-26). If you store the total value of a series of orders in the range L2:L586, you can create the formula =COUNTIF(L2:L586,">10000") to find the number of orders valued at $10,000 or more.

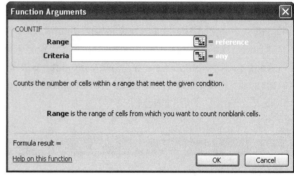

Figure 3-26. You can find the number of cells with values that meet a criterion using the COUNTIF function.

COUNT NONBLANK CELLS IN A RANGE

The Annoyance: I have a worksheet in which each order placed with my company is stored on a single row. Is there some way to count the number of orders in my worksheet without scrolling to the bottom of the list and losing track of my count halfway down?

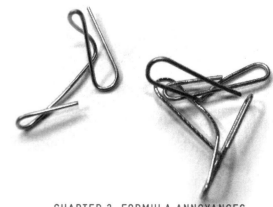

The Fix: You can count how many cells in a list contain numerical values with a COUNT formula. The COUNT formula requires you to tell it the range of cells you want to examine for values. If you want to count the number of cells in column C that contain a value, place the formula =COUNT(C:C) in the cell where you want the result to appear. If you want to count the number of cells in row 6 that contain a numerical value, enter the formula =COUNT(6:6) in the cell where you want the result to appear.

COUNT BLANK CELLS IN A RANGE

The Annoyance: I write magazine articles for a living, so I track the names of the commissioning editors at magazines I'd like to market to. These names are important because you never want to send off an article pitch with the salutation "To whom it may concern." What I'd like to do is find out how many rows in my worksheet have no value in the EditorName column. Is there some way to count blank cells in a column?

The Fix: Much like its close cousin the COUNT formula, the COUNTBLANK formula looks at a range and counts the number of cells that contain no values. If you know your list of magazines is 300 rows long and that the editor names are in column H, you can use the formula =COUNTBLANK(H2:H301) to determine the number of names you need to fill in. Just enter the formula in the cell where you want the result to appear.

COUNT THE NUMBER OF UNIQUE VALUES IN A RANGE

The Annoyance: I'm interested in how many different customers have placed orders with my computer company over the last month. I have all the orders in the same worksheet, and all the customer names in the same column. Can I count the number of different customers in the column?

The Fix: I was about to give up on this problem until I found Microsoft Knowledge Base article #268001, which offered the following two array formulas. (Remember, array formulas require you to press Ctrl-Shift-Enter instead of Enter when you're done typing. For more information, see "Deploy Array Formulas," earlier in this chapter.) To count the number of unique text and numerical values, use the formula =SUM(IF(FREQUENCY(MATCH(*range*,*range*,0), MATCH(*range*,*range*,0))>0,1)).

The range arguments are the cells that contain the list of names in which you want to find the number of unique values. For example, if the list of names were in cells A2:A308, your formula would be =SUM(IF(FREQUENCY(MATCH(A2:A308,A2:A308,0),MATCH(A2:A308,A2:A308,0))>0,1)).

If you're happy using the formula as a recipe, go for it. If you'd like to know how it does what it does, read on. Be warned, though...it's a complex process.

OK, let's work from the inside out. The MATCH() function returns the relative position of an item in an array, defined by the range *argument*. The 0 at the end of the MATCH() functions tells Excel that the items must match exactly. The FREQUENCY() function calculates how often specific values occur within a cell range and then returns a vertical array of numbers (that's why you have to enter this formula as an array formula). The FREQUENCY() function takes two arguments: data_array, which is the cell range that contains the raw values (in this case, the position of each customer name), and bins_array, which defines the number of "bins" the function uses for its counting. In this example, the MATCH() functions provide those values. The FREQUENCY() function takes only numbers, which is why you need to use the MATCH() function to find the numerical value of each name's place in the array.

The next step in the formula is to determine whether the frequency for a name is greater than zero (that's what the IF() function does). If a name occurs at least once, the IF() function outputs the value *1* (that's what the *1* in front of the last two parentheses means). Finally, the SUM() function counts the number of times the IF() function generated a *1*, which is the number of unique names in the list. Phew.

To count the number of unique numerical values, use the formula =SUM(IF(FREQUENCY(*range*,*range*)>0,1)). In this case, you don't need to count the number of text values to make the FREQUENCY() function work, which it does as described earlier. You can find the Knowledge Base article at *http://support.microsoft.com/support/kb/ articles/Q268/0/01.ASP*.

TETRIS IS BACK

If the United States' leading economic indicators drop suddenly after *Excel Annoyances* hits the store shelves, blame it on this sidebar. *Tetris*, the classic shape-arranging game from Russia (shown in the following figure), is available, in Excel, for free. You can find it at *http://www.xl-logic.com/xl_files/ games/tetris.zip*. Unpack the file and open the workbook in Excel 97 or later. You'll find all the instructions you need to play the game.

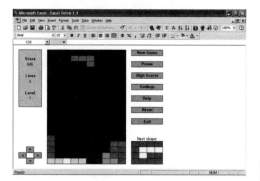

I'll probably regret this, but it's hard to turn my back on an old friend.

Manipulating Data
ANNOYANCES

4

Chapters 1 through 3 were all about getting data into Excel, summarizing it, and making it look pretty. In this chapter, you'll make your data tell you what you need to know—to run a business, to manage a sports team, or to figure out how much money you'll need to make those mortgage payments.

I'll start out by showing you how to make your life easy by sorting and filtering your worksheet data. For example, you'll learn how to create a formula that operates on visible cells only, master multilevel filters, and run sorts that whittle down your data to a manageable size.

Although Excel isn't a database, you can use it to find values in data lists thanks to the lookup family of formulas. Finally, I'll dig into PivotTables, the most versatile and useful Excel tool in the book, but one that's tricky for beginners and annoying for pros. You'll learn how to avoid the pitfalls when setting up your data, creating PivotTables, analyzing your data, and more.

SORTING AND FILTERING ANNOYANCES

SORT BY VALUES IN MULTIPLE COLUMNS

The Annoyance: Sorting the data in a single column is so easy, even I figured it out. I just click any cell in the column I want to sort, and then click the Sort Ascending or Sort Descending buttons on the toolbar. But look at my worksheet (Figure 4-1). I recorded my sales data by department (Accessories, Cars, Service), which is a handy enough view. But it doesn't help me see how I'm doing on a daily basis overall. How can I view my sales data by day?

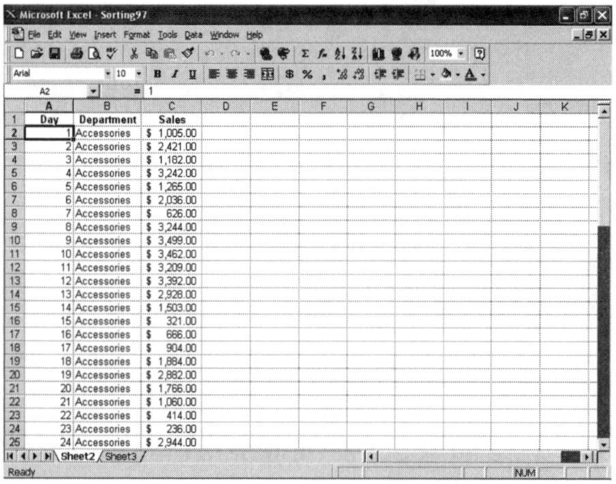

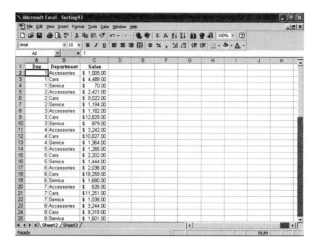

Figure 4-2. In this result, you see all sales, by type, per day.

Figure 4-1. Your sales data is recorded by department—but you need to see sales by day. That means sorting the worksheet by more than one column.

The Fix: What you need to do is sort the data list by the values in more than one column. Select Data → Sort and use the controls in the Sort dialog box—notably the "Then by" drop downs—to determine the order of the fields and whether to sort each field in ascending or descending order. Sorting by the Day column (in ascending order) and then the Department column (in ascending order) would result in the sorted data list shown in Figure 4-2.

WHAT'S A DATA LIST?

A *data list* is a set of data in an Excel worksheet in which each column has a unique name and each row represents a unique datum (for example, a salesperson's total sales on a given day). There can be no blank rows and no blank columns in the data list, no blank rows between column titles and the data, and no extraneous data in cells neighboring the list. That means you need at least one blank column to the right, at least one blank column (or the edge of the worksheet) to the left, and one blank row at the bottom of the data list. In essence, a data list looks and acts very much like a table in a database. See Figure 4-2 for a typical data list.

SORT DATA BY A CUSTOM SORT ORDER

The Annoyance: I hate the fact that Excel limits me to sorting data in alphabetical or numerical order! My boss at the car dealership insists the order of importance of our three departments is Cars, Service, and Accessories. He expects the data in my worksheets to reflect that priority, with Cars at the top of the list, Service a close second (if we don't sell cars, we won't have anything to fix), and Accessories third. The problem is that Excel insists on sorting the departments only in ascending alpha order (Accessories, Cars, Service), or descending alpha order (Service, Cars, Accessories). I spend a lot of time reordering the data to meet my boss's requirements. Is there some way I can make Excel sort the department names in an order I define? It would save me hours of work every month.

The Fix: You'll probably still have to work the same number of hours per week, but maybe this trick will help you devote those hours to selling cars instead of sorting data. The trick is to create a custom list of values Excel can use as the basis for the sort. The first task is to create a custom list. Here's how:

1. Type the values you want to sort by in a group of contiguous cells, in a single column or row, in the order you want to sort by. In your case you might type Cars, Service, and Accessories in cells A1, A2, and A3, respectively.

2. Select the cells that contain the values you just typed. Then choose Tools → Options, and click the Custom Lists tab.

3. Verify that the cell range you selected appears in the "Import list from cells" field.

4. Click the Import button and then click OK.

Now you can sort your data in the order of the values in your custom list, but you must use the custom list as the first sorting criterion. To sort your data by the values in your custom list, follow these steps:

1. Click any cell in the data list and press Ctrl-Shift-8 to select the entire list.

2. Choose Data → Sort, and in the Sort dialog box open the "Sort by" drop down and select the column you want to sort using your custom sort order.

3. Click the Options button and in the Sort Options dialog box open the "First key sort order" field, select your custom list from the list, and click OK.

4. If desired, you can set additional sorting criteria. Click OK, and when you return to the Sort dialog box click OK again to sort your data.

SORT DATA LEFT TO RIGHT

The Annoyance: Excel assumes everyone's data is arranged in columns, so all the sort functions work that way. However, sometimes I want to sort a row of values. How do I do that?

The Fix: To sort a row of values, select the row and choose Data → Sort, click the Options button, and in the Orientation section select "Sort left to right," and click OK. Then open the "Sort by" drop down, select the row you want to sort, select either Ascending or Descending, and click OK.

FILTER WORKSHEET DATA

The Annoyance: I create huge worksheets. In fact, I have one worksheet that is three columns wide and more than 1,000 rows long. You can see a sample of what I mean in Figure 4-3.

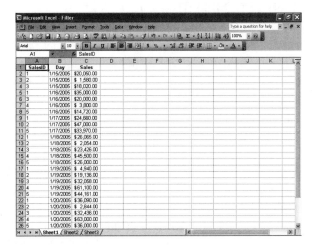

Figure 4-3. This data needs a serious trim.

For today, all I want to see are the sales for the rep with SalesID 1. That's all. Nothing more. *Nada mas.* Zip. How do I do that?

The Fix: To display just those rows that contain a certain value, click any cell in the data list. Then select Data → Filter → AutoFilter; a series of down arrows will appear in the first cell of every column in the list. (They hide the values in those cells, too.) These are filter arrows, and clicking one displays a drop-down list of filtering options. Click the value you want to use as your filter. All the rows in which *that* value does not occur in *that* column disappear. To refilter the results, click the filter arrow again and select a new criterion from the drop-down list. Incidentally, a filter arrow turns blue when the filter is active.

When you start this process, be sure not to click a column header (Excel's gray markers that denote column A, B, C, and so on). If you do and then you choose Data → Filter → AutoFilter, Excel will add a filter arrow only to the selected column.

To cancel all the filters, choose Data → Filter → Show All. To get out of filtering mode altogether and remove the filter arrows, choose Data → Filter → AutoFilter again. In Excel 2003, these filtering capabilities are included in the new List feature. For more information on Lists in Excel 2003, see the section "Excel 2003 List Annoyances" in Chapter 9.

DISPLAY TOP OR BOTTOM VALUES

The Annoyance: I use a long, complicated worksheet that shows hourly sales results for the auto dealership where I work. Instead of spending hours with a calculator to find the top 10 car-sales hours in the list, I was hoping there was some way I could get Excel to do that for me. Is there?

The Fix: When you click the filter arrow in the top row of your data list (see previous item), you'll see a set of filtering options. One of those options is Top 10, which displays the Top 10 AutoFilter dialog box (shown in Figure 4-4). You can use the controls to determine whether you want to display the top or bottom values from the list, and the number of values to display. You also can choose whether the number in the middle box represents a number of list entries to display, or the percentage of

entries to display. For example, if you type 10 in the middle box, and in the far right box you select Percent, Excel will display the top 10% of the values in that column.

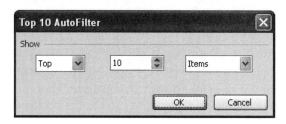

Figure 4-4. Find the best and worst in a list using a Top 10 AutoFilter.

CREATE A MULTILEVEL FILTER

The Annoyance: The other day, when I was giving a presentation based on the same auto dealership worksheet, one of the owners wanted to see a list of just those hours during which accessory sales were more than $2,500. I ended up sorting the list by department and then by sales in descending order, but it took forever and my boss was drumming his fingers by the end. Isn't there a faster way to filter list data by a criterion?

The Fix: To filter your data by a criterion, choose Data → Filter → AutoFilter, click the filter arrow at the top of the column to which you want to assign the criterion, and choose Custom to display the Custom AutoFilter dialog box (shown in Figure 4-5).

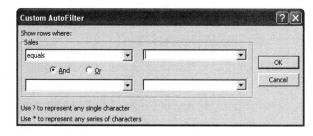

Figure 4-5. Filter your data by values in more than one column? Sure!

You can use the controls in the Custom AutoFilter dialog box to create two criteria by which you want to filter your data. When you open the top-left drop down, you'll see a list of Boolean operators (less than, greater than or equal to, and so on) to use on your data, while the top-right drop down contains a list of values taken from the column. (You can type in your own value if you want.) For example, if you wanted to find all hours during which sales were more than $2,500, you could choose "is greater than" in the top-left drop down and type 2500 in the top-right drop down.

If you want to create more complex criteria, dig into the second set of fields in the Custom AutoFilter dialog box and select the And or the Or radio buttons. For example, to find all sales hours with totals of more than $2,500 or less than $500, you would select the Or option, then choose "is less than" in the bottom-left drop down and type 500 in the bottom-right drop down.

The Custom AutoFilter you create filters values from only one column at a time, but you can use another filter to further hone the results the AutoFilter displays. To limit the results to the Accessories department, for example, you would click the Department filter arrow, choose Accessories from the value list, and then apply the custom filter.

FIND DUPLICATE ENTRIES IN A DATA LIST

The Annoyance: I am frustrated! I have a spreadsheet with 8,500 addresses that I'm going to use for an upcoming postcard mailing, but I need to pare the list to about 5,000 or I'll blow my postage budget. A lot of those 8,500 entries are duplicates, but Excel stubbornly refuses to find them for me. A friend told me I could export the data list to Access and run a Find Duplicates query. Please don't tell me I have to learn Access!

The Fix: Although finding duplicate entries per se requires a VBA macro, you can use the Advanced Filter dialog box (shown in Figure 4-6) to copy the unique rows from a data list to another location in your workbook—handily leaving all the duplicate entries behind.

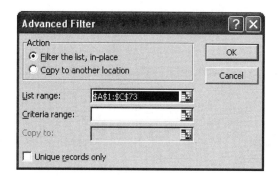

Figure 4-6. The Advanced Filter dialog box: not nearly as advanced as you might think, and quite useful.

To copy just the unique records in a data list, follow these steps:

1. Choose Data → Filter → Advanced Filter.

2. Select Copy to Another Location.

3. Click the Collapse Dialog button in the "List range" field and highlight the cells you want to filter, then press Enter.

4. Click the Collapse Dialog button in the "Copy to" field and click the cell at the top left of the range where you want to paste the filtered list (I suggest cell A1 of a blank worksheet). Press Enter.

5. Check the "Unique records only" checkbox and click OK.

Excel must find an exact match, including all punctuation, for two entries to be considered the same. If this doesn't whittle down your list much and you suspect there might be some undetected duplicate entries, try sorting the address list by last name, first name, and postal code to help simplify your job of spotting duplicates.

COPY ONLY VISIBLE CELLS FROM A FILTERED LIST

The Annoyance: I filtered a data list (shown in Figure 4-7), but when I try to copy the filtered rows and paste them into another worksheet, Excel pastes the hidden rows as well. I can tell I've selected more than the visible cells because as I select the cells, the Name box tells me I've selected an area that's 74 rows by 5 columns.

How do I copy and paste just the visible rows in my data list?

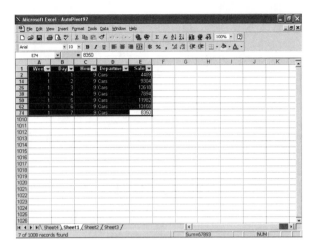

Figure 4-7. If you want to copy just the visible cells, use the Select Visible Cells button.

The Fix: To copy just the visible cells to the clipboard, you need to add the Select Visible Cells button to your toolbar. To add this button, choose Tools → Customize, select the Commands tab, select Edit from the Categories list, scroll down in the righthand Commands list until you find the Select Visible Cells button, and drag the button to any toolbar. Then, to copy and paste just the visible cells, follow these steps:

1. Filter the data list and highlight the visible cells.
2. Click the Select Visible Cells toolbar button.
3. Select Edit → Copy.
4. Choose Edit → Paste.

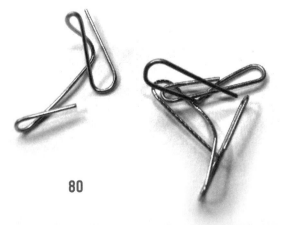

RUBIK'S CUBE IN EXCEL

If you ever played with a Rubik's Cube, raise your hand. Wow, a lot of hands are in the air!

If you feel funny about having toys lying around your office, but would enjoy an occasional diversion that tests your visualization and problem-solving skills, download the free Rubik's Cube emulator (written by Robin Glynn) from *http:// www.xl-logic.com/xl_files/games/cube.zip*. All you need to do is unzip the zip file and open the *cube.xls* workbook. As you can see in the figure, you manipulate the cube by clicking the renderings of the cube at the bottom of the screen representing the move you want to make. Buttons on the right side of the workbook save your position, restore a saved position, shuffle the cube's position randomly, and solve the cube automatically. You also can control how quickly the computer manipulates the cube in auto-solve mode. Don't change the time between moves while the algorithm is running, though. I managed to freeze my computer for two minutes when I tried.

In the great tradition of workplace entertainment, there's a Panic button that closes the workbook immediately. You'll lose your position in the game, but you'll keep your position at work.

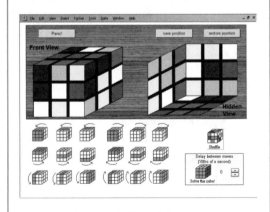

Twist your mind by twisting a cube.

SUMMARIZE VISIBLE CELLS ONLY

The Annoyance: Filters work for me, but I can't figure out how to create a formula that only summarizes the visible data in a worksheet. For example, let's say I'm working with sales data. I need to total the sales for each representative, but I can't find a way to add the cells for each representative without creating formulas that pinpoint individual cells. For instance, when I worked with the worksheet shown in Figure 4-3, I needed to create a formula that added cells C2, C5, C9, C12, C17, and C22 to find out the total for the salesperson with the SalesID 1. Then I had to add the values in cells C3, C10, C13, C18, and C23 for salesperson 2, and so on. I can filter the data list to show just one sales rep's sales. Can't I create a formula that totals just those cells?

The Fix: Figuring out what to do when your data doesn't behave is one of the most annoying aspects of working with Excel. Fortunately, in this case, the fix is actually fairly straightforward. You can create a filter that enables you to pick the sales representative whose data you want to summarize, and then create a Subtotal formula in a cell below the sales data. Here's the procedure in more detail:

1. Click any cell in the data list (in Figure 4-3, the data list is the cell range A1:C26).

2. Choose Data → Filter → AutoFilter.

3. Click the SalesID down arrow and click a SalesID number.

4. Click a cell in the Sales column that is below the data.

5. Click the AutoSum button on Excel's standard toolbar and press Enter.

Usually when you click the AutoSum toolbar button, you create a vanilla Sum formula that adds the data in every cell in your selected range and places the result just below. But if you click the AutoSum toolbar button in a cell below a filtered column of data, Excel creates a Subtotal formula. What's the difference? If you create a Subtotal formula below a filtered list when the filter is in place,

the formula only calculates its total (or average, or minimum, or maximum, or whatever) based on the cells that are visible in a filtered list.

The Subtotal formula has the syntax =SUBTOTAL(*function*, *range*), where *function* is the number of the summary calculation to be performed on the data and range is the range of cells in the filtered column. Table 4-1 lists the summary operations available to you when you create a SUBTOTAL() formula.

Table 4-1. Summarizing data with a SUBTOTAL () formula.

Number	Function
1	AVERAGE (the numeric average of the visible cells)
2	COUNT (the number of visible cells)
3	COUNTA (the number of visible cells that contain a value)
4	MAX (the maximum value in the visible cells)
5	MIN (the minimum value in the visible cells)
6	PRODUCT (the multiplicative product of the values in the visible cells)
7	STDEV (the standard deviation of the values in the visible cells)
8	STDEVP (the standard deviation of every cell named in the formula)
9	SUM (the arithmetic sum of the values in the visible cells)
10	VAR (the variance of the values in the visible cells)
11	VARP (the variance of every cell named in the formula)

LOOKUP FUNCTION ANNOYANCES

LOOK UP VALUES IN DATA LISTS

The Annoyance: I know Excel isn't a database... that's Access. And I know I shouldn't expect miracles, but I'm hoping you can help me look up a value in a table. For example, I have a list of sales reps, sorted by their employee ID number (as in Figure 4-8). If I see a transaction report with an employee ID, isn't there some way I can look up who belongs to that number without using the Find function?

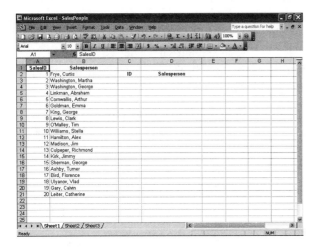

Figure 4-8. You can find corresponding values in a data list.

The Fix: Sure, you can do it. The process involves some pretty fancy footwork with advanced Excel functions, but once you grasp what's going on you'll be fine.

The first function you can use to find a value in a worksheet is the LOOKUP() function. Basically, the LOOKUP() function identifies a row in your worksheet by looking in, say, column A for a value you specify. Once it identifies the row that contains that value in column A, it looks in, say, column C of that same row, snatches the value it finds there, and "returns" it, or displays it, in whatever cell holds your formula.

The LOOKUP() function has this syntax:

```
=LOOKUP(lookup_value, lookup_vector, result_vector)
```

whereby:

- *lookup_value* is the cell (or value) to find in the table. It could be an employee's ID number, a Social Security number, or another unique identifier.

- *lookup_vector* is the range to search for the *lookup_value*. If a list of employee IDs were stored in the

range A2:A34, you would type **A2:A34** in the *lookup_vector* spot.

- *result_vector* is the range within which to look, find, and return the corresponding value. If the employees' names are stored in the range B2:B34, that's the range you'd type here.

In other words, you're telling the LOOKUP() function what to look for, where to look for it, and where to find the corresponding value you're really interested in. In the worksheet in Figure 4-8, if you enter the formula =LOOKUP(C3,A2:A21,B2:B21) into a blank cell, it will take the value you enter into C3, locate the matching value in column A (looking from row 2 to 21), and return the value in column B that corresponds with the value found in column A. Typing **5** in cell C3 would return *Cornwallis, Arthur*, while typing **16** in cell C3 would return *Ashby, Turner*.

The LOOKUP() function is somewhat limited in that the *lookup_vector* and *result_vector* can consist of only one row or column each. There's also the possibility of getting an incorrect result: if LOOKUP() can't find the *lookup_value* in the *lookup_vector* table, it matches the largest value that is less than or equal to *lookup_value*. In the case of the worksheet in Figure 4-8, if you hired a new sales rep who was assigned SalesID 21, but you didn't enter the rep's information into the worksheet, searching for the value would return *Leiter, Catherine*, which is incorrect.

If you don't mind going to a little more trouble, you can avoid bogus matches *and* go beyond the two-column limit by using the VLOOKUP() function instead. The VLOOKUP() function has the following syntax:

```
=VLOOKUP(lookup_value,table_array,col_index_num,range_lookup)
```

whereby:

- *lookup_value* is the value to be found; it can be a value (the number 14), a reference to a cell where the value appears (cell D2), or a text string (the part identification code GRO83). VLOOKUP always looks for the *lookup_value* in the first column of the array.

- *table_array* is the cell range in which Excel should search for the *lookup_value*. The *table_array* in Figure 4-8 is the range A2:B21.

- *col_index_num* is the column number in *table_array* in which the matching value will be found and returned. A *col_index_num* of 1 returns the value found in the leftmost column in *table_array*, a *col_index_num* of 2 returns the value found in the second column in *table_array*, and so on. If *col_index_num* is greater than the number of columns in the range named in the *table_array* argument, VLOOKUP() displays a #REF! error code.

- *range_lookup* is an optional argument. When set to TRUE or left blank, VLOOKUP() works like the LOOKUP() function and returns the largest value that is less than the *lookup_value*. If set to FALSE, the function must find an exact match or it will display an #N/A error code.

The VLOOKUP() function that's equivalent to the =LOOKUP(C3,A2:A21,B2:B21) formula I discussed earlier is =VLOOKUP(C3,A2:B21,2,TRUE).

Incidentally, VLOOKUP() doesn't distinguish between uppercase and lowercase text. If you need to create a lookup function that distinguishes between uppercase and lowercase, see the annoyance "Perform a Case-Sensitive Lookup" later in this chapter.

The VLOOKUP() function is short for *vertical lookup*, which means Excel assumes your data is arranged in columns. If your data happens to be arranged in rows, as is the case in Figure 4-9, you can use the HLOOKUP() function to search for corresponding values.

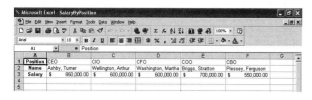

Figure 4-9. Excel also can look for values in horizontally oriented data sets.

> ### WHY USE A COL_INDEX_NUM VALUE OF 1?
>
> You probably noticed that the VLOOKUP() function lets you return values from the first column of the table array. Why would you do that, as that's where you're looking for values in the first place? One case where it would be helpful is if you have a list of dates in the first column, such as 3/15/2005, 3/17/2005, and 3/28/2005. You could use the formula =VLOOKUP(C3,A2:B200,1,TRUE) to find the date that's closest to, but not later than, the date in cell C3. If you typed 3/27/2005 in cell C3, for example, the =VLOOKUP(C3,A2:B200,1,TRUE) formula would return 3/17/2005.

The HLOOKUP() function uses this syntax:

    =HLOOKUP(lookup_value,table_array,row_index_
    num,range_lookup)

And it works exactly the way VLOOKUP() does, except at right angles:

- *lookup_value* is the value to be found in the first row of the table.

- *table_array* is the cell range to be searched.

- *row_index_num* is the row number in *table_array* from which the matching value will be found and displayed as the formula's result. In other words, if your worksheet had a series of employee IDs in the first row, the employees' names in the second row, and the employees' salaries in the third row, a *row_index_num* value of 2 would find a name, while a *row_index_num* value of 3 would find the salary. If *row_index_num* is less than 1, HLOOKUP() returns a #VALUE! error; if *row_index_num* is greater than the number of rows in *table_array*, HLOOKUP() returns a #REF! error.

- *range_lookup*, if set to TRUE or omitted, allows HLOOKUP() to find an approximate match. If set to FALSE, HLOOKUP() must either find an exact match or display an #N/A error.

For this table, the formula to look up the salary associated with the position (CEO, CIO, COO, etc.) entered into cell B12 would be =HLOOKUP(B12,B2:F3,3,FALSE).

LOOK UP A VALUE IN ANY COLUMN

The Annoyance: The VLOOKUP() function is neat. But you can't use it to look up a value in any column except column A. That means if I want to look up a value in the fifth column and return the corresponding value from the third column, I'm out of luck. Is there a way around this limitation of the VLOOKUP() function?

The Fix: You can search for values in an arbitrary column and return a corresponding value from another column, but you need to use a combination of the INDEX() and MATCH() functions to do it. The INDEX() function, which finds the address of a cell that meets a criterion, has the following syntax:

=INDEX(*reference, row_num, column_num, area_num*)

whereby:

- *reference* is a reference to one or more cell ranges that contain the values you want the function to look for and return. If you want to search a noncontiguous group of cells, you'll need to enclose the references in parentheses—e.g., (A1:B6, C3:D8, F1:G6).

- *row_num* is the number of the row in the range named in the *reference* argument where you want the function to look for the value.

- *column_num* is the number of the column in the range named in the *reference* argument where you want the function to look for the value.

- *area_num* is the cell range named in the *reference* argument where you want the function to look for the value. The first area selected or entered is numbered 1, the second is 2, and so on. If *area_num* is omitted, INDEX() uses area 1. For example, if INDEX() searched the ranges A10:B14, C12:D16, and F14:G18, A10:B14 would be area 1, C12:D16 would be area 2, and F14:G18 would be area 3.

The MATCH() function, by contrast, returns the relative position of a value in a cell range. For example, if the

target value were in the third cell down in a single-column range, MATCH() would return the value 3.

The MATCH() function has the following syntax:

=MATCH(*lookup_value, lookup_array, match_type*)

whereby:

- *lookup_value* is the search term you use to find the value you want in a table.

- *lookup_array* is a contiguous range of cells that contains a set of lookup values.

- *match_type* is the number -1, 0, or 1. If *match_type* is 1, MATCH() finds the largest value that is less than or equal to *lookup_value*. If this argument is set to 1, the values in *lookup_array* must be sorted in ascending order. If *match_type* is 0, MATCH() finds the first exact match to *lookup_value*. If this argument is set to 0, the values in *lookup_array* can be in any order. If *match_type* is -1, MATCH() finds the smallest value that is greater than or equal to *lookup_value*. If *match_type* is set to -1, the values in *lookup_array* must be sorted in descending order. If you don't specify a value for the *match_type* argument, Excel assumes it's 1.

The INDEX() and MATCH() functions work well together because the MATCH() function supplies the cell location that the INDEX() function needs to do its lookup. As an example, consider the data set in Figure 4-10.

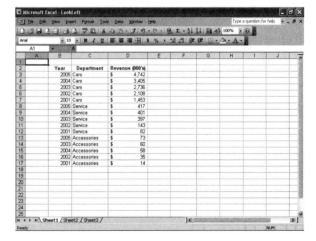

Figure 4-10. Searching to the left? It's possible, just not with VLOOKUP().

If you want to find the first instance when any department exceeded the $500,000 sales mark, first you would sort the sheet so that the Sales column is sorted in descending order, and then you'd use the formula =INDEX(C3: C17,MATCH(F3,D3:D17,-1)) to find the department, and the formula =INDEX(B3:B17,MATCH(F3,D3:D17,-1)) to determine the year when the sales mark was broken. Here's a rundown of what these compound formulas do:

- The INDEX() function's first argument defines the range with the potential values to be returned as C3: C17 (the auto dealership's departments).

- The INDEX() function derives its second argument from the MATCH() function. The MATCH() function uses the value in cell F3 to search the range D3:D17 for the smallest value that is larger than the value in F3; then it returns the cell's position in the range (in this case, 5) to the INDEX() function.

- The INDEX() function, which now looks like =INDEX(C3:C17,5), returns the value from cell C7, the fifth cell down in the sorted range.

CORRECT AN INCORRECT VLOOKUP( ) RESULT IN EXCEL 97

The Annoyance: I track my company's orders using an Excel 97 workbook that I converted from Lotus 1-2-3. I keep the orders on one worksheet and the actual products on another worksheet, but when I try to look up the product that corresponds to an order number, sometimes I get the wrong result. How come?

The Fix: Excel 97 has a bug that rears its ugly head when your lookup table and the cell with the VLOOKUP() formula are on different worksheets, *and* you use the Transition Formula Evaluation option to have Excel resolve its formula as Lotus 1-2-3 would. (The two programs evaluate VLOOKUP() formulas differently.) To fix the problem, click the worksheet with the products lookup table, choose Tools → Options, click the Transition tab, and uncheck the "Transition formula evaluation" checkbox.

TEXT-NUMBER MIX OVERWHELMS LOOKUP

The Annoyance: I track the car and truck parts we stock at the auto dealership where I work. The part descriptions vary by manufacturer, of course, as do the codes—and many part codes, such as A3000 or T1648B, contain letters. Anyway, I just imported my list of part codes into Excel (see Figure 4-11) and was looking forward to using a manufacturer's part code to look up the part's name and other information, but when I tried I got an #N/A error. I typed A2000 instead of A3000 into the "search-for" cell, so why did the formula generate an error? If I type in part number 9815 instead of 9816, the VLOOKUP() formula returns "Spark Plug," which is the previous entry in the table. Why didn't the formula skip back to part number 9816, the entry *before* part A3000, and return "Headlight?" I'm totally confused.

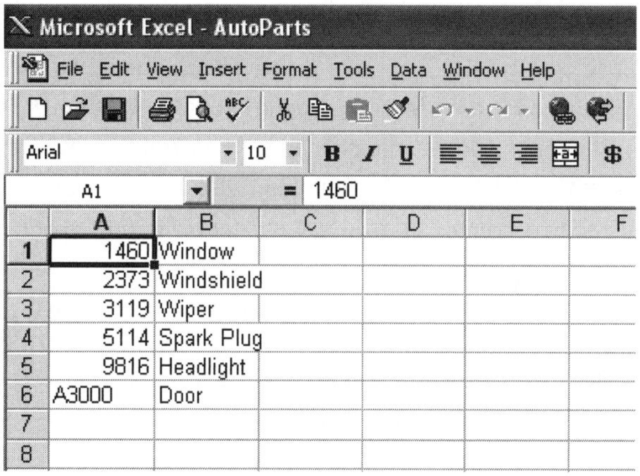

Figure 4-11. This parts list mixes numbers and letters, befuddling the usual lookup formulas.

The Fix: Excel doesn't react well when you mix text and numeric values in a lookup table. Excel tries to help you out by searching only for text values when you enter a text value, and only for numbers when you enter a number, but that can lead to problems. For instance, your sample worksheet contains a set of numeric values before the A3000 row, so the VLOOKUP() formula generates an error because the search made Excel try to go to a cell before the first text value.

The best way to prevent this error from occurring is to avoid mixing text and numeric values in a lookup list. If you can't do that, format the cells as text (select Format → Cells, click the Number tab, and select Text from the Category list) before you import or enter the data. If the data is already in the workbook, you can use an array formula to treat the values in the part code list as text (changing the formatting of the list cells after the data is entered won't work). Here's the formula, which assumes the value you want to look up is in cell D2 and the part code list is in cells A1:A3:

```
{=VLOOKUP(TEXT(D2,"@"),TEXT(A1:A3,"@"),1)}
```

Remember to press Ctrl-Shift-Enter to create this as an array formula; you'll get an #N/A error if you just press Enter.

PERFORM A CASE-SENSITIVE LOOKUP

The Annoyance: I own a martial arts supply business, and I've run into a problem with one of my employees. Jo is a wonderful employee, but her name, when spelled in lowercase, happens to be the word for a type of stick we use around the dojo (and also a great word for Scrabble). When I try to use a lookup function to find a match for *jo*, sometimes I get a match for *Jo*. There's gotta be a way to make a lookup function case-sensitive.

The Fix: Well, if you're doing just a simple search, you can require Excel to match the case of the search term by checking the "Match case" checkbox in the Find dialog box (Edit → Find). If you're planning to use one of the lookup functions (HLOOKUP(), LOOKUP(), VLOOKUP(), INDEX(), or MATCH()), there isn't an easy way to force them to require a case-sensitive match.

However, if you combine the IF() and EXACT() functions, you *can* make it happen. For example, assume you're working with the worksheet shown in Figure 4-12.

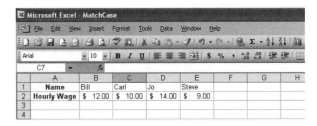

Figure 4-12. Sometimes the only difference between two values is the case of the letters.

If you typed the formula =IF(EXACT(B7,HLOOKUP(B7,A1:E2,1))=TRUE,HLOOKUP(B7,A1:E2,2),"No match") into cell C7 and typed jo into cell B7, the formula would return No match because the lookup value in cell D1 is not in the same case as the entry in the table. However, if you typed Jo in cell B7, you'd see her hourly pay rate of $14.00.

The same technique works with a LOOKUP() formula, but you need to change the parameters a bit to match the LOOKUP() function's syntax. In this case, the data is arranged so that it can be used in a LOOKUP() function (as shown in Figure 4-13). In this case, the formula should be =IF(EXACT(A7,LOOKUP(A7,A1:A5,A1:A5))=TRUE,LOOKUP(A7,A1:A5,B1:B5),"No match").

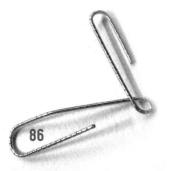

Figure 4-13. It's important to give your formulas the input they expect.

You also can use a VLOOKUP() formula with the data in Figure 4-13, which would be =IF(EXACT(A7,VLOOKUP(A7,A1:B5,1,FALSE))=TRUE,VLOOKUP(A7,A1:B5,2,FALSE),"No match").

WORK WITH INCORRECT TIMES SERIES

The Annoyance: I'm a marine biologist, and lately I've been studying the growth rate of a particular strain of bacteria in a fish habitat. I track the hourly growth rate in an Excel worksheet (shown in Figure 4-14), but occasionally I'll get an error when I try to look up the values with a VLOOKUP() formula. I've never had any trouble with this function before, so why doesn't it like this particular data now?

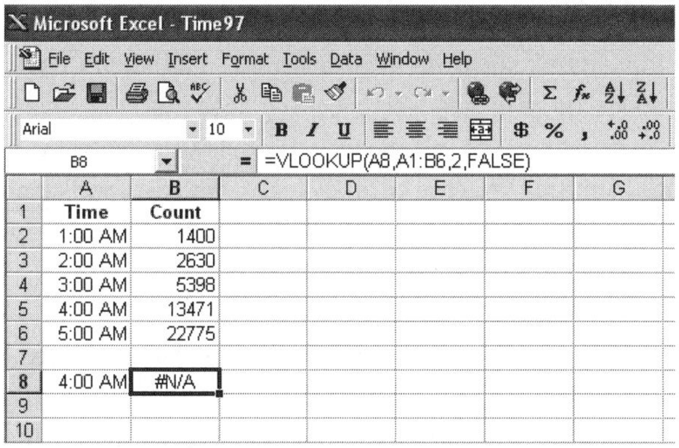

Figure 4-14. These times look normal. Why won't Excel let me use them in a VLOOKUP formula?

The Fix: The problem, which occurs in every Excel version up to and including Excel 2003, kicks in when you use the fill handle to extend a sequence of times. In the worksheet shown in Figure 4-14, you probably typed 1:00 AM in cell A2, 2:00 AM in cell A3, and then extended the series using the fill handle into cells A4, A5, and A6. You can avoid the problem by entering the times manually, but that's not a good solution if more than three or four entries comprise a series. One possible solution is to choose Tools → Options, click the Calculation tab, and check the Precision as Displayed box. After you click OK, you'll see an error message that says *Data will permanently lose accuracy*, which applies to all the data in your workbook, not just in the current worksheet. In other words, if you have a set of numbers with five digits after the decimal, but you've formatted the cells to display

only the first two digits, Excel will truncate the actual values and forget the original cell value. If that's going to be a problem for you (and if you're a scientist, it probably will), you need to keep your data as is (that is, with full precision), and if you want to use a VLOOKUP() formula that uses time values, you will need to enter all those time values by hand. Z–Z–z–z–z....

SPEED UP MULTIPLE LOOKUPS

The Annoyance: I maintain a master Excel 97 workbook that summarizes data from all the projects in my department—all 35 of them. I need to update the values in my summary workbook to keep up with new purchases and person-hours spent on the various projects, and, yes, that does mean my workbook contains quite a few VLOOKUP() formulas that rely on importing data from other workbooks. The problem is that when I ask Excel to update those links and formulas, it takes forever (well, several minutes) for the workbook to open. These delays didn't happen in Excel 95! Is something broken?

The Fix: The problem is that Excel has to open all the files you're linked to before it can pull in the updated values. Excel 97, Excel 2000 (before Service Pack 1), and even Excel 2002 (before Service Pack 3) didn't handle opening the linked files well. The best way to get around the problem is to upgrade to Excel 2000 or 2002 and install the appropriate Service Pack—or just bite the bullet and upgrade to 2003. You can download the most recent service pack for your version by visiting *http://office.microsoft.com/OfficeUpdate/default.aspx.* Click the Check for Updates link at the top of the page and the site will detect your version of Office and list the available downloads.

If you can't do any of those things for some reason, just make sure you open the files that you've linked to *before* you update the values in your summary workbook.

FIND THE FIRST OR LAST MATCH IN AN ARRAY

The Annoyance: I track orders from my customers in a database, and I import the data into an Excel worksheet so that I can create a PivotTable. The worksheet (shown in Figure 4-15) has the customer's ID number in the first column and the order details in the next few columns. Whenever I use a LOOKUP() or VLOOKUP() formula to search the table, the formula finds the last occurrence in the table. That's handy for finding the last time a customer placed an order, but what I'd like to do is find the *first* time a customer placed an order. Is there a way to find the first occurrence of a value in a list instead of the last?

![Microsoft Excel - LastOccur spreadsheet showing Customer ID and Order Date columns](image)

	A	B	C	D	E	F
1	Customer ID	Order Date				
2	000802	10/18/2004				
3	000802	10/19/2004				
4	001354	10/15/2004				
5	001354	12/1/2004				
6	001354	1/5/2005				
7						
8						

Figure 4-15. Want to find the last time a customer placed an order? Or the first? Both are possible, if you know how to ask.

The Fix: You can use a combination of the INDEX() and MATCH() functions to find the first occurrence of a value in a list. In the workbook shown in Figure 4-15, if the customer ID number 001354 were typed in cell D2, the formula =LOOKUP(D2,A1:A6,B1:B6) would return 1/5/2005, while the formula =INDEX(A1:B6,MATCH(D2,A1: A6,0),2) would return 10/15/2004. This particular combination of the INDEX() and MATCH() functions lets you perform the operation without sorting the list's first column into either ascending or descending order.

WHAT-IF ANALYSIS ANNOYANCES

CREATE A SCENARIO

The Annoyance: I have two bosses, which means I'm asked a lot of "What if" questions. For example, when I put together a project cost summary worksheet, each boss asked about *different* sets of variables: what would be the effect if one component or another cost more or less? Could I drive down labor costs through productivity gains? All good questions, but when I try to include them in one worksheet my head starts spinning. What I really need is some way to display alternative values in certain selected cells, such as labor costs and component prices, and a way to switch back and forth between them. Is that possible?

The Fix: You have only two bosses? Luxury. When I worked in Washington, DC, I had two official bosses and three "dotted-line" bosses who could reach across the corporate organization chart to order me around. Needless to say, I developed a few survival strategies, and one of them is the *scenario*.

A scenario is an alternative data set you can store as part of a worksheet. When you want to display the alternative values, just call up the alternate scenario and keep right on going with your presentation. Here's how you create a scenario:

1. Choose Tools → Scenarios to display the Scenario Manager dialog box.

2. Click the Add button, and give your new scenario a name.

3. Click the Collapse Dialog button in the "Changing cells" field, select the cells you want to change, and press Enter. Remember that you can select noncontiguous groups of cells by holding down the Ctrl key when you select the cells. Click OK when you're done.

4. In the Scenario Values dialog box (shown in Figure 4-16) enter the new values for your selected cells. Click

OK to close the dialog box and then click the Close button to close the Scenario Manager dialog box.

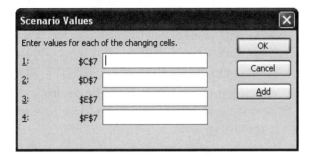

Figure 4-16. Enter your new scenario values here…

To apply a scenario, follow these steps:

1. Choose Tools → Scenarios to display the Scenario Manager dialog box (shown in Figure 4-17).

Figure 4-17. …and display them here.

2. Click the name of the scenario to display, and click the Show button.

3. Click Close to close the Scenario Manager dialog box.

When you want to hide the scenario, just click the Undo button on Excel's standard toolbar.

Warning: never use scenarios in any workbook that holds the only copy of your data. Instead, make a backup copy of the workbook to use for your scenario what-if analyses. Here's why: unless you carefully undo the scenario change, Excel leaves the values from the last-active scenario in place. If you close your worksheet without restoring the original values by clicking the Undo button, Excel will overwrite the original values! As a second safety measure, create a Normal scenario that contains the original values of every cell affected by one of your scenarios. Scenarios are limited to 32 cell changes each, so you might need to create more than one scenario to hold your original values, but the work is worth it to make sure your original data remains intact.

FIND A VALUE THAT GENERATES A SPECIFIC RESULT

The Annoyance: I created a summary table that lists the total revenue from the Accessories, Car, and Service departments at my auto dealership (see Figure 4-18). I'm disappointed that the Service department isn't pulling its weight; in most dealerships the Service department makes up at least 20% of the total revenue. So, how much more do I have to make from Service to get its total up to 20%? I probably could create some complicated formula, or fake it by plugging in dozens of different service revenue numbers until I finally got the share to exactly 20%, but is there some way Excel can do it for me?

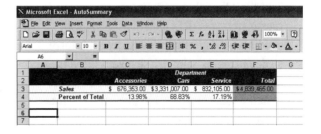

Figure 4-18. Don't chase your data's tail! Let Excel do the work for you.

The Fix: To find a value that will generate a specific formula result, follow these steps:

1. Choose Tools → Goal Seek to display the Goal Seek dialog box (shown in Figure 4-19).

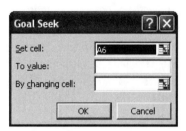

Figure 4-19. Set your goals, and Excel will see if it's possible to meet them.

2. With your cursor in the "Set cell" field, click the Collapse Dialog button on the right side of the field and click the cell with the formula that you want to generate a specific result (in the example, that's cell E4).

3. In the "To value" field, type the value you want the formula to generate (in this example, that would be either .2 or 20%).

BEWARE OF PERCENTAGES IN GOAL SEEK

When you're working with percentages in Goal Seek, it's easy to type in the wrong value. In this case, you might mistakenly type 20 in the "To value" field instead of .2 or 20%. If you make this mistake, Goal Seek will attempt to find a value for cell E3 that made it 20 times larger than (or 2000% of) the value in F3. This is impossible, of course, because cell E4 generates its value by dividing one department's sales by the total of all departments' sales, which means the value in cell F3, the grand total, always will be larger than the value in cell E3, one department's total.

---

4. With your cursor in the "By changing cell" field, click the Collapse Dialog button on the right side of the field and click the cell in the worksheet that holds the formula input you want to change (in this example, that would be cell E3). Then click the Expand Dialog button, and click OK.

5. Excel displays the solution, if any, to the problem. You can either click OK to replace the existing worksheet values with the result, or click Cancel to return to the original values.

To find out how to use Goal Seek with Excel charts, see the annoyance "Seeking Your Goal with a Chart" in Chapter 5.

USE SOLVER TO SOLVE MULTIVARIATE PROBLEMS

The Annoyance: I believe my annoyances extend far beyond the abilities of Goal Seek, but hey, maybe I'm wrong. Basically, I'm trying to figure out the best mix of advertisements for my company:

- I want to put my ads in front of as many people as possible.
- I have an advertising budget of $200,000.
- I must buy at least 15 ads on the backs of buses ("bus butts") to fulfill my end of a deal with the city.
- I must buy at least three ads in the lowest-circulation magazine to keep the editor (my brother-in-law) happy.
- I don't want to buy more than 30 ads in any venue.
- I can't buy a fraction of an ad, so the varying cells must contain integer values.

So, given the venue, price, and viewership figures in Figure 4-20, how do I figure out the best advertising mix for my business?

The Fix: Goal Seek works only when you want to vary the value in a single cell. To solve problems where you might need to vary the value in multiple cells, you need to move up to Solver, which is an Excel add-in produced by Frontline Systems and included for free with Excel. To check if Solver is installed, click Tools and see if there's a Solver item about halfway down the menu. If there isn't, choose Tools → Add-Ins, check the Solver Add-In box, and click OK to install Solver. If Solver is not listed in the Add-Ins dialog box, open the Windows Start menu, choose Search → For Files or Folders (or Find, depending on your OS), and search for the file *Solver.xla*. If you find it, in Excel choose Tools → Add-Ins, click the Browse button, and navigate to the file. If you can't locate the file, you might need to run the Office setup program to add the Solver component.

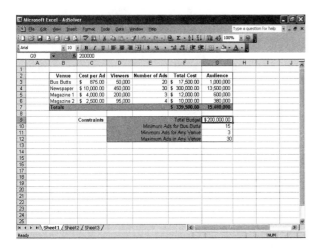

Figure 4-20. Make your assumptions clear so that Excel can understand them.

Once Solver is installed, choose Tools → Solver to display the Solver Parameters dialog box (shown in Figure 4-21).

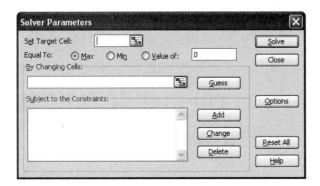

Figure 4-21. The base station for Solver in its natural state.

You'll use the Solver Parameters dialog box to enter the rules for your problem. Put your assumptions in the worksheet along with your data—they'll be easier to find in the Solver Parameters dialog box.

Here are the steps to create the model described in the annoyance:

1. Select cell G7, which is the cell with the value you want to maximize (total audience), and choose Tools → Solver. The Solver Parameters dialog box will appear with cell G7 already indicated in the Target Cell field.

2. In the By Changing Cells field, click the Collapse Dialog button, select cells E3:E6, and click the Expand Dialog button.

3. Click the Add button to display the Add Constraint dialog box (shown in Figure 4-22).

Figure 4-22. Don't let your data get out of line...constrain it!

4. To add the rule that the number of ads bought must be an integer value, click the Collapse Dialog button, select cells E3:E6, and click the Expand Dialog button. Then open the middle drop down in the dialog, select "int," and click the Add button. *Note: if you plan to use this constraint, always add the rule first.* When I first entered this solution, I created the "every ad buy must be an integer" rule last and, for some reason, got the value 29.065 for the Magazine 1 ad buy. When I deleted the scenario and reentered it, creating the "must be an integer" rule first, the solution came out all integers, the way I wanted it to. The lesson? Excel processes constraints in the order you enter them, so you always should put your formatting constraints (e.g., this value must be an integer) before the value-related constraints.

5. With your cursor in the Cell Reference field, click the Collapse Dialog button, select cell F7, and click the Expand Dialog button. Then select "<=" in the middle drop down, in the Constraint field select cell G9, and then click the Add button.

6. With your cursor in the Cell Reference field, click the Collapse Dialog button, select cells E3:E6, and click the Expand Dialog button. Then open the middle drop down, select ">=", in the Constraint field select cell G11, and then click the Add button.

7. With your cursor in the Cell Reference field, click the Collapse Dialog button, select cell E3, and click the Expand Dialog button. Then open the middle drop down, select ">=", in the Constraint field select cell G10, and then click the Add button.

8. With your cursor in the Cell Reference field, click the Collapse Dialog button, select cells E3:E6, and click the Expand Dialog button. Then open the middle drop down and select "<=". In the Constraint field, select cell G12, and click OK to display the Solver Parameters dialog box with your constraints.

9. Click Solve.

If you make a mistake while creating any of the criteria, you can click the rule in the "Subject to the Constraints" section of the Solver Parameters dialog box and click the Change button to edit the rule.

If Solver can find a solution to your problem, it will change the values in your worksheet and display a success message in the Solver Results dialog box, shown in Figure 4-23.

You can elect to keep the Solver values, or restore the original values, by selecting the appropriate option. If you want to save the Solver values as a scenario, click the Save Scenario button and type in a name for the new scenario.

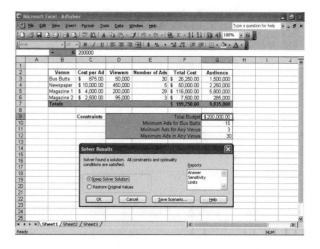

Figure 4-23. Another happy ending—Solver returns just the results you needed.

PLACE DATA ANALYSIS ON A MENU

The Annoyance: I'm trying to do some advanced data analysis (regression and such), and the boss left me instructions to "open the Tools menu and click Data Analysis." But there *is* no Data Analysis item on my Tools menu. And please don't tell me I have to buy something extra!

The Fix: You don't have to buy anything extra, but you do need to install the Data Analysis add-in that comes standard with the program. To do so, choose Tools → Add-Ins, check the Analysis ToolPak and (for good measure) the Analysis ToolPak-VBA boxes, and click OK. Excel will add the Data Analysis item to the Tools menu, so you can use the additional statistical functions to analyze your data.

PIVOTTABLE ANNOYANCES

LEARN TO USE PIVOTTABLES

The Annoyance: I've heard Excel aces talk about PivotTables as if they were some great gift to spreadsheet users. Then, the owner of a chain of local pet stores asked

me in a job interview if I knew how to make and manipulate the darned things. I didn't know and, rather than lie, I told him no, but that I was willing to learn. He hired me, but if I want to get past my probation period, I'm gonna have to learn how to use them. So, I ask: what the heck *is* a PivotTable, and how do I create one?

The Fix: A PivotTable is a dynamic data table (sort of a report, actually) that you can manipulate to emphasize different views of a data list stored in Excel. As an example, consider the worksheet shown in Figure 4-24.

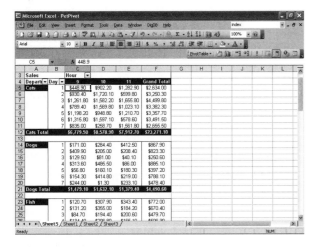

Figure 4-24. This configuration emphasizes days over hours.

This PivotTable shows a sampling of the hourly sales for the departments in your boss's four pet stores. The rows are grouped by department and then by day, while each column represents an hour of the day. You could produce exactly the same worksheet without using the PivotTable feature, but then you wouldn't be able to change it without rearranging all the data by hand to produce a different look, such as the one shown in Figure 4-25.

The PivotTable configuration in Figure 4-25 shows each department's sales, but instead of arranging it by day, it emphasizes sales during specific hours of the day (9:00

AM, 10:00 AM, and so on). That's the power of the PivotTable: you can change from one data arrangement to another quickly, perhaps as part of a presentation, and show how your sales break down by department, week, day, or even hour.

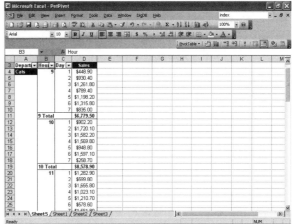

Figure 4-25. This configuration emphasizes hours over days.

To create a PivotTable, your data needs to be arranged as a list, as shown in Figure 4-26. The order of the columns isn't important, but it's easier to read your data if you arrange the columns in a logical order.

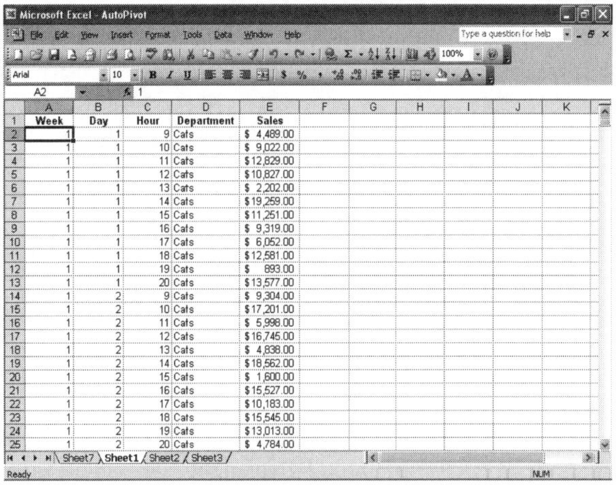

Figure 4-26. This data is ready to be made into a PivotTable.

Although the order of your columns doesn't matter, your data list must follow a few rules before Excel can use it to create a PivotTable:

- There can be no blank rows and no blank columns in the list.
- Each column must have a unique name.
- There should be no extraneous data in cells neighboring the list. That means you must have either the left edge of the worksheet or a blank column adjoining the list on either side, and you need at least one blank row at the bottom.
- There can be no duplicate keys.

Please note that each row denotes a unique bit of information. As an example, consider the data in row 2 of Figure 4-26 (the row just below the column headers). This row provides the sales total for the Week (1), the Day (1), the Hour (9), and the Department (Cats). The next row provides the sales total for the Week (1), the Day (1), the Hour (10), the Department (Cats), and so on, row by row. Each row in the data list corresponds to a cell in the PivotTable.

It's absolutely vital that each row provides a unique data point. In this example, the first four columns (Week, Day, Hour, and Department) combine to form a unique value, or *key*, for each row in the column. It wouldn't make any sense to have the two rows shown in Figure 4-27.

	G	H	I	J	K
	1	1	9	Cats	$ 4,489.00
	1	1	9	Cats	$ 9,022.00

Figure 4-27. These rows compete to see which value is used in the PivotTable. It's a fight no one will win.

Those rows attempt to set a different value for sales on Week: 1, Day: 1, Hour: 9, and Department: Cats, and it's the sort of error that will bring the PivotTable Wizard to a screeching halt. The Sales column, which provides the data displayed in the body of the PivotTable, doesn't matter...

Excel wouldn't care if every value in the Sales column were the same. What you can't have are two or more rows in the list where the nondata fields are an exact match.

CREATE A PIVOTTABLE

The Annoyance: OK, I followed all those complicated rules and I thought my data list was ready to make into a PivotTable. So, I chose Data → PivotTable Report in Excel 97 and tried to work my way through the PivotTable Wizard, but I didn't understand some of the questions, and Excel didn't seem to recognize the data list I wanted to use. Help!

The Fix: To create a PivotTable in Excel 97, follow these steps:

1. Select any cell in your data list and choose Data → PivotTable Report.

2. Select the "Microsoft Excel list or database" option and click Next.

3. Verify that the proper data range appears in the Range field and click the Next button to display the third page of the PivotTable Report Wizard, as shown in Figure 4-28. (If the data range in the Range field is not correct, click the Collapse Dialog button next to the Range field. Then select the cells from your worksheet, click the Expand Dialog button at the right of the field, and click the Next button to display the third page of the PivotTable Report Wizard.)

4. Drag the field headers to the desired positions in the PivotTable. The order of the field headers determines how Excel will group the PivotTable's data. To duplicate the layout seen in Figure 4-29, drag the Week, Department, and Day fields (in that order) to the Row area, the Hour field to the Column area, and the Sales field to the Data area. Click Next when you're done.

5. Verify that the New Worksheet option is selected and click Finish.

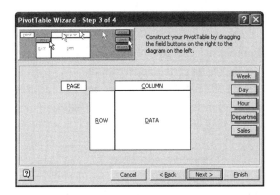

Figure 4-28. Create the initial layout of your PivotTable here.

To create a PivotTable in Excel 2000, 2002, or 2003, follow these steps:

1. Select any cell in your data list and choose Data → PivotTable and PivotChart Report.

2. Select the "Microsoft Excel list or database" option, and then the PivotTable option, and click Next.

3. Verify that the proper data range appears in the Range field, click Next, and then click the Layout button.

4. Drag the field headers to the desired positions in the PivotTable. The order of the field headers determines how Excel will group the PivotTable's data. To duplicate the layout seen in Figure 4-29, drag the Week, Department, and Day fields (in that order) to the Row area, the Hour field to the Column area, and the Sales field to the Data area. When you're done, click OK.

5. Make sure "New worksheet" is selected, and click Finish.

You can find out how to create Pivot-Charts in Chapter 5.

PIVOT A PIVOTTABLE

The Annoyance: I created a PivotTable, and it looks pretty good in its base configuration (shown in Figure 4-29), but I guess I missed the meeting in which they described how to rearrange my data on the fly. How

do I change its groupings to emphasize other aspects of the data?

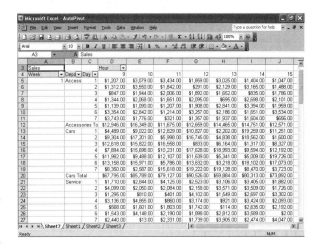

Figure 4-29. This is only one way to look at your PivotTable data.

The Fix: To pivot a PivotTable, choose Data → PivotTable Report (or Data → PivotTable and PivotChart Report, depending on your version), and drag a field header to the new position in the PivotTable. When you drag the field header over the row, column, or page area, you'll see a gray *I-bar* appear, as in Figure 4-30. When you release the left mouse button, Excel regroups the PivotTable data.

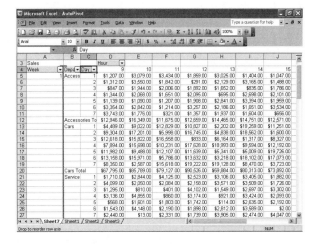

Figure 4-30. The gray bar tells you where your PivotTable header will end up when you release the left mouse button.

FILTER PIVOTTABLE DATA

The Annoyance: My PivotTable contains much more data than will fit on one screen. I see what appear to be filter arrows at the right edge of each field header. Can I use them to limit the data that appears in my PivotTable?

The Fix: To filter a PivotTable in Excel 2000 and later, click the filter arrow at the right edge of a field header and select the values you want to appear. If the Show All box at the top of the list is checked, unchecking it deselects all the values in the list; if the Show All box *isn't* checked, checking it selects every item in the list.

To filter an Excel 97 PivotTable, double-click a field header to display the PivotTable Field dialog box (shown in Figure 4-31). Select the values you want to hide in the Hide Items drop-down list, and click OK. To redisplay the items double-click the field header and deselect the items.

Figure 4-31. PivotTables are based on data lists. Just as you can filter a list, you can filter a PivotTable.

Filtering the data in your PivotTable won't affect the source data.

CREATE ADVANCED PIVOTTABLE FILTERS

The Annoyance: I created a PivotTable, and I want to emphasize certain aspects of the data, such as the top 10 (or bottom 10) sales days for my auto dealership's service department. I know how to do it using an AutoFilter in a regular data list; is there a way to do it in a PivotTable?

The Fix: Starting with Excel 97, you can use the equivalent of the AutoFilter Top 10 feature to display the top or bottom values in your PivotTable's data field. The specific method you use to activate the filter has changed as PivotTables have evolved, but it's there if you know where to look. For the purposes of this fix, assume you're using the PivotTable in Figure 4-32.

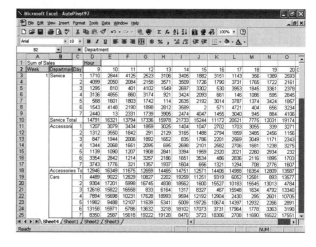

Figure 4-32. It's possible to find the top or bottom values in a PivotTable, but how you do it depends on the version of Excel that you're using.

To display a number of top or bottom values in an Excel 97 or 2000 PivotTable, follow these steps:

1. Click any cell in the PivotTable and choose Data → PivotTable Report (that's Data → PivotTable or Pivot-Chart Report in Excel 2000).

2. Double-click the row or column field header you want to use to find the top or bottom subset of data. The PivotTable Field dialog box appears. Click Advanced to display the PivotTable Field Advanced Options dialog box (shown in Figure 4-33).

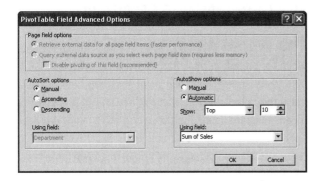

Figure 4-33. These advanced options include filtering your data.

3. Select the Automatic option.

4. Select Top or Bottom from the Show pull-down list, and specify the number of items to display in the field just to the right.

This same technique I just explained for Excel 97 and 2000 works perfectly well in Excel 2002 and 2003, but there's a faster way to invoke the top/bottom 10 feature in these later versions of the program:

1. Click any cell in the field by which you want to sort. For example, if you wanted to sort the PivotTable in Figure 4-32 by day, you could click cell C5 (or C6:11, etc.).

2. If necessary, right-click a blank spot on any toolbar and choose PivotTable to display the PivotTable toolbar.

3. Choose PivotTable → Sort and Top 10.

4. Select the On option, and use the Show field to set the number of values at the top or bottom of the list to display.

FILTER A PIVOTTABLE BY ANY FIELD

The Annoyance: I created a PivotTable with all the fields I wanted to use to group and filter my data, but now I'd like to filter my PivotTable using values from a field I *didn't* use in the grouping. For example, I'd like to create a PivotTable, such as the one in Figure 4-34, that doesn't use the Week field values to group the data, but I'd still like to be able to use the Week field to limit the data shown in the PivotTable. Is there a way to do that?

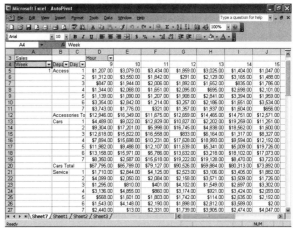

Figure 4-34. You don't need to sort your data by week, but you might need to filter it by week. No problem.

The Fix: To filter a PivotTable using a field that isn't used to group the PivotTable data, move the field header to the Page area in the PivotTable layout box, as shown in Figure 4-35.

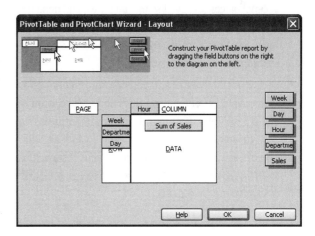

Figure 4-35. The Page area is your repository for fields you want to use just to filter your PivotTable data.

To display the layout box in Excel 97, click any cell in the PivotTable and choose Data → PivotTable Report. In Excel 2000 and later choose Data → PivotTable and PivotChart Report → Layout. In Excel 2000 and later, you also can drag a field header to the Drop Page Fields Here area of the PivotTable report. Once the field header is in the Page area, you can filter the PivotTable as if the header were in the Row or Column area.

FIND PIVOTTABLE ADD-INS

The Annoyance: I like using PivotTables, but I don't have time to learn how to do everything. Are any add-ins available that can help me do things such as set the print area, freeze the rows at the top of the Pivot-Table, and so on?

The Fix: The following add-ins are available:

- PivotTable AutoFormat XL records and applies custom formats for your PivotTables. You can download it from *http://www.ablebits.com/excel-pivottables-autoformatting-addins/*, for $39.95.

- PivotTable Helper is a free add-in for Excel 2000 and later that extends the capabilities of the PivotTable Auto-Format XL add-in. It adds buttons to the AutoFormat toolbar that enable you to quickly perform tasks such as selecting an entire PivotTable, changing the number of decimal places displayed in the data area, and adding or removing Grand Total rows. Download it from *http://www.ablebits.com/excel-pivottables-formatting-assistant-free-addins/index.php*.

- With PivotTable Assistant, you can resize columns for easier viewing, set the print titles and area for printing out a PivotTable, freeze title rows and columns for easy viewing, and add borders to the bottom and right side of each printed page of a PivotTable. It's available at *http://www.ozgrid.com/Services/Excel-pivot-table-assistant.htm* for $29.95.

APPLY AUTOFORMAT TO A PIVOTTABLE

The Annoyance: My PivotTables look great, but when I try to add formatting, such as displaying a value in boldface or italic, and then pivot the table, the cell formats don't pivot with the values. They stay in place, which means they are applied to the wrong cells. I know you can apply an AutoFormat to a table in an Excel worksheet. Is there a way to apply an AutoFormat to a PivotTable?

The Fix: To apply an AutoFormat to a PivotTable, click any cell in the PivotTable, choose Format → Auto-Format, and select the AutoFormat you want to apply. If you want to create your own PivotTable AutoFormats, you can use the Pivot Table AutoFormat XL add-in discussed previously.

STOP PIVOTTABLES FROM PIVOTING!

The Annoyance: I created several PivotTables in Microsoft Excel 2000 to analyze sales data, but changes I make to one PivotTable seem to affect the others I've created from the same data. What's going on?

The Fix: The problem is that you followed Excel's advice when you created the second (and subsequent) PivotTables based on the same data. When you create a second PivotTable from the same data source, Excel displays the advisory message *Your new PivotTable will use less memory if you base it on your existing PivotTable [WorkbookName]SheetName!PivotTableName, which was created from the same source data. Do you want your new PivotTable to be based on the same data as your existing PivotTable?* It seems like a reasonable thing to do, but it is, in fact, a very bad idea.

When you create a PivotTable, Excel creates a cache that contains the data and structure (that is, field groupings) for the PivotTable. When you use one PivotTable as the data source for a second PivotTable, any changes to any of those PivotTables that share the same memory cache will affect all the other PivotTables. You can avoid this behavior by clicking No when Excel asks if you want to base your PivotTable on the same data as an existing PivotTable. Then Excel will create a separate memory cache for the new PivotTable, and your PivotTables will pivot independently.

PIVOTTABLE DATA DISPLAYS AS NUMBER SIGNS

The Annoyance: I don't have a huge data list, so I created my PivotTable on the same worksheet as the original data. The problem is that Excel now displays some of my source data as number signs (#####). What's going on, and how do I fix it?

The Fix: What's happening is that Excel is reformatting the width of your worksheet columns to fit the contents of your PivotTable—and if there's no room in a cell to display the source data, Excel uses number signs. You can prevent Excel from changing your columns' widths by turning off the Autoformat Table option in the PivotTable Wizard. The procedure you follow depends on your version of Excel.

To turn off the Autoformat Table option in Excel 97, follow these steps:

1. Select a cell contained in your PivotTable and choose Data → PivotTable Report.

2. Click Next to get to the fourth step of the PivotTable Wizard, click the Options button, and uncheck the "Autoformat table" box.

In Excel 2000, follow these steps:

1. Select a cell contained in your PivotTable and choose Data → PivotTable and PivotChart Report.

2. Click Next twice to advance to page 3 of the Pivot-Table and PivotChart Wizard.

3. Click Options, and then uncheck the "AutoFormat table" box.

In Excel 2002 and 2003, right-click any cell in the Pivot-Table, choose Table Options, and uncheck the AutoFormat table box.

"PIVOTTABLE IS NOT VALID" ERROR

The Annoyance: I support a large mail order retail sales firm where the IT folks get the fancy software and we get very old versions of Office. I was so frustrated I brought in my own, unopened copy of Office 2000, but I'm the only person in my section that has anything that recent—everyone else uses Office 97. I created a Pivot-Table from something called an OLAP (Online Analytical Processing) cube in Excel 2000, went to our meeting room (which has a PC running Excel 97), and tried to use the PivotTable in a presentation. I got a "PivotTable is not valid" error message. Because I couldn't find the "Yes, it is!" button, I ended up having to wave my hands instead of doing the cool stuff I had planned. What happened?

Online Analytical Processing

Online Analytical Processing (OLAP) is technology that makes large collections of data easier to analyze and present by summarizing and arranging the data in response to user queries—and if you're using it, you probably know what you're doing. Excel PivotTables can handle the data summaries, but would choke on the massive database tables generated by most large business systems.

The Fix: As you probably guessed, Excel 97 simply can't handle PivotTables based on data in OLAP cubes. That functionality wasn't introduced until Excel 2000. Excel 97 will display the PivotTable in the state in which it was saved in Excel 2000, but you can't pivot it or re-fresh its data. You can work around this problem in two ways. The first workaround is to create a new PivotTable for each configuration you want to display on the Excel 97 computer. I recommend putting the PivotTables in separate worksheets and renaming the worksheets to reflect the emphasis of each PivotTable. The other workaround is to import the OLAP data into an Excel 2000 workbook, open the workbook in Excel 97, and create a new PivotTable.

PIVOTTABLE LOSES FORMATTING

The Annoyance: When I created the worksheet I use to track sales, I formatted the numbers in the Currency style, but when I create a PivotTable from that data, Excel loses the formatting. Is there any way I can retain data formatting when I create the PivotTable, or at least add the formatting quickly afterward?

The Fix: It's a sad fact of life that you lose your data field's formatting when you create a PivotTable. Microsoft Knowledge Base article #214021 offers a fix—you're supposed to click Options on the next-to-last (Excel 97 and 2000) or last (Excel 2002 and 2003) PivotTable Wizard page, and check the Preserve Formatting checkbox—but it didn't work for me in any version of Excel. What I *can* tell you is that there's a quick way to format your data in every version since Excel 97. To format the data field of a PivotTable quickly, right-click any cell in the data area and choose Field (Excel 97 and 2000) or Field Settings (Excel 2002 and 2003) to display the PivotTable Field dialog box (shown in Figure 4-36).

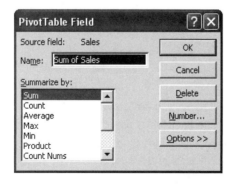

Figure 4-36. Here's where you go to find the Format Cells dialog box for your PivotTable.

Once in the PivotTable Field dialog box, click the Number button and use the Number page of the Format Cells dialog box to define your data's format.

USE CALCULATED FIELDS IN A PIVOTTABLE

The Annoyance: PivotTables are fine as far as they go, but I'd like to do more with the data in the table. For example, 3% of my company's revenue goes to a corporate overhead fund that pays the light bill, office supplies, and environmental cleanup for antifreeze spills. I'd like to have a field riding alongside the body of the PivotTable (as shown in Figure 4-37) that lists the overhead deduction associated with the data in the table. Is there any way to do that?

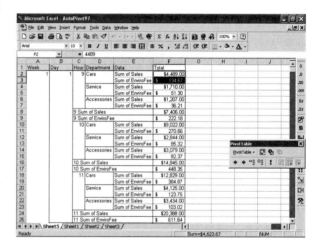

Figure 4-37. This PivotTable answers your questions.

The Fix: Excel 97 introduced the *calculated field* (a user-defined field that derives its value from a formula you create) and the *calculated item* (a user-defined field that derives its value from a particular entry in a column—e.g., the "Cars" entry in the Department column). For example, if you wanted to determine the amount of the 3% overhead fund deduction from hourly sales, you could create a calculated field with the formula =Sales * .03 to display the amount.

To add a calculated field to a PivotTable, follow these steps:

1. If it isn't already on, turn on the PivotTable toolbar by selecting View → Toolbars.

2. Select any cell in the PivotTable, and then, on the PivotTable toolbar, choose PivotTable → Formulas → Calculated Field to display the Insert Calculated Field dialog box, shown in Figure 4-38.

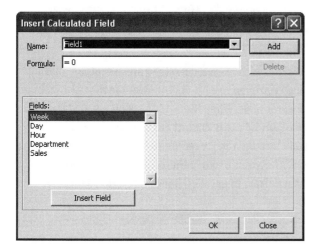

Figure 4-38. Create additional fields based on any formula you want.

3. Type the name of the calculated field in the Name field, type your formula (such as =Sales * .03) in the Formula field, click the Add button, and then click OK.

4. The calculated field appears in the PivotTable data area.

To delete a calculated field, follow these steps:

1. Display the PivotTable toolbar.

2. Choose PivotTable → Formulas → Calculated Field to display the Insert Calculated Field dialog box.

3. Open the Name drop down, select the calculated field you want to whack, click Delete, and then click OK.

Creating a calculated item is similar to creating a calculated field, except you need to decide at which grouping level to create the calculated item. For example, in the PivotTable shown in Figure 4-37 you could create a calculated item named NonCarSales that added sales from the Accessories and Service categories and included those results in the body of the PivotTable. You would need to create the formula using the format =Column[Value1] + Column[Value2] so that Excel can identify which elements you want to calculate. For example, the formula to add Accessories and Service sales would be =Department[Accessories] + Department[Service].

To add a calculated item to a PivotTable, follow these steps:

1. Click the field header that corresponds to the field you want to use in your calculations (in this case, click Department).

2. On the PivotTable toolbar, choose PivotTable → Formulas → Calculated Item to display the Insert Calculated Item dialog box, shown in Figure 4-39.

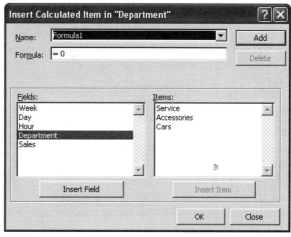

Figure 4-39. You also can create fields that pivot along with the rest of your PivotTable data.

3. Type a name for the calculated item in the Name field, type the formula for the calculation in the Formula field, and then click Add.

PIVOTTABLES WITH SUPERPOWERS

I thought I was pretty good with PivotTables until I saw what the *XLSTAT-Pivot* add-in from Addinsoft can do. It's a powerful program that helps you quantify the effect that different variables, such as the hour of the day or the day of the week, have on your business. The PivotTables you can create using *XLSTAT-Pivot* (shown in the following figure) are mind-blowing. You can have the program look at how closely variables are correlated, chart the percentage contribution each variable makes to your business, and determine the likelihood that the data model is correct by using measures of robustness.

There's only one catch. Well, two catches. OK, actually, there are three. First, *XLSTAT-Pivot* requires Excel 2000 or later, which is no biggie. Next, it requires you to have already installed *XLSTAT-Pro*.

The third catch is the big one: between them, these two applications run a cool $1,385 ($395 for *XLSTAT-Pro*, $990 for *XLSTAT-Pivot*). The good news is that you can download 30-day trial versions of both programs from the company's site at *http://www.xlstat.com/*, so you'll get a chance to try before you buy. You also can run through the *XLSTAT-Pivot* tutorial at *http://www.xlstat.com/demo-pivot.htm*, which gives you a good idea of how the program works.

The trial versions you download are executable files, so all you need to do is double-click the files to install the programs. When it comes to trying out *XLSTAT-Pivot*, my advice is to print out the tutorial and walk through the procedure to check your progress. *XLSTAT-Pivot* is a tool for hard-core analysts who aren't afraid to get their hands dirty; that's for sure.

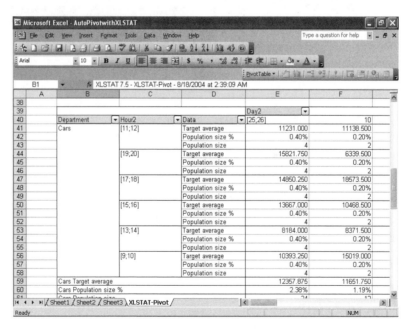

If you're serious about analyzing your data using high-powered tools, consider adding *XLSTAT*-Pivot to your arsenal.

CHANGE SUMMARY CALCULATIONS IN A PIVOTTABLE

The Annoyance: I used a PivotTable in a presentation the other day, and one of my company's senior partners asked if there was any way to change how the PivotTable data is summarized. Specifically, she asked if I could display average sales instead of total sales in a PivotTable. Is there any way to change how Excel summarizes PivotTable data?

The Fix: You can, in fact, change the summary operation Excel uses in a PivotTable. To do so, right-click any cell in the PivotTable's data area and choose Field to display the PivotTable Field dialog box (shown in Figure 4-40).

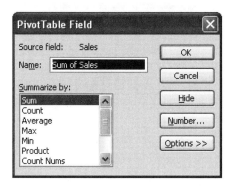

Figure 4-40. Sums and totals aren't your only options when summarizing PivotTable data.

Select the summary calculation you want to use from the drop-down list, and click OK to apply it to the PivotTable. For example, if you wanted to find the average hourly sales over a week, you would select Average. When you click OK, you'll see the PivotTable shown in Figure 4-41.

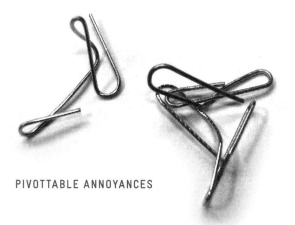

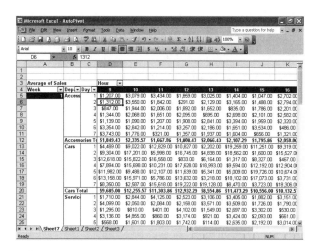

Figure 4-41. Here's where you find what you can do with your summaries.

HIDDEN DATA DOESN'T APPEAR IN THE SUMMARY

The Annoyance: My boss uses the PivotTables I create to show how much each department contributes on a daily and weekly basis to our bottom-line profits. One thing he doesn't like, however, is that Excel doesn't display a "filtered" total for a column when you filter it—it displays only the total for the visible values (as shown in Figure 4-42). Is there any way to have Excel display the total for all items, both visible and hidden?

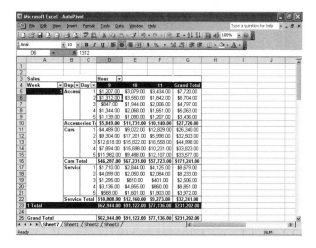

Figure 4-42. You control whether a PivotTable bases its calculations on all the values, or just the visible ones.

The Fix: To have Excel include hidden values in its subtotals, right-click any cell in the PivotTable's data area, choose Table Options (Options in Excel 97), and place a check in the "Subtotal hidden page items" checkbox.

"REFERENCE NOT VALID" ERROR

The Annoyance: I used a data form to enter the values for my PivotTable's data list, but now when I try to create a PivotTable based on that data, I get an error message saying "Reference is not valid." I know the reference is valid—it's just a data list, like dozens of data lists I've used before. Sheesh! One thing I *did* notice is that for some reason Excel is displaying the reference *Database* in the second page of the PivotTable Wizard (see Figure 4-43). I can select the range before I run the Wizard, but I'd rather let Excel detect the data list automatically. What's going on?

Figure 4-43. The data list looks like it should work, and it should—except for one detail.

The Fix: The problem is that when you create a data entry form to enter data into a list, Excel creates a named range called Database. What's worse, the Database named range is invisible, and doesn't show up in the Define Name dialog box. To delete the Database named range, follow these steps:

1. Select any cell in the worksheet and choose Insert → Name → Define to display the Define Name dialog box.

2. In the "Names in workbook" field, type Database.

3. Click Add, and then click Delete.

Excel will now detect the data list in the usual manner.

DISPLAY PIVOTTABLE DATA AS A PERCENTAGE OF A TOTAL

The Annoyance: I'd like to display my sales data as a percentage of a total, not just as a value with a running total in the far-right column of my PivotTable. For example, assuming the data in Figure 4-44, how can I display each day and hour as a percentage of a column and how do I change the display so that I see percentages of days and weeks instead of a percentage of the entire column?

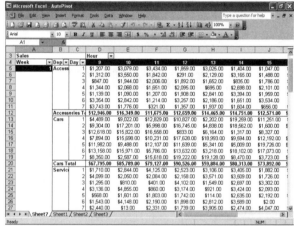

Figure 4-44. If you can't figure percentages in your head, you'll need to change how Excel displays this data.

The Fix: To display the values in an Excel 97 Pivot-Table as a percentage of a column total, follow these steps:

1. Click any cell in the PivotTable and choose Data → PivotTable Report.

2. On the third page of the PivotTable Wizard, double-click Sum of Sales and then, in the PivotTable Field dialog box, click the Options button (the result is shown in Figure 4-45).

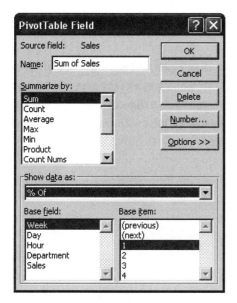

Figure 4-45. Use the controls in this dialog box to change how Excel summarizes your PivotTable data.

3. Click the down arrow at the right of the "Show data as" field and choose "% of Column" from the drop-down list.

In Excel 2000 and later, double-click the Sum of Sales field header in the body of the PivotTable to display the PivotTable Field dialog box and follow the same procedure. Then you can filter the data in the PivotTable, which will cause Excel to update the percentage calculations (as shown in Figure 4-46).

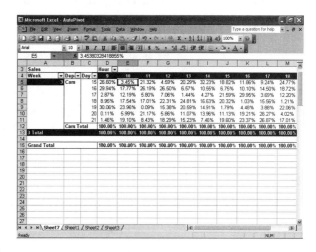

Figure 4-46. The end result answers your questions.

CRYPTOGRAM GAME

If you like the CryptoQuote decryption game in the newspaper, you'll enjoy Aaron Blood's free cryptogram generator, which you can download from *http://www.xl-logic.com/xl_files/games/cryptogram.zip*. You have to enter the text to be encrypted, as shown in the following figure, but you can have a group of friends rotate who generates the next cryptogram so that everyone gets a chance to play. If you want to be really sneaky, misspell one of the words. Drives people crazy.

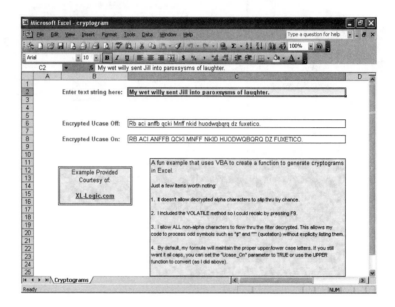

Cryptograms are a fun single substitution for work.

Chart
ANNOYANCES

5

Confucius *actually* said a picture is worth *10,000* words. Yes, 10,000. The modern interpretation shorts you by 9,000 words. In Excel, you use charting tools to make those valuable and pretty pictures that summarize your data visually. A good chart can make your data infinitely more comprehensible. In this chapter, I'll guide you past the many shoals along the way to creating charts quickly and efficiently. You'll also learn how to add error bars, change the scale of an axis, replace stodgy bars and columns with images of your choice, and more.

There are more than a few twists and turns when it comes to manipulating charts in Excel, from moving a chart to a new location to pasting a chart into Word. This and other seemingly basic operations can send Excel to Crash Central, but fear not—crash-proof solutions *do* exist. We'll show you those solutions and give you the scoop on some great third-party tools that help you create bigger and better charts than Excel can dream of.

CHART CREATION AND FORMATTING ANNOYANCES

INSTANT CHARTS

The Annoyance: I've got a meeting in five minutes, and I need to create a column chart that shows how the operating costs of our auto dealership (utilities, rent, and taxes, as shown in Figure 5-1) have changed over the past few years. How do I create the chart and still have time for a cup of coffee before my meeting?

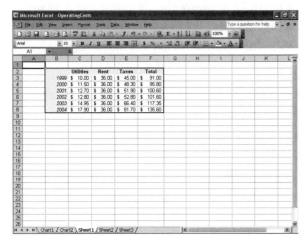

Figure 5-1. This data needs a chart…now!

The Fix: To create a chart quickly, select the data, including row and column labels, and press F11. Bingo! Excel creates a default chart, which—if you haven't changed the default type—is a column chart.

SPIFF UP A CHART QUICKLY

The Annoyance: OK, the boss is running a few minutes late, so I have time to do one or two *more* things. The chart Excel creates when you press F11 is a bit spare. Can I dress it up with a title, legend, and axis labels?

The Fix: If you have a few more minutes, use the Chart Wizard to step through the process of creating a more sophisticated and informative graphic. To create a chart using the Chart Wizard, select the data you want to summarize and choose Insert → Chart. The first page of the Chart Wizard, shown in Figure 5-2, lets you select the type of chart you want to use for your data. To preview your chart, click and hold the "Press and Hold to View Sample" button. Click Next when you're done.

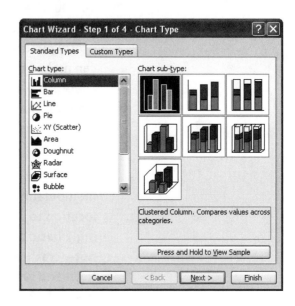

Figure 5-2. Your chart appears here, in miniature.

The second page of the Chart Wizard displays the cell range you selected before you ran the wizard, and gives you the opportunity to select a new range if you selected the wrong one, or didn't select one at all. This wizard page also lets you decide whether your *data series* (sets of related data points) will be in the selection's columns or rows. The four data series in Figure 5-1 (utilities, rent, taxes, and total) are in the worksheet's columns. If you don't see the desired data range in the Data range field, click the Expand Dialog button at the right end of the field, select (or reselect) the data you want to chart, and press Enter. Now the correct data range should appear in the Data range field. You also can use the second Chart

Wizard page to make some choices about the data series by clicking the Series tab, but I'll come back to this later. For now, click the Next button.

The Titles tab on the third Chart Wizard page, shown in Figure 5-3, lets you add information to your chart, including a title (usually displayed at the top of the chart) and labels for the horizontal (X) and vertical (Y) axes. The other tabs on this Wizard page let you change the characteristics of the axes, add or remove gridlines, and so on. I'll come back to them later. For now, click Next.

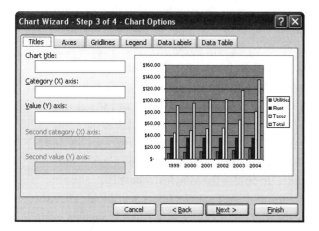

Figure 5-3. Add descriptive axis labels and a title to make your chart easier to read.

The final Chart Wizard page lets you choose whether you want to place your chart on the existing workbook sheet as an object, or on a new sheet all by itself.

UPDATE A CHART TO INCLUDE NEW EXCEL DATA

The Annoyance: I track the hourly water usage at a string of golf courses in Las Vegas. My apprentice types the data into an Excel worksheet, but she's tired of having to select the new range and re-create the chart every time. I want my colleagues to have a premium-quality work experience, so I tried to help by creating two dynamic named ranges (one for the hours, the other for

gallons of water used). But the Chart Wizard won't let me define a named range as the source for the data on the X or Y axis. Surely if I can use dynamic named ranges in formulas, I can use them in charts, but Excel won't tell me how. Will you?

The Fix: You're actually very close to solving the problem. While you have the Chart Wizard open to the second page (Step 2 of 4), click the Series tab, click a data series in the Series box, and then type a named range as the series' reference in the Values field. You can do the same thing for the X axis by typing a named range as a reference in the "Category (X) axis labels" field. The trick is using the proper format: first you must type an equals sign, followed by the workbook's name, followed by an exclamation point, and finally the range name. For example, if your workbook is named *WaterUsage.xls* and the range name for the X axis's values is Hours, you would type =WaterUsage!Hours (yes, you can leave out the .xls). Now Excel will update your chart whenever you add or remove data from the named range.

Create a Dynamic Named Range

If you haven't created a dynamic named range for each column you want to use in your chart, follow the procedure in "Create a Self-Extending Named Range" **in Chapter 3.**

POWERFUL CHART CREATION

If you're an engineer or scientist and you're tired of fighting with Excel to create the complex charts you require, you should convince your department chair, technical lead, or project manager to sign a purchase order for DeltaGraph, a charting program from statistics software giant SPSS. With it, you can create all the charts you can in Excel, plus many more. One cool example is the polar chart, which you can use to chart a quantity measured in degrees (such as wind direction) against a second, linear value (such as inches of rain). You can find a list of the 59 chart types in DeltaGraph that *aren't* in Excel at *http://www.redrocksw.com/ deltagraph/DeltaGraphvsExcel.htm* (in Appendix A, near the bottom of the page). The DeltaGraph Chart Wizard closely resembles the Excel Chart Wizard, but you don't have to use the wizard if you don't want to. DeltaGraph works just fine with data from Excel, SPSS (surprise, surprise), and delimited text files—but not with Access. What's more, DeltaGraph is available in Mac and Windows versions. The file formats for the most recent Mac and Windows versions of DeltaGraph aren't compatible (that is, you can't open Windows files in the Mac version, and vice versa), but the company claims it's going to fix the incompatibilities.

One aspect of DeltaGraph I really like is the gallery of sample charts you can browse through to learn exactly what types of charts and graphs you can create. Unlike the Excel sample gallery, this gallery is full-size and in vibrant color. To display the samples, choose File → Open, double-click the *Examples* folder, and double-click any of the example files. The program also lets you use the Pantone color definition system, so you can create charts using colors that exactly match your logo and corporate color scheme. You have to pay for such power, of course. The standard price for DeltaGraph 5.0 is $299, but the academic price is $199. You can download a fully functional demo from the Red Rock Software web site at *http:// support.redrocksw.com/downloads/.* (Red Rock Software is SPSS's distributor for this program.) The demo comes as an executable file. Just download it and run it. To display the samples, choose File → Open, double-click the *Examples* folder, and double-click any of the example files (one such example appears in the figure). If you're into heavy-duty charts and graphs, DeltaGraph is money well spent.

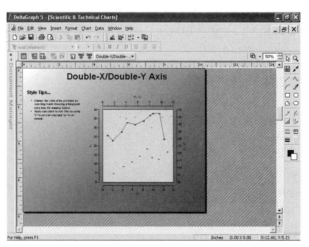

Finally, you can have different scales on each X and Y axis!

CREATE AND UPDATE CHARTS FROM QUERY DATA

The Annoyance: At the request of my boss, we're supposed to track the water usage at our brewery in Access—but I still need to get the data into Excel so that I can create the charts in my established workbooks. I know how to create a query, but how do I create a chart based on the data returned by that query? I'm presenting the reports to my boss tomorrow, and the last two words I want to hear are "You're fired."

The Fix: You won't get canned. This fix is very straightforward; you don't even need to create named ranges to accelerate data references. Query results are like any other cell data, so you just need to select any cell in the query results range, click the Chart Wizard toolbar button, and walk through the wizard. When you want to update the chart to reflect the current data the query generates, select any cell in the query results range and choose Data → Refresh Data. Poof! You're done! Excel also will update your workbook every time you open it, so you won't need to remember to refresh your data every morning.

EXPLODE YOUR PIE CHART

The Annoyance: My project undergoes its annual review in two days, so of course I'm writing my report right now. I have a one-column data series that represents the percentage of total cost for 10 expense categories (labor, parts, administrative, and so on), so I'd like to create a pie chart from that data. The problem is that two-dimensional pie charts are slightly less exciting than driving across Kansas. Flat. Dry. Darn near lifeless. Three-dimensional pie charts are a little more interesting to look at, especially if I can figure out how to separate one slice of the pie from the rest. Can I separate a wedge from a 3D pie chart in Excel?

The Fix: It is, in fact, quite easy to create a pie chart with one of the slices separated from the main body. Excel calls it the Pie Explosion chart type, which, you must admit, is a pretty colorful name for an Excel chart. To create a Pie Explosion chart, select the data to be summarized and choose Insert → Chart. Click the Standard Types

tab, then select Pie in the "Chart type" list on the left. Thumbnails of different pie chart types appear in the window to the right. The first two types on the bottom row are the 2-D and 3-D Pie Explosion charts. Select the one you want, click the Next button, and proceed through the steps of the wizard to define the data range for the body of the pie and the piece labels (which you can do on the Series tab of the second wizard page). After you create your chart, click the chart to activate it, then click the piece of the pie you want to "explode," make sure it's highlighted separately, and drag it away from the center.

TWO CHARTS FOR THE PRICE OF ONE

The Annoyance: My boss has an interesting idea for a chart to display the overhead costs paid by our auto dealership. She'd like something that shows the individual categories (utilities, rent, and taxes) as columns on a chart, but that also displays the total as a line instead of a bar. I looked through the Chart Wizard and found that a combination line and column chart is available on the Custom Types tab on the Wizard's first page (shown in Figure 5-4).

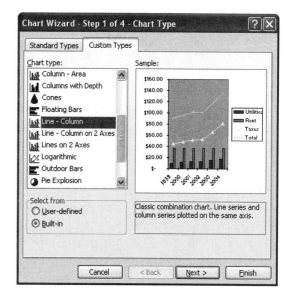

Figure 5-4. You're not stuck with just two lines and two columns; it just seems that way.

But when I try to create a chart of that type, my four data series appear as two lines and two columns. Is there any way to create a chart in which just one series is graphed as a line while the other series are graphed as columns?

The Fix: Sure there is. Start by creating a column chart from the data displayed in Figure 5-5.

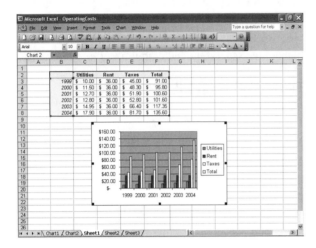

Figure 5-5. Here's the before picture…

The Total series contains the largest values, so that's the series you should plot as the line so that it will ride clearly above the columns and be more visible. First, create a column chart to display the Utilities, Rent, Taxes, and Total costs. Then, to change how one of the series is plotted, right-click the chart element representing the series you want to change (the Total column, in this case), choose Chart Type, and select the one you'd like to use for that series. If you choose Line, your chart will look like the one in Figure 5-6.

Incidentally, this type of chart (columns with a single line overhead) plays a visual trick on the viewer. Because the line forms a sort of ceiling over the columns, the total appears smaller than it would if the same value were displayed as a fourth column on the chart. I wonder if the boss figured that out, too.

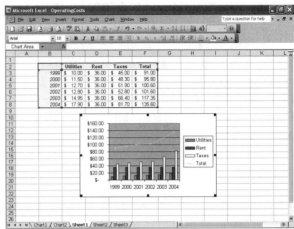

Figure 5-6. …and here's the after.

CHART DATA SERIES PROPERLY

The Annoyance: Something weird is going on. I sent the worksheet shown in Figure 5-1 to my boss so that she could review the data and include it in her own reports. She just sent me an email saying she created a chart by pressing F11, but the years in the lefthand column of the worksheet show up in the chart as values—they aren't being used to label the horizontal axis (as shown in Figure 5-7). If she's working with the same data, and she assures me she is, why are the years plotted in her chart and not used as the values for the horizontal axis?

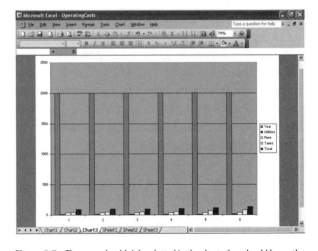

Figure 5-7. The years shouldn't be plotted in the chart; they should be on the horizontal axis.

The Fix: What probably happened is that your boss added the word *Year* in cell B2 as a label above the first data column, as shown in Figure 5-8. When the Chart Wizard sees a column label, it assumes the data in the labeled row or column is meant to be plotted in the chart, and not to be used as labels on an axis.

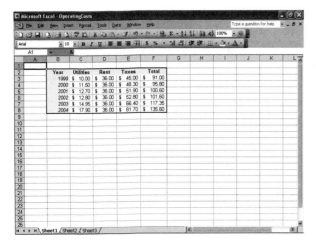

Figure 5-8. One stray label makes all the difference.

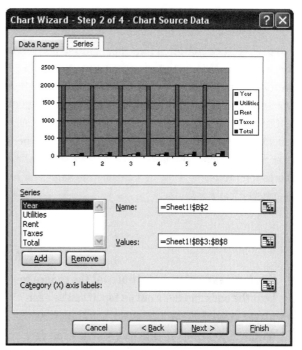

Figure 5-9. Here's where you fix the problem. You can keep the column label, but you need to tell Excel what to do with the data.

You can tell the Chart Wizard to treat a series as the horizontal (X) axis's labels, though. Click the chart and then click the Chart Wizard button on the Standard toolbar. Then, on the second page of the Chart Wizard, click the Series tab (which appears in Figure 5-9).

The data series appears in the Series list at the bottom left in the dialog box. In the Series list, click Year and then click the Remove button to exclude that data from the body of the chart. To assign the Year series to the horizontal axis, click the Collapse Dialog button at the far right in the "Category (X) axis labels" field and select the cells that contain the year values. Do not include the Year column label in your selection, or the first value on the horizontal axis will be Year, the second will be 1999, and so on. Press Enter and proceed.

FORMAT CHART ELEMENTS

The Annoyance: I'm so tired of the Arial font, I could scream. Please tell me I can change this default font that the Chart Wizard uses for chart legends and other text. Or at least show me how to change the size so that all the labels can appear. And while you're at it, tell me how I can get rid of those boring colors the wizard assigns to my bars and columns, too.

The Fix: The standard charts Excel creates are a reasonable compromise in terms of color and font, but in the final analysis they aren't the most eye-catching things in the world, are they? The good news is that you can change a chart element by right-clicking it and choosing the "Format *Whatever*" item on the shortcut menu. For example, to change the font used in the chart's legend, right-click the legend, choose Format Legend, click the Font tab, and dig through the various dialog boxes and other controls to modify the legend's text. You can use the same process to change bar colors, and so on.

TAKE CONTROL OF YOUR AXES

The Annoyance: I track standardized test scores for my school district, and as you might imagine I see a pretty wide range of data. The scores can range anywhere from 400 to 1,600, with the majority falling in the 900–1,100 range. When I create a chart using the Chart Wizard, Excel creates gridlines every 200 points. What I need is a gridline every 50 points so that I can show where scores tend to clump. How do I change the values on my chart's vertical axis?

The Fix: To change the values on your chart's vertical axis, right-click the axis, select Format Axis, click the Scale tab (shown in Figure 5-10), change the Maximum field to 1600 (indicating the top of your range), and change the "Major unit" field to 50 (for setting the gridline). The resulting chart is in Figure 5-11.

The Major unit value indicates where the tick marks and associated horizontal gridline should cross the Y axis, while the Minor unit value indicates the increment at which other gridlines cross the Y axis. Minor unit–based

---

PLAY BLACKJACK IN EXCEL

What makes gambling so attractive? The chance to beat the odds and come out on top. If you've ever played craps, blackjack, or poker, you know how quickly a good run can turn bad—or how, on very rare occasions, you can parlay your last $5 into a grand. When you play against other people, as in poker, you have a decent chance to win. When you play a game such as blackjack, which has a built-in house advantage, you can make the game close to an even proposition, but you still have to hope luck is on your side. If you want to tune up your big-money game before you hit the casino, try Rob van Gelder's blackjack game for Excel 2000 and later versions.

As shown in the figure, the program uses built-in toolbar buttons (for card suits, numbers, and letters) to display the cards, so the code is very interesting to read if you're a programmer. You can download the code from Rob's site at *http://www.vangelder. co.nz/excel* and follow the directions to copy it into a module.

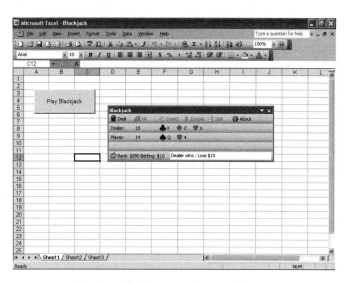

Play blackjack in the comfort of your own home.

---

gridlines clutter up the graph, but if you want to turn them on, you can select the chart, click the Chart Wizard button, move to the third page of the Chart Wizard, click the Gridlines tab, and check the "Minor gridlines" box.

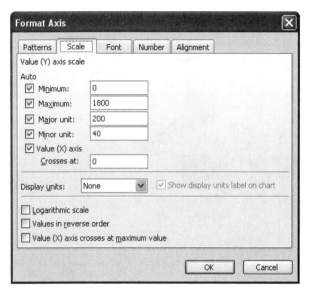

Figure 5-10. You can change far more than the font and color of a chart axis.

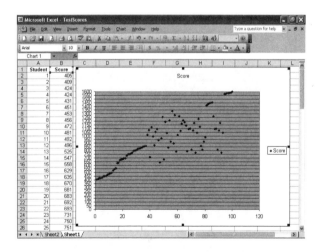

Figure 5-11. More lines sometimes can make your data easier to interpret.

With regard to your chart's design, you should use a consistent set of axes for every similar graph. If the minimum score is 400, you should consider setting the Minimum

value to 400 for review with the faculty. But you also might consider setting it to 0 (so that the bottom scores aren't at the very bottom of the graph) if you plan to show the summary chart to the students.

Be sure to uncheck the Auto box next to any fields you change. If the Auto box is checked, Excel will ignore the value in the field to the right and make its own determination as to the appropriate value for that parameter.

ADD TEXT TO A CHART AXIS

The Annoyance: I work for a nonprofit theater group, and we have to scale our production budget based on how successful our fund-raising efforts are. I'd like to substitute words for some of the values on our fund-raising schedule. For example, if we can raise $10,000, we'll be able to stage *Merchant of Venice*. If we get another $5,000, we also can do *Our Town*. Can I drive home my point by changing some of the numeric values on the vertical axis to words?

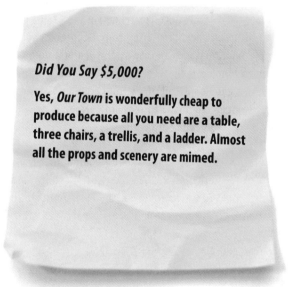

Did You Say $5,000?

Yes, *Our Town* is wonderfully cheap to produce because all you need are a table, three chairs, a trellis, and a ladder. Almost all the props and scenery are mimed.

The Fix: You always can add text values to a chart axis by masking the existing value with a borderless white square and creating a text box with the new value. But if you *really* want to change a numeric value to a text string on the axis itself, you can do that, too. The trick is to create a custom format that substitutes a text string for a target value. Here's how you would do it in this example, substituting *Merchant of Venice* for $10,000 and *Our Town* for $5,000:

1. Right-click the Y axis, choose Format Axis, click the Number tab, and select Custom from the Category list.

2. In the Type field, enter `[=10000] "Merchant";[=5000] "Our Town"`.

t i p

For more information on creating custom formats, see Chapter 2.

GLITZ UP YOUR COLUMNS

The Annoyance: My newspaper runs a recycling program that offers our readers a credit for every pound of newspapers they bring to our center. I thought it would be a neat idea to display the yearly amount recycled on a column chart, but I'd love to use a stack of recycling symbols instead of a boring column. Is it possible to replace columns with recycling symbols, or whatever other image I come up with?

The Fix: It's easy to represent a column or bar with an image or series of images; you just need to know where to look. To use an image as the basis for a column or bar, first create the column or bar chart. Then right-click any column or bar in the series, choose Format Data Series, and click the Fill Effects button and then the Picture tab (shown in Figure 5-12 with a picture selected).

Click the Select Picture button and navigate to the folder with the image you want. Click the image file, then the

Insert button. Then you can use the controls in the Format section of the Picture tab to determine whether you want one image stretched, a series of images stacked, and, if they're stacked, the value of each full image. One possible chart appears in Figure 5-13.

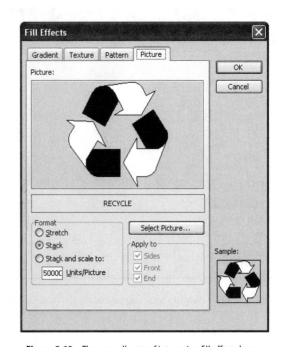

Figure 5-12. There are all sorts of interesting fill effects here.

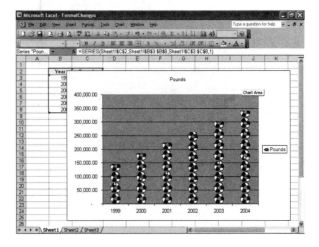

Figure 5-13. Environmentally conscious charts, at your disposal!

ADD ERROR BARS TO A GRAPH

The Annoyance: I'm a graphic artist at a newspaper, where one of my jobs is summarizing sales, stock market, and polling data for our readers. Because polls derive national trends from a smaller sample of the population, there's always a margin of error—usually anywhere from three to five percent, if you believe the statisticians. My boss won't let me put a note at the bottom of the page saying "The margin of error for this survey is *x* percent." That would be too easy. She wants me to add error bars to the line graph I've created so that our readers will have a visual cue as to how far the results of a survey might be off. She's the boss, so I do what she says. But how in the world do I add error bars to a graph?

The Fix: Usually the statistics are less of a problem than the tricky questions the pollsters ask. Too bad there's no way to measure the validity of a questioner, or his/her motives. But I digress. To add error bars to a line in a chart, follow these steps:

1. Create the chart, right-click the bar or line to which you want to add error bars, choose Format Data Series, and click the Y Error Bars tab, which appears in Figure 5-14.

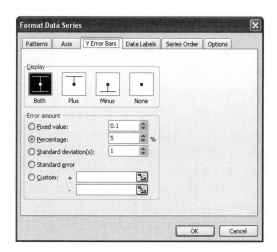

Figure 5-14. Demand well-defined areas of uncertainty and doubt.

2. Select the type of error bar to add (plus, minus, or both).

3. In the "Error amount" section, click the radio button next to the type of error that applies to your data (in this example, it's Percentage) and type the value by which the data could be in error into the field to the right.

Figure 5-15 shows the approval ratings for a nationally celebrated book editor. If you'd like to include a "margin of error" notification in the chart, you can add a text box to the body of the chart. Here's how: right-click any toolbar and choose Drawing. On the Drawing toolbar, click the Text Box button. Click anywhere on the body of the chart and type your text. To format the contents of the text box, right-click it and choose Format Text Box.

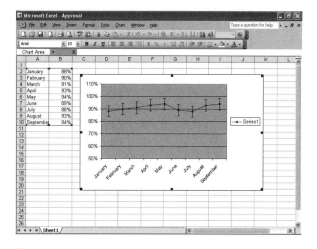

Figure 5-15. My editor's approval ratings, plus or minus a bit.

CHART MANIPULATION ANNOYANCES

COPY CHARTS AS PICTURES

The Annoyance: I want to include one of my charts in a Word document, but not as a full-blown chart someone can edit. I want to include just a *picture* of the chart. Is there a way to do that?

The Fix: There is, but you won't find it on any of the standard Excel menus. Not many people know you can get at some alternative menu commands if you hold down the Shift key when you open a menu. That's what you'll do here:

1. Select the chart.
2. Hold down the Shift key and choose Edit → Copy Picture, then select the "As shown on screen" and Picture radio buttons. Click OK.
3. Go to your Word document and select Edit → Paste.

MOVE A CHART TO A SEPARATE SHEET

The Annoyance: I created a chart and left it on the worksheet that supplied the data—which I'm beginning to think was a mistake. I have to drag the chart around to look at my data! Is it too late to move the chart to its own sheet?

The Fix: To move a chart to its own sheet, right-click any spot in the Chart Area, choose Location, and select the radio button for "As new sheet." Then name the sheet if you want (otherwise, it comes up as Chart1) and click OK to move the chart. The Chart Area is any part of the chart that isn't claimed by the values on an axis, the legend, or the plot in the middle of your chart. If your chart has a legend, plenty of Chart Area space usually is available above or below it (as shown in Figure 5-16).

In any event, just move your pointer around on the chart; a tool tip saying "Chart Area" will appear when it's in the right place.

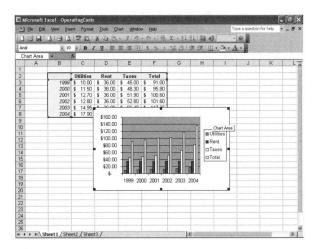

Figure 5-16. Look for the Chart Area tool tip to know you're in the right place.

PRINT A CHART WITHOUT SURROUNDING DATA

The Annoyance: I placed a chart on the same page as the data I used to create it. I don't need to print out the data; there's too much of it to fit on one page anyway. Can I print just the chart?

The Fix: Simply click the chart to select it, and then choose File → Print to print it. In the Print dialog box you'll see the Selected Chart radio button has been selected. Click OK, and the chart prints. All the other radio buttons will be inactive, so if you want to print any other part of your worksheet you'll need to deselect the chart and choose File → Print again.

CHOOSE YOUR AXIS

The Annoyance: I'm a graduate student in my university's psychology department, and I spend a fair amount of time tabulating and summarizing data from my advisor's experiments. On one particular experiment we're measuring the subjects' ability to recognize whether the text on a screen is a word. We've decided to compare average response times and accuracy rates (the data is shown in Figure 5-17), and I want to create a scatter plot (what Excel calls an XY Scatter graph). The problem is that Excel always puts the time data on the horizontal axis, and there doesn't seem to be a way in the Chart

Wizard to choose which parameter goes on which axis. Or if there is, I can't find it.

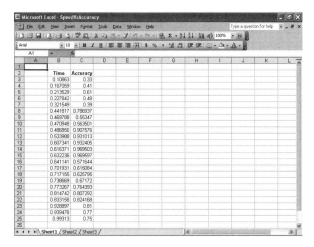

Figure 5-17. It's hard to tell if response time and accuracy correspond just by looking at the data.

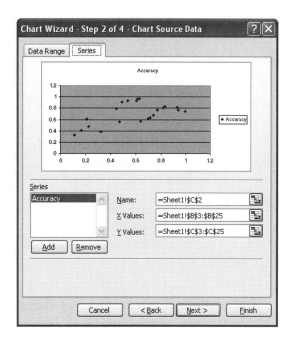

Figure 5-18. You can tell Excel where to map which data.

The Fix: You *can* control which series the Chart Wizard assigns to which axis in an XY plot, but to do so you must visit the Series tab of the second Chart Wizard page, as shown in Figure 5-18. Here's how:

1. Click the chart to activate it, and then click the Chart Wizard button on the standard toolbar.

2. Click Next to move to the second wizard page, and click the Series tab.

3. Erase the contents of the X Values field and then, with the cursor still in the field, click the Expand Dialog button at the far right in the field, select the cells that contain the values you want to map on the X axis, and press Enter.

4. Erase the contents of the Y Values field and then, with the cursor still in the field, click the Expand Dialog button, select the cells that contain the values you want to map on the Y axis, and press Enter.

5. If you don't want to make any other changes to your chart, click Finish.

SEEKING YOUR GOAL WITH A CHART

The Annoyance: I'm still obsessing over that meeting at the auto dealership where I work (see the "Instant Charts" annoyance earlier in this chapter), but this time I want to streamline my presentation a bit. I like using Goal Seek to show how much a single value has to change to meet a goal, such as how much revenue from the Service department would need to grow to account for 20% of the dealership's revenue. What I hate, however, is having to flip back and forth between the data and the chart to *use* Goal Seek. Is there any way I can use Goal Seek from inside my chart?

The Fix: There sure is, so long as you're using a two-dimensional column, bar, pie, doughnut, line, XY (Scatter), or bubble chart—*and* the charted value you're changing wasn't generated by a formula. (For everything else you *will* need to make the change in the worksheet.) For the chart types that work, however, all you have to do is click the data point (such as a column or bar) you want to change, and drag until its data marker displays the desired value (the mouse pointer changes into a multiheaded arrow once you start dragging). The data marker's form depends on the type of chart you're working with:

- If the chart is a bubble, line, or XY (Scatter) chart, drag the data marker.

- If the chart is a bar or column data marker, drag the top-center (or right-center) selection handle.

- If the chart is a pie or doughnut chart, drag the largest selection handle on the outer edge of the slice representing the value you want to adjust.

This change affects your data! When you change a value by dragging its data marker, Excel also changes the underlying value in the worksheet.

If the charted value you're changing comes from a formula, the Goal Seek dialog box will appear after you drag the data marker. The good news is that it will be filled in completely, except for the cell you'd like to vary to generate the new result. Click the worksheet cell with the formula value you want to adjust, and click OK to complete the operation.

PIVOTCHART ANNOYANCES

PIVOTCHARTS AND PIVOTTABLES GO TOGETHER LIKE …

The Annoyance: I frequently use PivotTables to summarize my data, but my boss likes to see charts. He says he finds my lack of graphics…disturbing. I looked through Excel 97, which I have on my home computer, but when I selected the PivotTable and created a graph, the graph didn't change when I manipulated the Pivot-Table. Am I stuck creating a chart for each interesting PivotTable configuration?

The Fix: PivotCharts were introduced in Excel 2000, so as long as you have that version or later, you can create a PivotChart when you create your PivotTable. You *do* have to create a PivotTable, though—it's what the PivotChart

relies on for its data. The only difference in the procedure is that you click the PivotChart Report (with PivotTable Report) radio button on the first page of the PivotTable Wizard. (In Excel 2000, it's the PivotChart (with PivotTable) radio button.) Then you create the PivotTable as you usually would, and after you click Finish, Excel creates both the PivotTable and the PivotChart. A sample PivotChart appears in Figure 5-19.

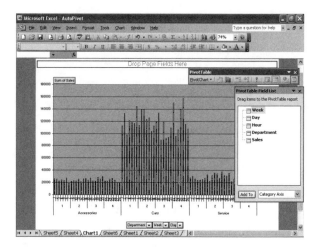

Figure 5-19. This PivotChart represents the dynamic data that forms its base.

As with a PivotTable, you can use the filter arrows on the field headers to limit the data that appears in your chart, which is a lot of help when you have a few hundred rows of data and a lot of subdivisions. That makes for a pretty busy chart. Any filters you set on the PivotTable also affect the PivotChart, and vice versa.

FIRST A PIVOTCHART, THEN A PIVOTTABLE

The Annoyance: I messed up! I created a Pivot-Table and forgot to select the PivotChart option. Am I out of luck? Do I need to create the PivotTable over again? Or can I create the PivotChart from the existing PivotTable?

The Fix: You easily can create a PivotChart from an existing PivotTable. Just select any data cell in the Pivot-Table and click the Chart Wizard button on the Standard toolbar, or choose Insert → Chart. You don't need to go through the Chart Wizard to define your chart's data series and such because Excel can derive that information directly from the PivotTable's configuration.

MAKE NORMAL CHARTS FROM PIVOTTABLES

The Annoyance: I found a PivotTable configuration I really like, and even better, I can use the same configuration to create a terrific PivotChart. But I don't want to create a PivotChart—I want to create an uncomplicated, simple, static chart that always will look the same and won't change when the PivotTable changes. I've tried to create a chart by running the Chart Wizard and selecting the visible PivotTable cells, but the Chart Wizard always creates a PivotChart. Is there any way to turn a PivotChart into a regular chart using the data in my PivotTable?

The Fix: Sure, but first you need to break the link between the data and the PivotTable. The easiest way to do that is to copy the PivotTable and paste the values into another worksheet. Pasting the values breaks the link between the data and the PivotTable it came from, which in turn lets you create a conventional chart. Here's the procedure:

1. Click any cell in the PivotTable and press Ctrl-Shift-8.

2. Choose Edit → Copy, flip to a blank worksheet, and click the cell at the upper-left corner of the range where you want to paste the data.

3. Choose Edit → Paste Special, select the Values radio button, and click OK.

4. Click any cell in the range you just pasted, press Ctrl-Shift-8, and choose Insert → Chart to run the Chart Wizard.

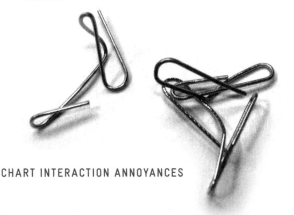

CHART INTERACTION ANNOYANCES

PRINT AN EXCEL 97 CHART FROM POWERPOINT

The Annoyance: I use Excel 97, and I tried to print out a PowerPoint 97 presentation that has an embedded Excel chart—but the page came out blank. This can't be a case of incompatible versions, because both programs were from Office 97. What's going on?

The Fix: I'll bet you were trying to print the chart at a resolution higher than your printer is capable of. To check, open PowerPoint, choose Tools → Options, and select the Print tab. If the "Print inserted objects at printer resolution" box isn't checked, check it now. You also should ensure that your embedded chart isn't selected when you try to print the slide. To deselect the chart, click any blank spot on the PowerPoint slide.

CHART MACRO CRASHES EXCEL

The Annoyance: I'm an impoverished technical writer running Excel 97 under a primeval Windows 95 OS, and I'm having consistent problems with a macro I wrote to create a chart on an existing worksheet. The error I get is singularly unhelpful: *This program has performed an illegal operation and will be shut down. If the problem persists, contact the program vendor.* When I click the Details button in the warning box, I get a similarly unhelpful message: *Excel caused an invalid page fault in module Excel.exe at 0137:30118912.* And then Excel quits; just quits. It doesn't mark the location in the macro where the error occurs, so I have no idea what I'm doing wrong. Any ideas?

The Fix: You might be trying to create your new chart on a worksheet that doesn't exist. One of the known bugs of Excel 97 is that it will crash when you try to create a chart on a nonexistent worksheet, so the first thing you should check is whether the worksheet name you specified in the Location method's Where argument is an existing worksheet. As an example, consider the following macro, which creates a column chart using the data in cells A1:B4:

```
Sub ChartTest()
 Charts.Add
 With ActiveChart
             .ChartType = xlColumnClustered
  .SetSourceData Source:=Sheets("Sheet1").
     Range("A1:B4"), PlotBy:= xlColumns
  .SeriesCollection(1).XValues = ""
      .SeriesCollection(1).Values =
         "=Sheet1!$A$1:$A$4"
      .SeriesCollection(1).Name =
         "=Sheet1!$B$1:$B$4"
  .Location Where:=xlLocationAsObject,
       Name:="Sheet1"
 .HasTitle = True
 .ChartTitle.Characters.Text = "A B C D"
 .Axes(xlCategory, xlPrimary).HasTitle = False
 .Axes(xlValue, xlPrimary).HasTitle = False
 End With
End Sub
```

The line displayed in colored type is the one that can cause you problems. If the Name argument's value were Shet1 instead of Sheet1, the invalid name would cause Excel to go belly-up. If you want to create a chart on a new worksheet, you must set the Where argument to the Excel constant xlLocationAsNewSheet. If you tell Excel you want to create a new sheet for the chart, it doesn't matter what you name it.

CHART GROWS WHEN MOVED TO TEXT BOX

The Annoyance: I'm using Word to draft a quarterly report for the manufacturing division I oversee, based on numbers I track and summarize in an Excel worksheet. I created a chart in the Excel worksheet to summarize some of the data, but I didn't think the axis labels, title, and legend of my chart provided enough information. So, I used Excel to create a text box within the body of the chart to hold a few more words explaining the chart. For instance, I added the text *$=000's* to indicate that all the dollar values on the chart should be multiplied by 1,000. Then, to ensure that the quarterly report always would display the most recent version of the chart, I pasted a link to the chart into the Word document. I did this by copying the Excel chart and pasting it into the

Word document by choosing Edit → Paste Special, and selecting Paste link.

The chart appeared in the Word document and looked fine. However, back in Excel, when I tried to move the text box in the chart to make it easier to read, Excel resized the chart *and* the text box. I know for a fact that I wasn't grabbing any of the size handles at the edges of the box. What am I doing wrong?

The Fix: You're not doing anything wrong; it's just one of those magic moments in which a combination of arbitrary circumstances makes Office handle your data improperly. In this case, the arbitrary circumstances that cause the problem are:

- You add a text box to an Excel chart.
- You change the chart's zoom level to something other than 100%.
- You paste link the chart into a Word document.

The upshot is that if you set the Excel zoom level to anything other than 100%, and then resize a text box within the body of a chart, the chart will expand dramatically in both Excel and Word. The only workaround is to change the zoom level on the chart's sheet back to 100%. To do that, click the Zoom control on Excel's standard toolbar and choose 100%.

DISAPPEARING SCATTER PLOT POINTS ON THE WEB

The Annoyance: I'm that graduate student who's graphing test data against the trial number in an XY (Scatter) plot chart, and I have another problem. As I was graphing the test data, I found a cute shortcut: if the data in my first series follows the sequence 1, 2, 3, and so on (in this case, Trial 1, Trial 2, Trial 3…), I can skip entering this series entirely and Excel still will create a horizontal axis with the number of the trial (the data and resulting chart appear in Figure 5-20). I saved myself the trouble of typing in a sequence of 100 trial numbers in column B, next to the scores in column A. The problem with my cleverness, however, is that the chart disappears when I publish the worksheet as an interactive web page on the Internet—only the data shows up. When I publish the page without interactivity, it looks exactly the same in Internet Explorer as it does in Excel. What's going on?

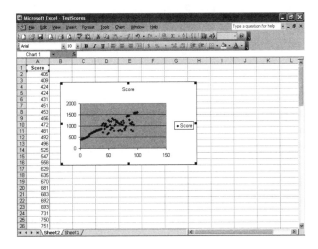

Figure 5-20. This chart appears in a regular Excel file, but not when it's published as a web page.

The Fix: The problem is that your shortcut is allowed in Excel, but not in the Office Web Components. The solution is to always create that second data series, even if it's as simple as 1, 2, 3.... For more information on entering a data series quickly, see "Extend a Numeric Series Automatically" in Chapter 1.

PASTED CHART TURNS INTO GRAY RECTANGLE

The Annoyance: I'm composing a report in Word, and I'd like to paste an Excel chart into the report. The problem is that when I copy a chart from Excel into Word, all I get in my Word document is a gray box. I tried double-clicking the chart object in Word, which would normally open Excel and display the chart in all its glory, but I still got a gray box. I also opened Word and chose Tools → Options, clicked the View tab, and checked the Drawings box, so I know Word will display my chart, but the gray box persists. What's going on?

The Fix: The first thing you need to do is ensure that you are viewing your Word 97 document in either Print Layout or Online Layout mode because you won't see the graphics in any other views. You made sure Word would display drawings, so that's fine. The problem is that someone (probably in your IT department) set up Excel to use minimal resources, probably because your PC doesn't have much RAM. The solution: you need to display the chart in Excel before you can copy it to Word. To display all the charts and other graphical objects in Excel, choose Tools → Options, click the View tab, and in the Objects section click the Show All radio button. When you're done copying, go back to the View tab and choose the Show Placeholders option again to save system resources.

RAM IS CHEAP

Incidentally, a great way to improve your computer's performance is to add RAM. In many cases, adding $100 worth of RAM can improve your computer's performance substantially more than buying a faster CPU or hard disk. The price of RAM varies somewhat, but usually you can buy a 256MB module for $50 or so. If your computer came with only 256MB or less and your motherboard can accommodate another 256MB module, you can't go wrong by adding it. Check your computer's documentation to verify which type of RAM you need to buy.

CAN'T PUBLISH A CHART FROM MULTIPLE SHEETS

The Annoyance: I'm running into problems trying to publish a chart on my company's intranet. I want to create an interactive web page with a chart that draws its data from multiple sheets, but when I try to do that I get the following error message: *Excel cannot publish the chart because the source data is on multiple sheets.*

Why not? The chart is just a graphical representation of the data, right? So it shouldn't matter where the data resides in my workbook. Is this a bug that I can download a patch for?

The Fix: The problem is that an *interactive* chart is more than just a graphical representation of the data. It actually *contains* the data from which it creates its graphical representation. Excel is built to handle sheets and charts based on multisheet data sources, but its web components aren't as flexible. If you want to publish an interactive chart on the Web, all the data needs to be accessible from a single worksheet. You can copy the data manually, or, if the data on the other worksheets might change, you can create links to those cells on the worksheet that serves as the chart's data source. Essentially, this means you must create a worksheet A that links to worksheets B, C, and D, but you must base your interactive Internet table only on the data displayed in worksheet A.

DRAGGING EXCEL CHART CRASHES WORD

The Annoyance: My auto dealership acquires used cars from auctions in other states. Part of my job is to track the states the cars come from, which broker sold them to us, and the cars' condition. I use Microsoft Map (shown in Figure 5-21) to help organize the data in Excel, but I've started having problems in both Excel 97 and 2000 when I try to drag any *other* chart (not the map) to a Word document.

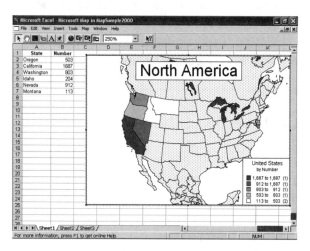

Figure 5-21. Use Microsoft Map when you want to associate your data with a geographical entity.

When I try to drag a chart from Excel to a Word document, I get this very "helpful" error message:

Microsoft Map
An error has occurred while retrieving data from Microsoft Excel.

I click OK (like I have a choice?) and then see this other very helpful error message:

WINWORD caused an invalid page fault in module GDI32.DLL at 014f:bff3501d.

And Word stops responding. I've tested the same workbook without a Microsoft Map added, and neither Excel nor Word crashes when I copy a chart from Excel to a Word document. Do I have to stop using Microsoft Map?

The Fix: Nope. You only need to change how you copy the chart from Excel to Word. If you want to copy your file from Excel to Word (or WordPad, for that matter), don't drag it—select the chart, choose Edit → Copy, go over to Word, click where you want to paste the chart, and choose Edit → Paste. It works every time.

CHART TITLES SHOW ONLY ONE LINE

The Annoyance: I'm putting together a chart showing how my theater's fundraising campaign is going and, OK, maybe I *can* be a bit overartistic at times, but I like long, descriptive chart titles that run vertically instead of horizontally across a page. I just feel that the more information I put into the chart, the fewer questions I'll have to answer down the line. Also, it looks cool. The problem I run into is that if I create a really long chart title, Excel 97 won't display all of it. Shouldn't Excel wrap the text?

The Fix: The problem (which is maddeningly intermittent—it doesn't happen to everyone, or even every time) is that you rotated the text in the title. When you rotate title text in Excel 97, Excel displays only the first line of the title. You can work around the problem in two ways. The first way is to click the title and choose Format → Selected Chart Title, click the Alignment tab (see Figure 5-22), and set the value in the Orientation field to 0 Degrees. If you absolutely must have a rotated title, you might need to export the chart as a graphic and add the title in a graphics program such as Microsoft Paint.

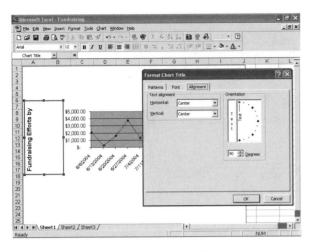

Figure 5-22. When you rotate text, only the first line shows. Be sure to set the Orientation field to 0.

PREVIEW A CHART, CRASH EXCEL 97

The Annoyance: It's been another bad day at the theater office. I'm putting together a grant proposal that requires a pie chart showing how our expenditures were distributed last year. The foundation's guidelines say I'm supposed to put the chart on its own page, so I did. Then I wanted to print a draft copy of the workbook, but when I tried to take one last look at the chart in Print Preview, I saw this message just before Excel 97 crashed: *EXCEL caused an invalid page fault in module EXCEL.EXE at 0137:302c5865.*

Does Microsoft have something against small theater companies? What happened this time?

REPLACEMENT FOR MAPPOINT

Until Office 2003 hit the stores, every version of Excel from 97 on included MapPoint, an Office helper application you could use to display geographic data, such as regional sales, on a map of the United States or the world. Today, MapPoint is sold separately for $259. Beyond being a good reason to keep old versions of Office installed on at least one computer in your organization, it's also an opportunity for the folks at Shale Software. You can use Shale's Xatellitesheet program to create custom regions and link to data in an Excel spreadsheet (see the figure). The program costs only $24.95, and if you'd like to try it with a U.S.-only map before you buy, you can download a trial version from *http://www.shalesoftware.com/xatellite-sheet-frame1.htm*. Xatellitesheet isn't as powerful as MapPoint, but it's a darn sight cheaper.

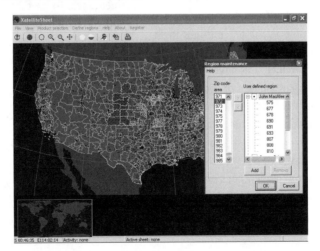

No more MapPoint in Office leaves a gap for others to step into.

The Fix: This issue, believe it or not, is more likely to affect small organizations than large ones because small organizations tend to print workbooks in draft quality, and they also tend to use older versions of Excel. Excel 97 will crash under these circumstances:

- You select the Entire workbook option in the Print dialog box.

- You preview a worksheet set to print as a draft, and then preview a chart.

There are two ways to make sure you're not trying to print a worksheet as a draft. The first method is to select the sheet tab of every worksheet you want to modify, choose File → Page Setup, click the Sheet tab, and uncheck the "Draft quality" box. The second method is to run the following macro (you can assign it to a toolbar button or a menu item if you want—for more information on how to assign a macro to a toolbar button, see Chapter 8):

```
Sub ChangeQuality()

For Each mySheet In Worksheets
 mySheet.PageSetup.Draft = False
Next mySheet

End Sub
```

FALSE PERCENTAGES IN PIE CHART

The Annoyance: I'm going into a meeting with my CEO in a few hours, and something is very wrong with the way Excel 97 is calculating the percentages in my pie chart. Our labor costs always are exactly 50% of our total expenditures for our product. This never changes because we base our employee bonuses on how well we do. The more we make as a company, the more the line workers make. The problem is that when I hover the mouse pointer over the labor wedge, Excel displays labor as accounting for 49% of our cost, not 50% (as shown in Figure 5-23). Also, the total of the percentages in cell C7 is 101%, which is impossible. What's going on?

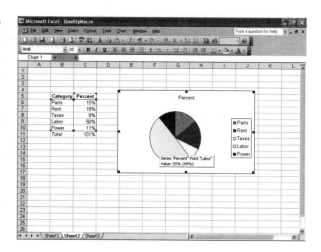

Figure 5-23. You can't give 110%, and you can't give 101% either.

The Fix: The percentage values (data labels) shown next to the pie slices can display incorrect values because Excel, and the Microsoft Graph helper application, round the values in a chart up or down, depending on the value. This means that about half the time, the total of percentages will be 101% and not 100%. When that happens, Excel and Graph subtract one percent from the largest value in the chart to make the numbers add up to 100. Yep, Excel changes your data for its own convenience. Annoying. But there is a way around it—you just need to increase the precision of the numbers used to represent the percentages. To do that, click any of the data labels you want to change. (If you can't see the data labels in your pie chart, right-click anywhere in the pie, choose Format Data Series, click the Data Labels tab, select the "Show percent" radio button, and click OK.) Then, click the data label, choose Format Data Labels, click the Number tab, and type 2 in the Decimal places field.

THE CASE OF THE DISAPPEARING AXIS LABELS

The Annoyance: I work in the seismology lab at my university. Naturally, part of our job is measuring earthquakes, and we plot most of our data on a logarithmic scale—which increases by powers of 10. (On the Richter scale, a 4.0 earthquake is 10 times more powerful than a 3.0, and a 3.0 is 10 times more powerful than a 2.0, and so on.) I use Excel 2000, but most of the folks I

work with use Office 97. And when I copy their Excel 97 workbooks into Excel 2000, the charts on those sheets lose their axis titles, and the scale on the vertical axis (where we measure the amplitude of the earthquake) becomes linear instead of exponential. What's going on?

The Fix: What's going on is that Excel 2000 has problems translating Excel 97 worksheets with charts. (You already guessed that, no doubt.) The problem was fixed in Microsoft Office 2000 Service Release 1/1a; download the service pack from *http://support.microsoft.com/default.aspx?scid=kb;EN-US;245025*.

CHART IMAGE CHOPPED

The Annoyance: I want to include one of my charts in a Word document—not the actual chart, just a picture of it. I copied the chart, but when I pasted the image into Word, big pieces of the chart disappeared. Is this something I have to live with, or is there a way around it?

The Fix: You can get around the problem by copying the image as a picture instead of as a bitmap. To do that, Shift-click the chart, hold down the Shift key, and choose Edit → Copy Picture. Select the "As shown on screen" and Picture radio buttons, and then click OK. You'll be able to paste the image without any trouble.

Keep the Original When You Drag a Chart from Excel to Word

When you drag a chart from Excel into another Office application, you remove the original chart from Excel. But all is not lost! To restore the chart in Excel without affecting the copy, choose Edit → Undo Clear.

CHART ADD-INS AND HELPER APPLICATIONS

MAGIC ADD-INS FOR CHARTS AND GRAPHS

The Annoyance: I can't believe how long it takes to do the simplest things in Excel! I mean, I'm not trying to create anything fancy in the charts and graphs department, but it takes forever to wade through the menus and toolbars to get at Excel's built-in capabilities. For example, I'd like to have a simple interface that lets me switch the axis on which values are plotted.

The Fix: Once again, OzGrid comes to the rescue. Its Chart Assistant add-in (one screen appears in Figure 5-24) lets you manage your charts much more easily. The Chart Assistant costs $29.95; you can buy it at *http://www.ozgrid.com/Services/excel-chart-help.htm*. John Walkenbach also has two handy utilities in his Power Utility Pak, which you can find at *http://j-walk.com/ss/pup/pup5/features.htm*. The Power Utility Pak costs $39.95 ($59.95 if you want the VBA code behind it).

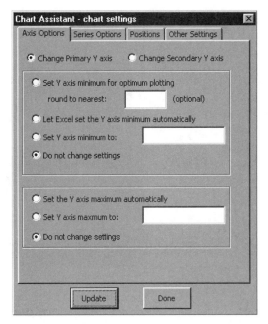

Figure 5-24. The Chart Assistant simplifies a lot of chart drudgery.

BETTER 2D AND 3D CHARTS

The Annoyance: I work with high-end customer relationship management and data mining companies, and Excel's charts, especially the 3D charts, just don't look good enough for the ballpark I'm playing in. I need professional software that turns out great-looking charts I won't have to massage before I put them on a slide. Are there programs that create nicer charts?

The Fix: Plenty of companies have stepped up to the plate and taken a swing at winning your charting dollar. One of the better programs is *XLSTAT-Pro*, which gives you the tools to do some very advanced statistical analysis and charting. The same company also makes *XLSTAT-3DPlot*, which you can use to create striking 3D graphs of the sort shown in Figure 5-25. *XLSTAT-Pro* costs $395. You can purchase the product (or download a 30-day trial) at *http://xlstat.com/products-xlstat-pro.htm*. *XLSTAT-3DPlot* costs $175, but you must have *XLSTAT-Pro* already installed.

HIGH-END VISUALIZATION AND PRESENTATION

I'm a sucker for Excel tools that help you visualize and present your data more effectively. Miner3D EXCEL Professional, an Excel-compatible program you can find on the Web at *http://www.miner3d.com/m3Dxl/index.html*, fits the bill. You get all the goodies you'd expect from a high-end visualization tool (customizable colors, a wide variety of chart and graph types, real-time summary statistics, and so on). But what makes Miner3D EXCEL Professional really cool is the ability to create data animations and record them as AVI files you can include in a presentation, or put up on the Web so that your colleagues can play them in Windows Media Player, RealOne Player, and others (as shown in the following figure). This is a professional tool, so you'll pay a professional price: $595. You can download a 15-day demo from the site, but you'll need to fill in your contact information to get it. Be sure your email address is correct—the company sends the download instructions to the account you list.

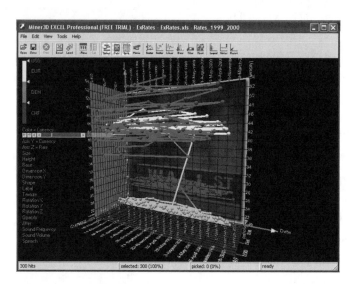

The ability to record a data transformation and play it back is good news for scientific and engineering presenters.

You can download a 30-day trial of *XLSTAT-3DPlot* from *http://www.xlstat.com/products-xlstat-3DPlot.htm*.

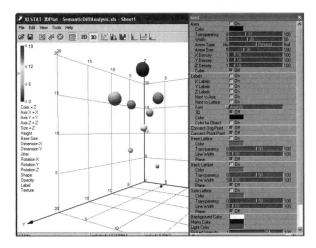

Figure 5-25. Create this chart in Excel? Don't count on it.

Here are some other chart add-ins you might want to consider:

- You can find a free gradient contour chart add-in on John Walkenbach's site, *http://j-walk.com/ss/excel/ files/gradcontour.htm*.

- Decision modeling software from Treeplan is available at *http://www.treeplan.com/sensit.htm*. It costs $29, but you can download a 15-day free trial.

- StatTools from Palisade, *http://www.palisade.com/ html/stattools.asp*, adds a more robust set of statistical analysis tools to Excel. It costs $350, but you can download a 10-day free trial from *http:// www.palisade.com/html/trial_versions.html*.

- CHARTrunner from PQ Systems adds statistical process control capabilities to Excel. You can find the program at *http://www.pqsystems.com/*. It costs $795, but you can download a 30-day free trial version at *http://www.pqsystems.com/products/SPC/ CHARTrunner/CHARTrunnerTrialForm.php*.

- Experience in Software's Project KickStart, a tool to produce Gantt and other project management charts, is available at *http://www.projectkickstart.com/html/ excel.htm*. It costs $129, but you can download a 20-day free trial.

- A set of 2D and 3D graphics packages from OzGrid is available at *http://www.ozgrid.com/Services/ 2D-3D-Graph-Chart-Software.htm*. The typical price for a license is $199.

3D CHART ANNOYANCES

CAN'T CHANGE 3D COLORS IN EXCEL 97

The Annoyance: My company is near the end of its fiscal year, which means for the next few months I'm stuck using Excel 97 to create 3D charts. I'm trying my best, but the darn program keeps getting in the way. For example, there's a cool bit of clip art called AMVICTOR on the Office 97 CD. (Choose Insert → Picture → From File and navigate to the *CLIPART\Popular* folder on the CD to find it.) I added the image to the floor of my 3D chart, and then tried to change the floor's fill color by clicking the floor, clicking the Fill Color button on the Formatting toolbar, and clicking a new color (actually a lighter shade of gray). Nothing happened. Why must Excel always make my life difficult?

The Fix: Sometimes it does seem like Excel is doing its best to frustrate you, but take heart: it does this to everyone. If you're using Excel 97 or 2000, adding a bit of clip art or pasting a drawing object into the floor or wall of a 3D chart prevents you from changing the color of the wall or floor using the Fill Color toolbar button. Go figure! But you *can* change the wall or floor fill colors by right-clicking the wall or floor, choosing Format Wall (or Floor), and clicking the square with the desired fill color. Bear in mind that changing the element's fill color removes the clip art or drawing object you pasted into the element, so you'll need to reinsert it into the floor or wall.

FLOOR TURNS BLACK IN 3D CHART

The Annoyance: One of my co-workers uses Excel 2000, and the floor of her 3D chart turned black after she pasted clip art into the floor. The kicker is that she specifically set the floor's area fill to None by right-clicking the floor, choosing Format Floor, and selecting the None radio button in the Area section of the Format Floor dialog box. What's going on?

The Fix: Believe it or not, the problem would not have occurred if your co-worker had *not* changed the floor's fill to None. It's a bug in Excel 2000. The fix: change the floor's fill to anything except None. Oh, yeah, if the floor of the graph is selected and you press the Delete key, you set the floor's fill to None. Make sure you don't do that by accident.

PIE EXPLOSIONS ARE NO FUN IN 3D

The Annoyance: Excel 97 is trying to make my life difficult—and is succeeding admirably. I created a three-dimensional pie chart that lets you explode one or more pieces by dragging them away from the center of the graph. Good enough. The problem is that my pie slices are all over the place in some uncoordinated mess. One slice appears inside another slice, and nothing moves rationally when I try to fix it. Do 3D pie charts work at all in Excel 97, or should I just call in sick until we have the money to buy a newer version?

The Fix: The problem is that your chart has a slice that crosses both the 0-degree and 180-degree marks (the top and bottom) of the pie. For some reason, that sometimes (but not always, go figure) makes 3D exploded pie charts behave erratically. Fortunately, the issue was fixed in Service Release 1 of Excel 97. You can download the patch from *http://support.microsoft.com/default.aspx?scid=kb;EN-US;172475*.

Exchanging Data
ANNOYANCES

Excel usually plays nice with other programs—but when something goes wrong, it goes *really* wrong. One troublesome area is getting data from external sources, such as databases. Sure, it's easy to cut-and-paste from Access to Excel, but that's a sledgehammer approach where you might need a little finesse. For example, what if you only want to find the addresses of customers from Oregon who placed an order in the last month? That's the sort of thing that's difficult to do with Excel's built-in tools, but it's easy if you use Microsoft Query, an Office utility designed to get data out of databases, text files, and other data sources. You'll learn how to use Query to solve this and other conundrums, tap into SQL to get data, and also make Excel make nice when exporting data to the Web.

MS QUERY AND
DATABASE ANNOYANCES

BRING IN SELECTED DATABASE RECORDS

The Annoyance: I'm pretty good at using Excel, but I've never had to do anything more than copy and paste rows from an Access database table into my worksheets. Now I'm faced with bringing thousands of database records into Excel. How do I get Excel to do the picking and choosing for me?

The Fix: First off, don't copy the entire table into Excel and then try to wrestle the data into some sort of shape! You want to narrow down the data to a manageable set, which is exactly what Microsoft Query was designed for. It lets you create and run queries in other database and spreadsheet programs, pull that information into Excel, and format it as you wish. You can find Microsoft Query on your Office installation disk. If you don't already have Query installed in Office 2002 (aka Office XP) or 2003, choose Data → Import External Data → New Database Query—normally the sequence to launch Microsoft Query. Put your Office installation CD into your drive when prompted and Office will do the rest. In Excel 97 and 2000, when you try to create a new query without Microsoft Query installed you'll get an error message telling you to install it yourself. Hmph...how rude. But here's how to do it in Excel 97:

1. Insert your Office CD into your CD drive. If the Setup program doesn't run on its own, open My Computer, right-click the icon that represents the CD drive, and click Open. Double-click *Setup.exe*.

2. Click the Add/Remove button.

3. On the next Wizard page, click the Data Access item and click the Change Options button.

4. Check the Microsoft Query box and click OK.

And here's how you do it in Excel 2000:

1. Insert your Office CD into your CD drive. If the Setup program doesn't run on its own, open My Computer, right-click the icon that represents the CD drive, and click Open. Double-click *Setup.exe*.

2. Click the Add or Remove Features button.

3. On the next Wizard page, click the tiny plus (+) sign to open the Office Tools item, click the Microsoft Query item, select Run from My Computer, and click the Update Now button.

4. Click Continue to acknowledge that you want the Wizard to install the new component, and then click OK after Setup verifies that it installed Query successfully.

To run Microsoft Query, select the cell you want to place at the top left corner of the imported data list and then choose Data → Get External Data → Create New Query (or Data → Import External Data → New Database Query, or Data → Get External Data → New Database Query, depending on your version). You'll see the Choose Data Source dialog box, shown in Figure 6-1. Then, follow these steps.

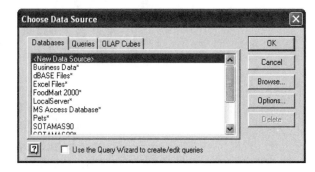

Figure 6-1. Select a source database or create a new one in this appropriately named dialog box.

1. First, uncheck the "Use the Query Wizard to create/edit queries" box. Now, look around the Choose Data Source dialog box for the database you want to use. If you see it, highlight it and click OK. You'll go directly to the Add Tables dialog box, so skip down and start reading the material just after step 7.

2. If you don't see the database you want to use, click <New Data Source> and click OK. The Create New Data Source dialog box opens.

3. Type a name for your data source (usually it will be the same as the name of the database) in Field 1.

4. In Field 2, "Select a driver," click the down arrow and select the appropriate driver from the drop-down list. In your case, it would be *Microsoft Access Driver (*.mdb)*. You will notice that, for some odd reason, the drop-down list seems to be in Portuguese. At least mine is. *Muito estranho, nao?* (If you don't see a list of database drivers in the "Select a driver" field, you might have to install the database drivers from your Office CD. After you run the Setup program, choose Add/Remove and add the database drivers from the Data Source section of the Wizard.)

5. Click the Connect button to open the ODBC Microsoft Access Setup dialog box. Click the Select button and navigate to the folder that holds your Access database. Highlight the database in the lefthand Database Name pane as shown in Figure 6-2, and click OK (I had you uncheck the "Use the Wizard" box so that Microsoft Query will show a preview of your actual data, not just a list of the fields you select. Once you've created a query, as explained in this fix, you can turn the Wizard back on if you want to use it.)

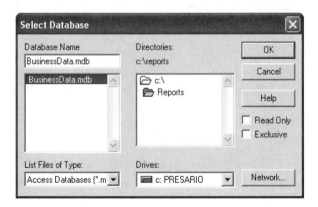

Figure 6-2. Use this dialog box to find the Access database that contains the data you want to import.

6. You will return to the ODBC Microsoft Access (or whatever) Setup dialog box, but now the name of your database will appear in the Database section. Click OK. You will return to the Create New Data Source dialog box. If your database contains multiple tables and you always want to draw data from the same table, open the "Select a default table for your data source (optional)" drop down and pick a table from the list. Whether you do or not, afterward click OK.

7. Your new data source now appears in the Choose Data Source dialog box. Highlight it, and click OK. The Add Tables dialog box will open.

Databases store their data in tables, so you need to identify the Access tables you're drawing data from. The Add Tables dialog box displays all the tables, as well as queries (which you can use because they refer to table data) you can bring into Excel (see Figure 6-3). To make a table or query available for use in the query just click its name, click the Add button, and click Close. This leaves you in the Microsoft Query program window with a query named "Query from *<datasource>*" displayed in a subwindow.

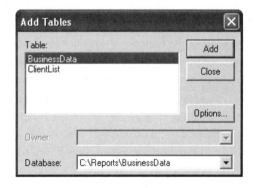

Figure 6-3. Select from a list of database tables.

If you realize you've forgotten to add a table or query you need, choose Table → Add Tables from Query's menu bar to redisplay the Add Tables dialog box. You also can remove a table; choose Table → Remove Table and select the table to remove.

Once you add a table, its field headings will appear in a small field box in the Microsoft Query dialog box.

Now you can bring in the fields that contain the particular data you're looking for (such as a customer ID number, any bonuses for a sale to that customer, and so on). To add a field to your query, drag the field from the Table pull-down list and drop it onto the grid in the larger Query from MS Access Database dialog box, as shown in Figure 6-4.

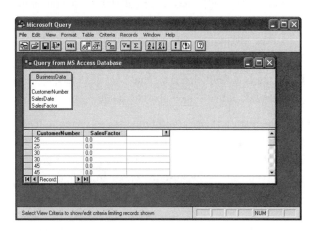

Figure 6-4. You can now build the query.

After you add a field, the data it contains will appear in the preview area at the bottom of the Microsoft Query program window. For example, if you added a States field you would see the states in the first few rows of the table. If you'd like to limit the data that appears in your database—for instance, to see just those customers with Oregon mailing addresses—click any cell in the column representing the field you'd like to limit and choose Criteria → Add Criteria. You can use the controls in the Add Criteria dialog box to limit the data your query returns. You also can use the buttons on the toolbar to sort your data based on the contents of one or more fields.

When the query you just created is showing the correct data, choose File → Return Data to Microsoft Office Excel. Back on the worksheet you will be asked to confirm the action (see Figure 6-5).

After you confirm the operation and the data's destination, Excel imports your data. As an added feature, Excel now recognizes this area as an *external data range*, which means Excel recognizes that the data comes from a source outside the current workbook. It also means you can create special handling instructions for the data, such as including row numbers in the query or refreshing the data every minute, with the External Data Range Properties dialog box, shown in Figure 6-6.

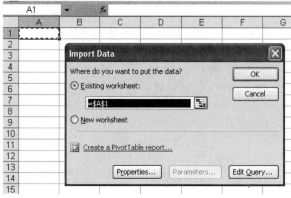

Figure 6-5. Confirm the data import to bring your data into Excel.

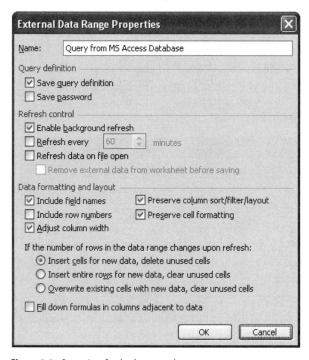

Figure 6-6. Set options for the data range here.

To open the External Data Range Properties dialog box, click any cell in the imported list and choose Data → Import External Data → Data Range Properties. Now, whenever you open the workbook, Excel will refresh the data. You also can refresh the query results by right-clicking any toolbar, choosing External Data, and clicking the Refresh Data button.

AVOID DUPLICATE RECORDS

The Annoyance: I use Microsoft Query to get data out of our customer database and into my Excel worksheets, but some customers are listed in the database twice. Is there a way to make Query return unique records only?

The Fix: To prevent Microsoft Query from returning duplicate records, choose View → Query Properties to display the Query Properties dialog box (see Figure 6-7) and check the Unique Values Only box. Bear in mind that Query will only eliminate records that are *exact* duplicates. If there are any differences between two records, they will be returned as unique listings. Once the data is in your Excel worksheet, you can sort it to get a better look at whether there are any duplicates. If you're working with addresses, sorting by city, last name, and then first name is a good strategy.

Figure 6-7. Duplicates? What duplicates?

CONTROL THE NUMBER OF IMPORTED RECORDS

The Annoyance: When I use Microsoft Query to pull my SQL Server data into Excel, I can't tell how many records there are—but obviously SQL Server tables can have more records than fit on an Excel worksheet because I get a message from Query telling me that not all records can be displayed (see Figure 6-8). Is there some way to tell Query how many records I want pulled into Excel?

Figure 6-8. You can't import more than 65,536 records into Excel.

The Fix: As you probably know, a worksheet can hold a maximum of 65,536 records (the maximum number of rows on a worksheet).

While you're creating a query in Microsoft Query, you can view the SQL code behind the query by clicking the SQL button on the toolbar. Figure 6-9 shows a sample SQL statement.

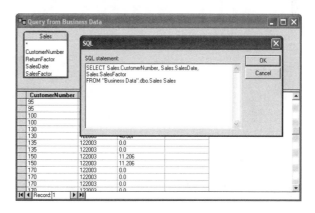

Figure 6-9. Here's the SQL statement, in all its glory.

Here's how this particular SQL query works:

```
SELECT Sales.CustomerNumber, Sales.SalesDate,
    Sales.SalesFactor
FROM `C:\Reports\BusinessData`.dbo.Sales Sales
```

The first line of this query tells Query to bring in the CustomerNumber, SalesDate, and SalesFactor values for every record in the Sales table of the BusinessData database, regardless of how many records that is.

To limit the number of records returned, you must add a function called the Top predicate to the first line of the SQL statement, which tells the system how many records to return. The Top predicate is similar to the Top 10 filter you can set in Excel. Both techniques limit the number of rows returned by an operation on a data table.

Here's the procedure you follow to add the Top predicate to an SQL statement:

1. Create the query and click the SQL button. You will see something like the SQL statement shown earlier.

2. On the first line, just after SELECT (the first word in the SQL query) and before the next word (for example, Sales.CustomerNumber) type Top *number*, where *number* is a value you enter representing the number of records you want the query to return. Figure 6-10 shows what the SQL should look like when you're done.

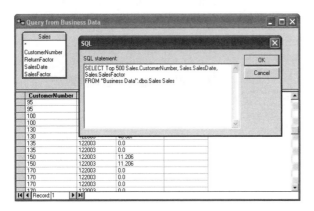

Figure 6-10. Alter the SQL statement to return a certain number of records.

3. Click OK twice, the first time to make the change and the second time to clear the message box shown in Figure 6-11.

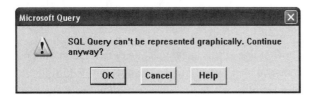

Figure 6-11. Ignore this warning.

4. Choose File → Return Data to Microsoft (Office) Excel to bring the records to your worksheet.

Isn't there an easier way to limit records? Yes, and no. In Query you can choose Edit → Options and use the controls in the dialog box to limit the number of records the query returns. The problem is that you can set a maximum value of only 32,767, so if you need to fetch more records (up to the 65,536 limit) you must use SQL.

In any case, Excel doesn't give you a lot of help composing SQL queries, and neither will this book. Fortunately, there are countless tutorials on SQL to be found on the Internet. For example, check out *http://www.w3schools.com*, or use the Transact-SQL reference at *http://msdn.microsoft.com/library/en-us/tsqlref/ts_tsqlcon_6lyk.asp*.

GET MORE THAN 65,536 RECORDS INTO EXCEL

The Annoyance: I work at a large call center where I track incoming toll-free calls. We use Access to record each incoming call, but now my boss wants me to export a month's worth of calls—that's 100,000 records' worth—into an Excel worksheet. How do I bring more than 65,536 records into Excel?

The Fix: The 65,536 rows per worksheet limit is set in stone, so your only option is to put the incoming database records on more than one sheet. The trick here is how to split the records between sheets, and the best approach will depend on the data.

If you're lucky, the database table will have an *auto-counter* or *autonumber record number field*—a number that is incremented record by record. When this type of field is present, it's easy to select exact ranges of data records. Figure 6-12 shows Microsoft Query with an Access table set to be queried, with the RecordNumber field as the sequential counter. To cull the desired number of records, in the Criteria Field you'd enter RecordNumber and in the Value field a range—1 through 65,536 in this example. In the Value field, make sure you enter the Between and And operators as shown here. Also, leave the comma out of any number with more than three digits.

To create this query, follow these steps:

1. Download *BusinessData2.mdb* from *http://www.oreilly.com/catalog/excelannoyances/downloads.csp*.

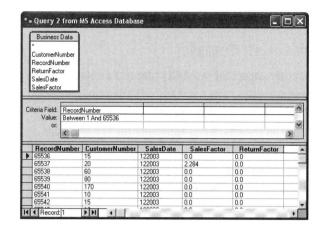

Figure 6-12. Create a criterion to specify which records to return.

2. Choose Data → Get External Data → Create New Query in Excel 97 (or Data → Get External Data → New Database Query in Excel 2000 or Data → Import External Data → New Database Query in Excel 2002 and 2003) to run Microsoft Query and display the Choose Data Source dialog box.

3. If you don't see the database you want, click <New Data Source>, click OK, and step through the process outlined earlier in the annoyance titled "Bring In Selected Database Records." Navigate to the directory where you saved *BusinessData2.mdb*. Select the database, and click OK.

4. In the Add Tables dialog box, select BusinessData, click the Add button, and then click the Close button to close the Add Tables dialog box.

5. Choose Criteria → Add Criteria to display the Add Criteria dialog box.

6. Open the Field drop down and select RecordNumber to assign the criteria to the RecordNumber field.

7. Open the Operator drop down and select the blank item at the top of the list.

8. In the Value field, type Between 1 And 65536.

9. Click the Add button, and then click the Close button.

10. Drag the RecordNumber field from the BusinessData table in the top pane of the Microsoft Query/Query From program window to an open rectangle in the bottom pane of the Microsoft Query/Query From

window. You just added the RecordNumber field to your query's results.

11. One field at a time, drag the CustomerNumber, Sales-Date, SalesFactor, and ReturnFactor fields to the next open space in the bottom pane of the Microsoft Query/Query From window. Doing so adds each field to your query's results.

12. Choose File → Save to display the Save As dialog box, type a name for your query in the File Name field, and click Save.

13. Choose File → Return Data to Microsoft Excel.

14. In the Returning Data to Microsoft Excel dialog box, type the address of the cell you want to be at the top left of your imported data range (if necessary), and click OK.

This first cut of the data can be pulled into one worksheet. Then, starting with another worksheet, create a query that returns the next block of values—in this case, the criteria for RecordNumber would be Between 65537 and 100000.

You're not limited to using a range of numbers as your selection criteria. The Add Criteria dialog box helps to establish how the records should be limited. Figure 6-13 shows the dialog with some of the options. For example, you can cull records by dates within a particular range, find orders of at least (or no more than) a given value, or limit the records returned to customers from a particular state.

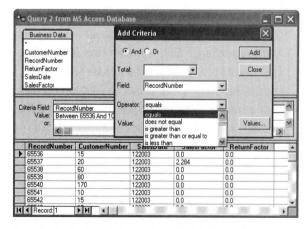

Figure 6-13. The Add Criteria dialog box helps limit the records that a query returns.

AND NOW...A QUICK OVERVIEW OF DATABASE TECHNOLOGY

The basic unit of a database is the table, which contains carefully structured information about a particular type of object, such as the auto parts in Table 6-1.

Table 6-1. This table is informative, but it's just the start of what you can do with a database.

PartID	PartName	PartCost
0000001	Platinum spark plug	4.95
0000002	Steering wheel	136.90
0000003	Gear shift lever	97.50

If you think a database table's structure is identical to that of an Excel data list, you're correct. A database table consists of columns representing different specific aspects of an object (in the sample table, it's PartID, PartName, and PartCost) and rows that represent different examples of the object (such as a platinum spark plug) and usually include information in every column. The entries in a database column are called *fields*, while the rows are called *records*.

The difference between a database program such as Access and a spreadsheet program such as Excel is the program's focus. Excel is good at creating formulas to summarize relatively limited data sets, while Access (and its big brothers MySQL and SQL Server) are good at managing larger data sets. Over time, Microsoft's Excel team has added limited database capabilities such as the LOOKUP() functions, so users who don't need a true database or who just don't want to learn one can search data lists stored in worksheets. The database equivalent of a LOOKUP() function is called a *query*. For example, if you maintained a table of 160,000 customer addresses that contained fields for the street address, city, state, and Zip Code, you could create a query to ask the database to list all the addresses in the Zip Codes starting with 972.

Another important capability that sets a database program apart from a spreadsheet program is the database's ability to create links between tables based on common fields and to use the combinations to answer a query, or create new tables based on the data. For example, suppose you had a list of customer order items, as shown in Table 6-2.

Table 6-2. This table also contains a PartID field, so it's possible to link it with the previous table.

Order Number	PartID	Quantity
0000015678	0000001	6
0000015679	0000002	1
0000015679	0000003	1

There are two orders in this list. The first order was for six spark plugs, while the second one was for a steering wheel and a gear shift lever—but you'd never know that unless you remembered each part's PartID value. Because the two tables have a common field, the PartID field, you can create an SQL query telling your database to create a relationship between the two tables based on that field. The benefit of combining the two tables is that you can create a new table, such as Table 6-3, that contains both the PartID value and the PartName without typing in the PartName value again. What's even better is that *the database did most of the work*. Sure, you had to create the table with a list of PartName values that correspond to PartID values, but you had to do it only once. As explained in Chapter 4, it's possible to convince Excel to do that sort of lookup, but you have to write a lot of custom formulas to make it happen. This capability is built into relational database programs such as Access, SQL Server, Informix, IBM DB2, Oracle, and so on, so why not use it to bring the data into Excel? Of course there are issues when you try to bring database data into Excel, but it's still a lot easier to keep hundreds of thousands of records in a database and bring a few of them into Excel. Why spend hours building a custom workbook that does what Access, a $200 program, does for you right out of the box?

Table 6-3. Having something in common is important in all relationships, particularly relationships between tables.

Order Number	PartID	PartName
0000015678	0000001	Spark plug
0000015679	0000002	Steering wheel
0000015679	0000003	Gear shift lever

So, how do you combine the two tables without importing them both into Excel and doing some magic? You use an Office helper application named Microsoft Query (much more on this program later in this chapter) and SQL. The language is quite complex, as you might imagine, but elementary queries drawing data from a single table aren't that hard to follow.

For example, consider the following SQL query:

```
Name,Customers.OpenDate
FROM 'C:\Reports\BusinessData'.Customers
    Customers
ORDER BY Customers.OpenDate ASC
```

Let's look at the second line first. This query line is going to draw data from the Customers table of the BusinessData database. The name of the database is enclosed in single quotes because it includes the full directory path of where the database is stored on your computer. The specific table you're drawing data from (Customers) is listed after the database name, separated by a period. The second Customers after the table name is the name of the table created by the query.

The first line of the query lists the database columns (fields) the query will cull from the Customers table. In this case, the query returns the CustomerNumber, Name, and OpenDate fields. You can create a query that draws data from more than one table at a time, which is why you need to put the table name in front of the field name.

The final line of the query describes how SQL should deliver the query results. In this case, the results will be sorted in ascending order by the contents of the OpenDate field. What does that mean? It means you'll get a list of your customers based on the date they first opened their account with your company.

There's a bit of art as well as science to good database design. You can find a lot more information in *Access Database Design and Programming*, Third Edition (O'Reilly).

ADD A COUNTING FIELD TO QUERY RESULTS

The Annoyance: OK, smart guy, I managed to bring in data from an order-tracking table where the rows had a sequentially numbered field. But now the only fields I have to work with are CustomerNumber, Sales-Date, and SalesFactor. Please tell me I don't have to learn SQL Server to bring this data into Excel...there's not enough time in the day!

The Fix: Good news! Using a few Query and SQL tricks, you still can break the data records into usable chunks. This example makes use of an Access database with a table named BusinessData, which contains 116,300 records. In the table are a few fields: CustomerNumber, SalesDate, and SalesFactor. Figure 6-14 shows the table in Access.

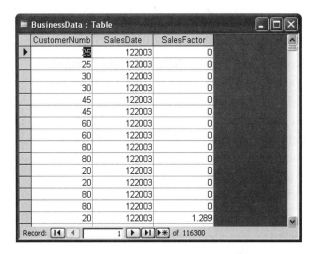

Figure 6-14. This Access table contains 116,300 records, more than you can put on one worksheet. You can still slice it and dice it to drop different chunks of the data in separate worksheets, but you'll need a revised SQL query to do it.

On the first worksheet, choose Data → Get External Data → Create New Query (or Data → Import External Data → New Database Query, depending on your version) to create a new database query. In Query, select the Business-Data table as the data source, and choose Records → Sort to sort the records by the value in the CustomerNumber field. In SQL, you can use the Top keyword, followed by a number, to limit the results of the query to that number of records as the query searches from the top of the table. For example, the following SQL query limits the results to the first 65,000 records in the BusinessData table; the query also uses the ORDER BY keyword to sort the query results by customer number. (The query you create will differ from this one if you stored the *BusinessData* database in a folder other than *C:\Reports*.)

```
SELECT Top 65000 BusinessData.CustomerNumber,
BusinessData.SalesDate, BusinessData.SalesFactor
FROM 'C:\Reports\BusinessData'.BusinessData
BusinessData
ORDER BY BusinessData.CustomerNumber
```

To create the query, follow these steps:

1. Select the cell you want to be at the top left corner of your imported data.

2. In Excel 97, choose Data → Get External Data → Create New Query. In Excel 2000, that's Data → Get

External Data → New Database Query. In Excel 2002 or 2003, select Data → Import External Data → New Database Query to run Microsoft Query and display the Choose Data Source dialog box.

3. Select New Data Source and click OK to display the Create New Data Source dialog box.

4. Type Bdata as the name for your data source. Then, open the "Select a driver" drop down and select Microsoft Access (*.mdb) Driver.

5. Click the Connect button and in the ODBC Microsoft Access Setup dialog box, click the Select button.

6. Navigate to the directory where you stored the *BusinessData* database, click the filename, and then click OK.

7. Click the fourth field's down arrow, select Business Data, and click OK twice.

8. Drag the CustomerNumber field from the Business-Data table in the top pane of the Microsoft Query window to an open rectangle in the bottom pane of the Microsoft Query/Query From window. One field at a time, drag the SalesDate and SalesFactor fields to the next open space in the bottom pane of the Microsoft Query/Query From window.

9. Choose View → SQL to display the SQL dialog box.

10. After the word SELECT at the start of the query, type Top 65000 followed by a space, and click OK. Click OK again to clear the warning box that indicates the edited query can't be represented graphically.

11. Choose File → Save, type BusinessDataQuery (or any other name) in the "File name" field, and click Save.

12. Choose File → Return Data to Microsoft Excel.

13. Click OK to import the data.

The query you just created ensures the query will return only the top 65,000 records. Figure 6-15 shows how the SQL query looks after you set the conditions.

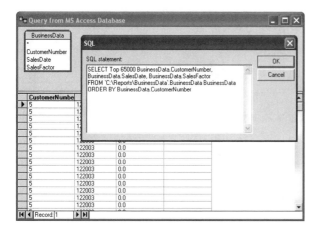

Figure 6-15. This query returns just the first 65,000 records.

The next part is just a little more involved. On the next worksheet, start another database query that uses the same database and table to return the remaining records. I mentioned earlier that the total number of records in this example is 116,300, but you might not always know ahead of time how many records there are. Luckily, Microsoft Query can tell you. In Query, choose Records → Add Column to display the Add Column dialog box (shown in Figure 6-16).

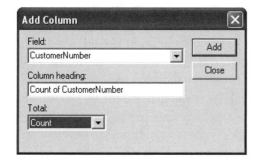

Figure 6-16. Tell MS Query to count the total number of records.

Select a field to summarize (in this case, it's CustomerNumber) and summarize it using the Count operation. Here's how:

1. Select the cell you want to be at the top left corner of your imported data.

2. In Excel 97, choose Data → Get External Data → Create New Query. In Excel 2000, it's Data → Get External Data → New Database Query. In Excel 2002 or 2003, select Data → Import External Data → New Database Query to run Microsoft Query and display the Choose Data Source dialog box.

3. Click Bdata (the data source you defined earlier) and click OK.

4. Choose Records → Add Column to display the Add Column dialog box (shown in Figure 6-16).

5. Open the Field drop down and select CustomerNumber.

6. Type `Record Count` in the Column heading field.

7. Open the Total drop down and select Count.

8. Click the Add button. Microsoft Query displays the value 116300 in the bottom pane of the Microsoft Query window. Make note of the value.

9. Click Close.

10. Choose File → Cancel and Return to Microsoft Excel.

When you create the query in Microsoft Query (but don't return the result to Excel), the column you added displays the total number of records (as shown in Figure 6-17). By no surprise, the count operation will match the number of records reported by Access in Figure 6-14.

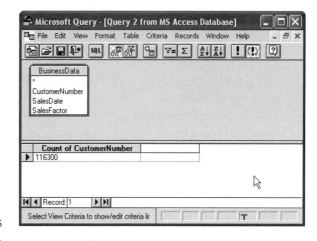

Figure 6-17. The field you added finds the total number of records.

Now crunch the numbers! 116,300 – 65,000 = 51,300. Now you know you need to bring in the remaining 51,300 records. You do this with the same techniques you employed for the first 65,000 records. Once again you use a Top statement to return the "first" 51,300 records—but this time you first sort the CustomerNumber field in descending order, not ascending order, so that it culls records 65,001 through 116,300. Here's how:

1. Display a new worksheet and select the cell you want to be at the top left corner of your imported data.

2. In Excel 97, choose Data → Get External Data → Create New Query. In Excel 2000, choose Data → Get External Data → New Database Query. In Excel 2002 and 2003, choose Data → Import External Data → New Database Query to run Microsoft Query and display the Choose Data Source dialog box.

3. Click Bdata (the data source you defined earlier) and click OK.

4. Drag the CustomerNumber field from the Business-Data table in the top pane of the Microsoft Query window to an open rectangle in the bottom pane of the Microsoft Query/Query From window. One field at a time, drag the SalesDate and SalesFactor fields to the next open spaces in the bottom pane of the Microsoft Query/Query From window.

5. Click any cell in the Customer Number data column and click the Sort Descending toolbar button.

6. Choose View → SQL to display the SQL dialog box.

7. After the word SELECT at the start of the query, type **Top 51300**, followed by a space, and click OK. Click OK again to clear the warning box that indicates the edited query can't be represented graphically.

8. Choose File → Return Data to Microsoft Excel.

9. Click OK to import the data.

The query you just created looks like the one shown in Figure 6-18.

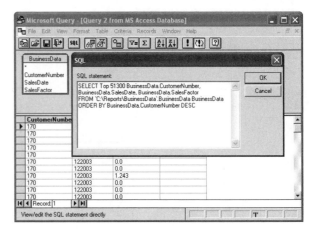

Figure 6-18. Here's the SQL to return the remaining records.

Here's the SQL statement:

```
SELECT Top 51300 BusinessData.CustomerNumber,
BusinessData.SalesDate, BusinessData.SalesFactor
FROM 'C:\Reports\BusinessData'.BusinessData
BusinessData
ORDER BY BusinessData.CustomerNumber DESC
```

OK, you're asking, what happens if you have *more* than two worksheets' worth of data *and* the table *doesn't* include a counter such as RecordNumber that you can use in a Between clause? In that situation, you might need to ask your database administrator (after all, what are you paying him for?) to add a stored procedure to the database to get a set number of records. If you show your database administrator the Select statement you are trying to perform (just cut/paste it from Query into an email message) and describe the 65,536 record limitation, he should be able to hook you up. Once a stored procedure is added to a database, you can call it from the SQL dialog box using the Exec statement as shown here:

```
EXEC CustomerSales @StartRecord=1, @EndRecord=1000
```

Those words after the @ sign are parameters passed to the stored CustomerSales procedure. In this case they tell the procedure which records to return. The mechanics of creating a stored procedure in a database vary depending on what database software you are using. Your database administrator should know how to do this.

IMPORT DATA FROM MORE THAN ONE TABLE

The Annoyance: In our company database, one table holds the names of clients, and another lists the automobiles they own. I have to make a report on who owns what cars. My problem is that the two tables don't have a field with the same name, so Query doesn't create a link between them. How can I get the right info from those two tables?

The Fix: Relational database programs often hold (surprise!) *relational* data—that is, data connecting two related tables. For example, you might have one table that lists cars sold by a dealership and another table that contains a list of clients and the cars they bought. What data might these two tables have in common? The unique vehicle identification number (VIN) assigned to each car. In the Cars table, the VIN is a *key* field, which means it contains a unique value for each table row and can be used to distinguish one table row from another. (In other words, no two cars can have the same VIN.) In the best case scenario, the fields with the common data will have the same field name. For example, the CustomerPurchase table might have three fields: a PurchaseID field that's unique for each row (the key for that table), the CustomerID, and the VIN. Note that the VIN field isn't necessarily a key in the second database...but the PurchaseID field is. The way to query related information from more than one table is to make sure key fields are used to indicate the relationship. Figure 6-19 shows a database that has a tblCustomers table and a tblVehicles table. A line connects the matching key fields: CustomerID. For each customer in tblCustomer, the CustomerID is a unique number. You can use that uniqueness to create a relationship between the tblVehicles table and the tblCustomers table. A customer can own more than one car, but a car can't be owned by more than one customer.

The scenario you have to worry about is when the two fields contain the same data but don't have the same name. One such example appears in Figure 6-19.

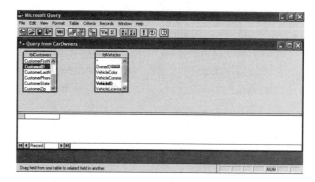

Figure 6-19. Both tables contain CustomerID data, but when the fields have different names you must relate the fields manually.

The good news is that this "worst case scenario" isn't all that bad. You can manually relate the two fields by following this procedure:

1. Select the cell you want to be at the top left corner of your imported data.

2. Choose Data → Get External Data → Create New Query in Excel 97; Data → Get External Data → New Database Query in Excel 2000; or Data → Import External Data → New Database Query in Excel 2002 and 2003; to run Microsoft Query and display the "Choose Data Source" dialog box.

3. Click the data source you want to use and click OK.

4. Click the first table you want to relate and click Add.

5. Click the second table you want to relate and click Add.

6. Drag the field name from the table where the related field is the primary key to the corresponding field in the second table.

7. Add the fields with the values you want to pull into Excel to the data area in the bottom part of the Query program window.

8. Choose File → Return Data to Microsoft Excel and click OK to import the data.

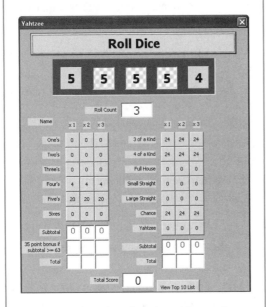
TRANSLATE ERROR MESSAGES INTO ENGLISH

The Annoyance: I've tried various Microsoft Query techniques for getting unique values, combining tables, and counting records, but sometimes Query gives me errors I don't understand, and then refuses to return the data. How do I fix the problem and get the data I want?

The Fix: Microsoft Query has to deal with many different databases, so when it encounters a problem its feedback isn't always very clear. What's worse is that if you click Help on the error message, you're liable to see the singularly unhelpful explanation: "Driver error."

Microsoft Query is really just a tool for connecting Excel and other Office applications to databases by composing queries in the SQL language. The tables, columns, and criteria you select are just added to the SQL Select statement, as you can verify simply by clicking the SQL button. The only problem you might run into is that not every database connection program, or driver, can handle every SQL statement. That's when you might get the dreaded database driver error.

Table 6-4 is a short list of some of the common errors you might see, along with their possible causes and solutions.

A few tips:

- The term *aggregate function* refers to SQL functions that return a single value from a set of data. Those functions include Avg, Count, Max, Min, and Sum. All of those functions require a Group By clause that Microsoft Query usually adds automatically.

- Not all field types are valid in a Group By clause. Long text fields and images (which you can't use in Excel anyway) can't be grouped.

- Not all SQL statements are valid in Microsoft Query. These limitations are set by the database driver, and by what Microsoft Query can interpret. For complicated queries, it's sometimes easier to create a stored procedure in the database and call it from Microsoft Query using the Exec statement.

Table 6-4. A short list of database driver errors.

Error message	Possible cause and solution
The text, ntext, or image data type cannot be selected as DISTINCT.	You are trying to get unique rows, but your query includes long text fields or images. Either remove those columns from the query or deselect Unique Values Only in the Query properties.
Column *columnname* is invalid in the selected list because it is not contained in either an aggregate function or a GROUP BY clause.	You are trying to use an SQL function, such as Count, but your query includes a long text field or image. This is similar to the preceding error. Either remove the column containing the long text field from the query, or remove the column that uses the SQL function.
You tried to execute a query that does not include the specified expression *fieldname* as part of an aggregate function.	You are using an SQL function that requires a Group By clause, but for some reason that clause wasn't added to the SQL statement. In Query, select View → Query Properties and check the Group Records box.
Incorrect syntax near *statement*.	You tried to edit the SQL statement directly, but made a mistake. Writing or editing your own SELECT statement can be tricky. You can restore the original statement generated by Microsoft Query by clicking Cancel.
Other errors after manually editing an SQL statement in Query.	Restore the original statement generated by Microsoft Query by clicking Cancel.

IMPORT AND EXPORT ANNOYANCES

MOVE DATA BACK AND FORTH FROM EXCEL TO ACCESS

The Annoyance: I've tried copying data from an Excel worksheet and pasting it into an Access database table, but the paste operation created errors. Is there an easy way to transfer data from Excel to Access? And vice versa, from Access to Excel?

The Fix: There are several ways to handle this. One of these options is to simply use the Get External Data feature in Access. This method will import your Excel data and either put it into a new Access table or append it to an existing table. Here's how.

Moving data from Excel to Access

1. In Access, select File → Get External Data → Import.

2. In the "Files of type" drop down, select Microsoft Excel (*.xls) from the list.

3. Navigate to and select the Excel workbook that has your data, and click the Import button.

4. The Import Spreadsheet Wizard starts up (see Figure 6-20). In the Wizard you can select the worksheet or range that has your data. Additional pages in the Wizard ask whether the data has a header row, whether to place the data in a new table or an existing one, which fields (columns) to import or not, and so on. When you've made all the appropriate choices, click Finish.

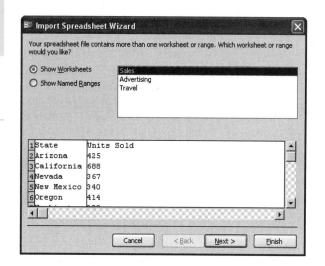

Figure 6-20. Import Excel data into Access with a few clicks!

An alternative way to transfer data from Excel to Access is to use Paste Append. This command is a special variation of the Paste command, and is available in Access only when you want to copy Excel data to an existing

Access table. To use Paste Append, select and copy the data in Excel just as you normally would, display the Access table to which you want to add the data, and choose Edit → Paste Append.

Don't copy Excel headers when using Paste Append. You're pasting into an existing Access table that, by design, already has field names—the equivalent of header rows in Excel. If you copy your Excel header row along with the actual data, that row will become just another data record in the Access table. Worse, an error could occur. For example, if you paste a column from Excel with numeric data and the header into an Access field that expects numeric data, you'll get an error for sure.

Moving data from Access to Excel

Transferring data from Access to Excel is usually a simple matter of copying the data from the Access table and pasting it into the Excel worksheet.

Another way to exchange data between Excel and Access is to use the XML data format. The advantage is that once you get the data into Excel you can set up an XML Map in your Excel workbook and easily update the data in the worksheet whenever you update it in the source Access database. You can select which fields will be displayed in your worksheet and preserve the format of the worksheet no matter how many times you refresh the data.

This technique is available only in the 2003 versions of Excel and Access. To export a table in XML from Access:

1. Select the table you wish to export and choose File → Export.
2. Select XML as the "Save as type" in the Export Table dialog box, name the file, and click Export All.
3. In the Export XML dialog box, click OK.
4. Excel exports the table as XML data and saves information about the fields in the table as an XML schema file (XSD).

To import the Access XML data into Excel for the first time:

1. Select Data → XML → Import. Excel displays the Import XML dialog box.
2. Choose the XML file you just generated from Access and click OK.
3. Excel creates an XML Map that it uses to map fields from the table to columns in a worksheet, and then asks if you want to import the data into an existing worksheet or create a new one.
4. When you click OK, Excel imports the data through the XML Map and displays it on a worksheet in a list.

After you import the data into Excel the first time and you make changes in the Access database file, you can update the data in the Excel worksheet by selecting Data → XML → Refresh XML Data. If you make changes to the data in Excel and you want the changes reflected in the Access database, you can export the data from Excel to an XML file and import that file as a new table in Access.

However, exporting changes made in Excel back into Access has a few gotchas:

- Only fields that are displayed on the Excel worksheet will be exported to XML. Excel ignores any data in hidden columns or rows.
- Exporting a table from Access adds an extra field you'll have to remove from the XML Map before you can export the data from Excel. To do that in Excel, choose Data → XML → XML Source and then, in the XML Source task pane, delete the table element that wasn't in your original table. (It's usually titled "generated.")
- Importing XML data into Access doesn't merge changes with existing records. You have to import the data as a new table.

Still, it's worth looking at using XML for data exchange if you need to frequently export or import data from the same Access tables.

TRUNCATED DATA IN ACCESS

The Annoyance: For several years now I have used an Excel worksheet in which I enter customer comments about our service department. But because it's unwieldy handling comments in a worksheet I also store the customer comments in an Access database, and link them to the relevant products and services in the Excel worksheet. To move the comments from the worksheet to Access, I established a link from the Excel worksheet to one of the tables in the Access database. Until recently, this worked perfectly: we would type in brief summaries of the customers' comments, and they would be imported perfectly into Access. But that was then and this is now. Recently, my boss decided we must enter a verbatim transcription of exactly what each customer says—which can be a pretty long chunk of text. There's no problem entering it into the Excel sheet, but Access imports only the first 255 characters of the customer comment into the customer comment field I set up. What's up?

The Fix: When you first linked your Access database to the Excel worksheet, Access assigned a field type for each column of Excel data. Remember, at that time the comments were fairly short. When Access saw textual data that did not exceed 255 characters for any cell in the column, it assigned the Text datatype. The Text datatype is used for alphanumeric text up to 255 characters. Once it assigns a field type, Access never checks back to ensure the datatype it set remains correct. Now that you're entering longer comments, any that exceed 255 characters are being truncated.

To correct this annoyance, reestablish the link. In Access, delete the link to the Excel worksheet. Then choose File → Get External Data → Link Tables to set up the link again. When Access realizes that some cells have more than 255 characters, it will classify the field as a Memo datatype, which can hold any number of characters.

UPDATE EMBEDDED POWERPOINT CHART

The Annoyance: I copied a chart from our monthly PowerPoint sales presentation to an Excel workbook. Now I need to add a new series to the chart, but when I click the chart to highlight it I don't see the Chart option on Excel's menu! I've always used Chart → Add Data to add an additional series. I never had this problem with regular Excel charts, and I don't want to have to use PowerPoint every time I want to update a chart I've plugged into Excel.

The Fix: When you copy a chart from PowerPoint and paste it into Excel, the chart behaves much as it did in PowerPoint, meaning you can format the chart by changing its colors, legend, axes, and so on. The difference between a PowerPoint chart and an Excel chart, however, is that an Excel chart uses data on a worksheet for its source, while PowerPoint charts use dedicated chart datasheets. So...you *can* add additional data to the chart, but you have to use the chart's datasheet, which comes along for the ride when you paste the chart into Excel. Just double-click the chart to display its datasheet and enter the additional data. Figure 6-21 shows an embedded PowerPoint chart with its datasheet.

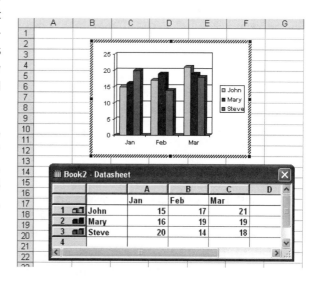

Figure 6-21. PowerPoint-based charts use a connected datasheet for their source data.

After additional data is keyed in, click anywhere on the Excel worksheet to close the datasheet. Be aware that there is no live link between the chart in Excel and the original chart in PowerPoint—changes you make to the datasheet in Excel won't change the original PowerPoint chart, and vice versa.

INCLUDE ANOTHER FILE IN AN EXCEL WORKBOOK

The Annoyance: I pride myself on my ability to create compelling reports in Microsoft Office. My secret? I don't just use Word, or Excel, or PowerPoint...I use *all* the Office programs to get my point across. What really gets my goat, though, is that I have to remember to bring my Word document, my Excel workbook, my PowerPoint presentation, and my Access database with me when I travel. I know it doesn't seem like a big deal, but if you've ever had 20 minutes to get your materials ready before you rush to the airport, you will understand why it can be a huge deal to copy all those files to my notebook. If I forget even one file I have to hold up my presentation for 20 minutes while I call the home office and have them put the file on a server I can get to. Never again! How do I put all my files into a single package?

The Fix: I feel your pain, but relief is at hand! You can include existing files in an Excel workbook using the Object Linking and Embedding (OLE) protocol. To embed a file in an Excel workbook, follow these steps:

1. Choose Insert → Object.
2. Click the Create from File tab and then click the Browse button.
3. Select the file you want to insert and click the Insert button.
4. Click OK to verify your choice.

You have just literally embedded the selected file in your Excel workbook (when you click the embedded file in the Excel sheet you'll see an =EMBED() formula on the Formula Bar). You need to have the source application (e.g., PowerPoint for a presentation) on the computer where you have the file, but you won't have to worry about keeping track of each individual file!

LINK TO ANOTHER FILE FROM AN EXCEL WORKBOOK

The Annoyance: I followed your advice and embedded my presentation files in an Excel workbook, but something strange happened when I updated the Word file on my office computer: nothing! The changes I made to the original files didn't appear in the files I embedded in my traveling workbook. Doesn't Excel create some sort of live link between the two files so that any change in one is reflected in the other? Did I skip a step somewhere?

The Fix: You didn't skip a step—but you're right that the procedure I just outlined doesn't create a link between the two files. When you embed one file in another file, you create a new copy of the file that's independent of the original. As you discovered, changes in one version of the file aren't transferred to the other version. If you want to create a link between your workbook and an external file, you need to use the linking half of the OLE protocol. To do so, follow these steps:

1. Choose Insert → Object.
2. Click the Create from File tab and then click Browse.
3. Select the file you want to insert and click the Insert button.
4. In the Object dialog box, check the "Link to file" box.
5. Click OK to verify your choice.

Unlike the situation when you embed a file, *linking* to a file doesn't create a new copy of the file...it simply creates a link to the original file—much as you'd expect. Now, when you double-click the linked file in Excel, Windows opens the original file, not a separate, embedded copy, in the source application. Any changes you make when you open the file in its application (or when you open it by double-clicking it in Excel) will appear in both places.

DATA FORMAT ANNOYANCES

PLACE EXCEL DATA ON THE WEB

The Annoyance: My boss wants our department's monthly figures to be available both in Excel *and* on a web page on the company intranet. It needs to be in both formats because we email the Excel file to outside vendors who cannot access the intranet. Each month I copy the data from Excel and paste it into a web editor to create a web page. This takes a while, and sometimes the information ends up in the wrong place. Is there some way I can just copy the whole worksheet to the web page?

The Fix: In Excel 2000 and later, you can put Excel data on the Web simply by choosing File → Save as Web Page. Selecting this option displays the Save As dialog box with a few extra features for optimizing the Excel data to be used on the Web (shown in Figure 6-22). An option in the dialog is to save either the workbook or the current selection. The current selection can be the active sheet, or a selected worksheet area or range.

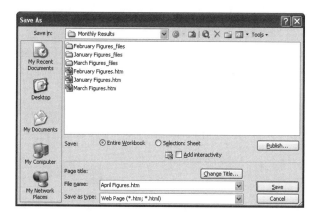

Figure 6-22. Save your Excel data in HTML format.

When you save Excel information as a web page, the program creates a set of *.htm* files in the specified directory, which you can then copy to a web server. You also can choose to publish the data directly to the Web, which gives you additional options relating to the page you're publishing. To publish a page, choose File → Save as Web Page → Publish to display the Publish as Web Page dialog box seen in Figure 6-23. The Publish as Web Page dialog box has an "AutoRepublish every time this workbook is saved" box. When you check this box, any changes you make to the file on your computer will be replicated automatically in the file you published to the Web. You don't need to do anything else!

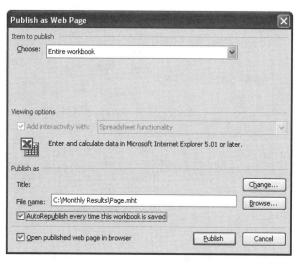

Figure 6-23. Now you can tell your friends you've been published!

PLACE A USABLE WORKSHEET ON A WEB PAGE

The Annoyance: The Save as Web Page feature is very handy for our needs—it lets us create a picture of our business information for all to see. But now some of my co-workers have asked if there's a way to use the information on the web page in a dynamic way. They want to be able to test what-if situations with the data on the web page. Is there any way to make the worksheets we publish interactive?

The Fix: To save an Excel workbook as an interactive document, choose File → Save as Web Page, and click the Publish button to display the Publish as Web Page dialog box (shown in Figure 6-24). Check the "Add interactivity with" box, then select either Spreadsheet functionality or Pivot-Table functionality from the drop-down list to the right.

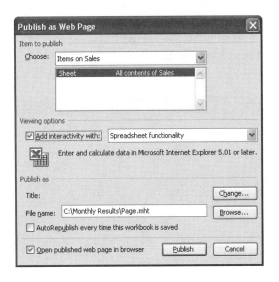

Figure 6-24. Create an interactive worksheet on a web page.

Figure 6-25 shows a web page with interactive worksheet capability. It is possible to add, edit, and delete information; format the worksheet; sort; filter; use functions; and so on—if you have Excel installed on the computer you're using to view the web page.

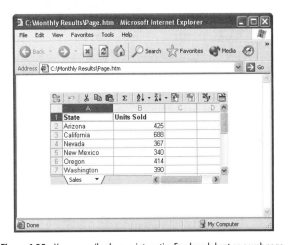

Figure 6-25. You can easily place an interactive Excel worksheet on a web page.

CONTROL THE WEB PAGE WORKSHEET

The Annoyance: We publish our worksheets to a web page using the interactive feature, but we can't seem to change one thing interactively—the sheet tab names. The only solution I've figured out is to change the tab names in the original workbook and republish it. There's gotta be a better way.

The Fix: It *is* possible to change the tab names on a workbook on a web page, but it involves hacking some HTML code. Figure 6-26 shows a workbook published on the Web with the worksheet tabs, as usual, at the bottom left of the window. What you want to do is search for each occurrence of the worksheet name you want to change and use your editor's find and replace mechanism to switch the old text for the new text.

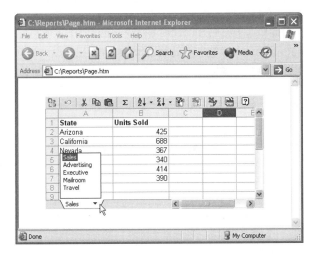

Figure 6-26. Hack the HTML code for a published worksheet and you can change its name.

To change the names of these worksheet tabs open the file in Internet Explorer and follow these steps:

1. Choose View → Source to display the HTML source code. The HTML source opens in your default text editor (probably Notepad).

2. Choose Edit → Find and search for one of the worksheet tab names using the following search term: *<x:Name>sheetname</x:Name>*, where *sheetname* is the name of the sheet. For example, for the sheet shown in Figure 6-26, you would type `<x:Name>Sales</x:Name>`.

3. When the Find feature finds the worksheet tab name, change it right there in the HTML code. If you like, you can use the Replace feature instead of the Find feature to change the name.

4. Still in Notepad, choose File → Save to save the changes.

5. Back in the web browser, refresh the display. In Internet Explorer you can choose View → Refresh or click the Refresh button.

Figure 6-27 shows the results of these steps. In this example, Sales was changed to Revenue and Mailroom was changed to Shipping.

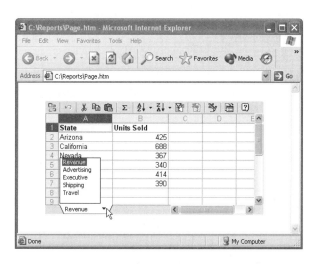

Figure 6-27. Worksheet names have been changed.

Make sure you're editing the right file! Changes made to the HTML code might not stay after the web browser is closed. The changes might have been made to either the original source, or a copy of the source. Make sure you save the changes to the web server where the published page is stored, not to the browser history cache on your computer. To do that, choose File → Save As and verify to which directory you're saving the file.

BREAK LINKS TO EXTERNAL DATA

The Annoyance: Talk about being annoyed! Every time I open one of my workbooks, I get a message that the workbook is linked to other data sources, with buttons for Update and Don't Update. I always click Don't Update, but doing this all the time is annoying. Isn't there a way to get rid of this link!?

The Fix: There are several ways to avoid having the Update/Don't Update question appear. First, you can instruct Excel not to check for links. After you open the workbook, choose Edit → Links to display the Edit Links dialog seen in Figure 6-28.

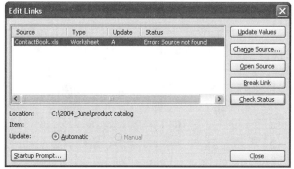

Figure 6-28. Control how links are handled.

Click the Startup Prompt button and in the dialog shown in Figure 6-29, select "Don't display the alert and don't update automatic links." This will prevent that annoying link update question from appearing in this workbook, regardless of who opens it. So, the good news is that you won't be bothered about updating links to external data, but the bad news is that your data could be out of date and you won't know it.

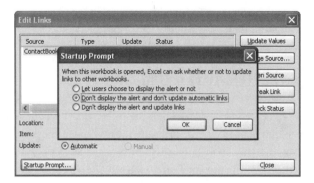

Figure 6-29. Kill the update links alert once and for all.

An alternative is to remove the link altogether—if you're sure you won't need it. In the Edit Links dialog box select the link in question, click the Break Link button, and confirm your choice.

Manipulate Data Tables in Excel

If you do a lot of database-related work in Excel and you want to combine Excel data tables based on common field values (called a *join* in database speak) without exporting the data to Access, pick up the DigDB add-in package for $69 from *http://www.digdb.com/*. The package lets you join tables, sort based on more than three columns of values, sort based on formatting characteristics such as font color, sort in random order, split tables into two or more tables, delete blank columns, and extract email addresses from a worksheet.

EXTERMINATE EXTERNAL LINKS

The Annoyance: I try not to link to other workbooks unless I have to. In my opinion, an external link is the Excel version of a moving part, and the more moving parts you have the more likely something will break. Sure enough, I recently opened a workbook one of my colleagues created, and Excel asked whether I wanted to update the workbook's links, only...there shouldn't *be* any links! I've gone through all the worksheets on the tab bar at the bottom left of the Excel window, but I haven't found anything. How can I find these links and get rid of them?

The Fix: There are a number of ways to sweep all the links out of a workbook. First, make sure the workbook contains no hidden worksheets. Choose Window → Unhide and in the dialog box reveal any hidden worksheets. Once you've displayed the hidden worksheets, right-click any sheet tab, choose Select All Sheets, and then choose Edit → Find. In the "Look in" drop down, select Formulas, and in the Find What field, type [*] (including the brackets). Then click the Find Next button until Excel doesn't find any more cells. The [*] search code finds any cells with links to external workbooks.

Next, check for any named ranges that refer to cells in another workbook. Choose Insert → Name → Define and see if any named ranges refer to external cells. If you do and they aren't being used in a formula, consider deleting the range. In a similar vein, see if any pictures, charts, or form controls draw on images or forms in other workbooks.

If Excel still tells you your workbook contains links, create a new, blank workbook and save it. Back in the workbook you're checking for external links (not the new workbook), choose Edit → Links, select a file in the Source File list, click Change Source, and click the new workbook you just created. Save your workbook, delete the link you just created, and save it again. This is a little convoluted, but it works. If none of this works, download the Microsoft link deletion utility, *Dellinks.exe*, from *http://support.microsoft.com/default.aspx?scid=kb;EN-US;q188449*.

IMPORT SELECTED FIELDS ONLY

The Annoyance: The mainframe system at work periodically creates a comma-separated value (CSV) file that I import into Excel. I don't mind using a CSV file, because I can open it like any normal Excel file. The only pain? I don't use all the fields in the file, so the first thing

I have to do is delete columns A, C, and D. Isn't there a way to tell Excel to give me just the data I want?

The Fix: Instead of opening the file, import it. Importing the file gives you the ability to control how the data comes in. To import a comma-delimited text file and exclude some of the fields it contains, follow these steps:

1. If your file has a *.csv* extension, change the extension to *.txt* in My Computer or Windows Explorer.

2. Choose File → Open, and in the "Files of type" field select Text Files.

3. Click the text file you want and click Open.

4. On the first page of the Text Import Wizard, select the Delimited option button (indicating that the file uses a character, such as a comma, to mark the boundaries between fields) and click Next.

5. Check the Comma box and uncheck the Tab box. Verify that your data looks right in the data pane at the bottom of the Wizard page, and click Next.

6. Click anywhere in the column you don't want to import and click the "Do not import column (skip)" radio button at the upper right of the Wizard screen. Repeat this step for all the columns you don't want to import.

7. Click Finish.

In Figure 6-30, the first column is set to be skipped on import.

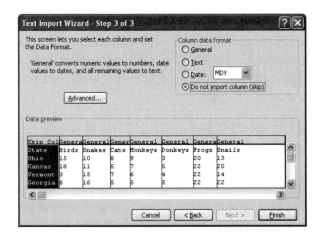

Figure 6-30. Skip columns on a text import.

If you're always importing the same file or files with the same column layout, record your actions as a macro, then run the macro to repeat the import whenever you need it.

PREPARE DATA FOR A DATABASE

The Annoyance: The president of my company requires all our salespeople to maintain a contact list—a list of the appointments they've had with those contacts—and to copy that data into a corporate database to prevent duplication. I don't know how to use that central database, and I'm not really interested in learning, so the programmer at my job put a button on my worksheet. All I have to do is click the button, and the names and appointment information from my sales calls go into our database. But I've been able to crash the routine by entering names such as O'Leary, O'Reilly, O'Shaunessey, and O'Rourke. Does my programmer hate the Irish?

The Fix: The likely culprit is the apostrophe in those Irish names. Most databases don't like apostrophes in the data. In fact, a typical programming task is to write code that checks for apostrophes in data and removes them just before they're inserted into a database table. In Figure 6-31, for example, the name Jack O'Leary probably would cause your magic button to crash.

	A	B	C	D	E
1	Client	Next Appointment			
2	Mike Prabaria	12/15/2004			
3	Steve Overlake	2/10/2005			
4	Brenda Winston	2/18/2005		Update Database	
5	Jack O'Leary	1/8/2005			
6	Jill Sillstone	1/22/2005			
7					
8					
9					

Figure 6-31. Clicking the button attempts to write the information to the database—causing an error.

Typically, attempting to enter data with apostrophes will cause the error seen in Figure 6-32. The programmer must have left out the code for handling apostrophes.

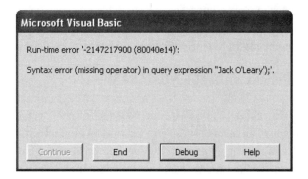

Figure 6-32. An apostrophe causes an insert to fail.

Luckily you can easily take care of this right in the worksheet! Wherever there is an apostrophe in the data, enter another apostrophe. (For example, make O'Leary into O''Leary.) That's all it takes! Really. As long as two apostrophes appear in the data, the records will be written to the database with one apostrophe in place. To add an accompanying apostrophe to your Excel data, follow these steps:

1. Choose Edit → Replace.
2. Type ' in the "Find what" field.
3. Type '' in the "Replace with" field.
4. Click Replace All, and then click the Close button.

EXPORTED DATA LOSES 100 YEARS

The Annoyance: I work in the oil industry, which means I'm quite concerned about our petroleum reserves and how long they will last. Honest. As a result, I often create worksheets containing dates that go 100 years or more into the future. The engineers I work with use a database program that isn't compatible with Excel, so I have to export my worksheets as text files so that they can suck them into their database. The problem is that when they send data back and I read the data into Excel, some of my dates, such as 12/5/2102, come back as 12/5/2002. What's going on?

The Fix: I suspect you're entering the date as 12/5/2102, but you have set Excel to display the date using a two-digit year, so it appears in the cell as 12/5/02.

When you export worksheet data to a text file, you export the data the way it's displayed, not the way Excel stores it internally. That means the date is exported as the string 12/5/02. This little quirk comes into play when you export a worksheet to any of the following formats:

- Text (tab-delimited) (*.txt)
- Unicode text (*.txt)
- CSV (comma-delimited) (*.csv)
- Formatted text (space-delimited) (*.prn)
- Text (Macintosh) (*.txt)
- Text (MS-DOS) (*.txt)
- CSV (Macintosh) (*.CSV)
- CSV (MS-DOS) (*.CSV)
- DIF (data interchange format) (*.dif)

When you read the date back into a worksheet from the text file, Excel sees a two-digit year and has to decide whether it means 2002 or 2102. The rule Excel uses is this: any two-digit year of 29 or less is treated as the current century, and any two-digit year of 30 or more is treated as the previous century. So, 12/5/02 is turned into December 5, 2002, while 12/5/32 becomes December 5, 1932.

To prevent Excel from misinterpreting future dates when you export your worksheets to text files and then reimport the data, choose Format → Cells. Then click the Number tab, highlight Date in the Category list, and in the Type list to the right, select any Date format that displays the year as a four-digit value.

If you prefer to create a custom date format, you can do so by following the custom formatting instructions in the "Create a Custom Date Format" annoyance found in Chapter 2. Just be sure that your custom format uses *yyyy* to represent the year.

OUTLOOK MESSAGE INCLUDES TOO MUCH WORKSHEET

The Annoyance: I have a colleague who copies cells from his worksheets into email messages and sends them to me. We both use Outlook and so far it's worked just fine. But now, suddenly, when I double-click the cells he pasted into his Outlook message, I see the entire worksheet, not just the pasted cells. What's changed?

The Fix: This problem can occur in Outlook 2000 when you send your email in the rich text format (*.rtf*). The rich text format doesn't carry detailed information about what you paste, so although it does understand that you pasted in some Excel worksheet cells, it can only represent the entire worksheet, not a selection of cells. The good news is that Outlook errs on the side of too much data, but the bad news is that you can get a huge worksheet coming down your slow dial-up connection when all you wanted were the first two rows.

To fix the problem, have your buddy change Outlook's default message format to something other than rich text. To do that, in Outlook choose Tools → Options → Mail Format and select either HTML or Plain Text. Do not, under any circumstances, choose Microsoft Word as your email editor; that opens up an entire raft of problems you don't want to know about.

PIVOTTABLE CONTAINS TWO FIELDS WITH THE SAME NAME

The Annoyance: I create PivotTables from customer relationship management data that my network administrator keeps in SQL Server. I use a query to bring the data into Excel, but when I built a new PivotTable last week and tried to publish it to my company's intranet, I got this error message:

> *An error occurred while trying to use a query published from Excel. Consult the creator of the Web page 0x800a6986: Cannot use a stored procedure, query or SQL command that does not have unique names or aliases for all output fields.*

I clicked OK and saw this second error message:

> *The PivotTable list "PivotTable1" could not connect to the data source "tblSatisfaction". For more information about the data source, consult the creator of the file. 0x80040e14: "[Microsoft][ODBC SQL Server Driver][SQL Server]Invalid object name 'tblSatisfaction'."*

What's going on? There aren't any duplicate field names in the database table!

The Fix: The problem isn't with the database table, but with how you imported it. When you see these kinds of errors, chances are you inadvertently added the same table field to your query twice. To rectify the problem, follow these steps:

1. Select a cell in the PivotTable and choose Data → PivotTable and PivotChart Report to display the third page of the PivotTable and PivotChart Wizard.

2. Click Back and then click Get Data. If you see an error box that says *This query cannot be edited by the Query Wizard*, click OK.

3. Microsoft Query displays the query used to create the PivotTable. You probably will see a duplicate field.

4. Click one of the duplicate fields, choose Records → Edit Column, and type a unique name for the column in the Column Heading box.

5. Choose File → Return Data to Microsoft Excel.

6. Click Finish to close the PivotTable and PivotChart Wizard.

PIVOTTABLE WORKS IN EXCEL BUT NOT ON THE WEB

The Annoyance: I've been having terrible luck publishing PivotTables to my company's intranet. The most recent catastrophe occurred when I tried to publish a PivotTable that used data from an Excel worksheet. Yes, I originally copied the data from a database table, but the data works just fine in my copy of Excel 2000. Anyway, after I published the PivotTable-enabled worksheet to the intranet, I saw this error message:

> *An error occurred while trying to open the data file "./ SatSummary_files/Dec2004Summary_9225_cachedata.xml". The file may be damaged or missing. Consult the creator of the Web page 0x800a65c7: The name Overall.Rating contains invalid characters.*

SatSummary is the name of my web page, *Dec2004-Summary* is the name of the Excel file I published to the Web, and Overall.Rating is the name of the column that Excel claims contains an invalid character, which I assume must be the period. But what's the big deal? The PivotTable works just fine in Excel! Shouldn't it be OK when I try to open it as a web page as well?

The Fix: You guessed right about the period. In a perfect world, every PivotTable that works in Excel would work on the Web, too, but that isn't the case. The difficulty lies with the Microsoft Office PivotTable Component, Version 9.0, which ships with Office 2000 and enables you to publish PivotTables to the Web. This version of the PivotTable Component can't handle periods in column or field names, so you can't use them in the column headings of the data list you use to create a PivotTable you publish to the Web. To change the heading and republish the worksheet, follow these steps:

1. Open the Excel workbook and remove the period from the field name that generated the error.

2. Click any cell in the PivotTable and choose Data → Refresh Data. Click OK to clear the info box that tells you the Refresh Data operation changed the Pivot-Table.

3. Drag the field from the PivotTable toolbar to the appropriate area on the PivotTable.

4. Choose File → Save as Web Page, and click the Publish button to open the Publish as Web Page dialog box. Check the "Add interactivity with" box, then open the "Add interactivity with" drop down and select PivotTable functionality.

5 . Type the name of your file in the "File name" field, and then click Publish.

FILE EXPORT MACRO IGNORES REGIONAL SETTINGS

The Annoyance: I share project and manufacturing data with some parts providers in Germany, but I've run into a problem. Their database system can't accept data in comma-delimited format; they use semicolons.

That's not the problem. I have a computer set up with German regional settings, so I can save my Excel file as semicolon-separated data. The problem? I wrote a macro to save the files and it absolutely refuses to write out the data with semicolons. Instead, it ignores my computer's regional settings and insists on delimiting the data with commas. What am I doing wrong?

The Fix: You're not doing anything wrong. As a matter of design, Excel's macro handler ignores a computer's regional settings and always uses the U.S. settings. There are two reasonable solutions here:

- You can still choose File → Save As and select the Comma-Separated Values (*.csv) type by hand, which, based on your regional settings, will save the file with semicolon delimiters.

- You can write a VBA procedure to replace the file's commas with semicolons after it's saved.

Here's the code for changing a *.csv* file's delimiters. Notice that most of the code is devoted to reading and saving the file. The actual conversion only takes one statement (Replace):

```
Sub DemoChangeDelimiters()
 Dim str As String
 str = QuickRead(ThisWorkbook.Path & "\book1.csv")
 str = Replace(str, ",", ";")
 QuickWrite str, ThisWorkbook.Path & _
  "\book1.csv", True
End Sub

' Reads a file into a string.
Function QuickRead(fname As String) As String
 Dim i As Integer, res As String, l As Long
 ' Get a free file handle.
 i = FreeFile
 ' Get the length of the file
 l = FileLen(fname)
 ' Create a string to contain the data.
 res = Space(l)
 ' Open the file.
 Open fname For Binary Access Read As #i
 ' Read the whole file into res.
 Get #i, , res
 ' Close the file
 Close i
```

```
' Return the string.
 QuickRead = res
End Function


' Writes data to a file.
Function QuickWrite(data As String, fname _
 As String, Optional overwrite As Boolean = False) _
 As Boolean
 Dim i As Integer, l As Long
 ' If file exists and overwrite is True, then
 If Dir(fname) <> "" Then
 If overwrite Then
 ' delete the file.
 Kill fname
 Else
 ' else, return False and exit.
 QuickWrite = False
 Exit Function
 End If
 End If
 ' Get a free file handle.
 i = FreeFile
 ' Get the length of the file
 l = Len(data)
 ' Open the file.
 Open fname For Binary Access Write As #i Len = l
 ' Read the whole file into res.
 Put #i, , data
 ' Close the file
 Close i
 ' Return True.
 QuickWrite = True
End Function
```

Printing
ANNOYANCES

Sooner or later, most worksheets get printed—providing tangible evidence of your hard work, as well as the real location of the paperless office (just down the block from Shangri-La). So it's important that the printed output do your efforts justice. If you spend hours or even days entering data and building elaborate workbooks, you should be able to print out that data without hassles. In this chapter, I'll look at the one class of annoyances that dogs all Excel users: controlling what prints. It might be multiple workbooks, a single worksheet, or even a small selection (as tiny as one cell). Then we'll move on to annoyances you bang into when you request a special layout or try to control where content appears on a skein of printed pages. Along the way, you'll discover how to control gridlines, page numbers, report titles, and so on. Finally, you'll learn how to pick a printer, dictate output quality, check the status of a print job, and more.

BASIC PRINTING ANNOYANCES

SQUEEZE THAT ENTIRE WORKSHEET ONTO ONE PAGE

The Annoyance: My worksheet prints with lots of its columns or rows scattered onto a second page. This makes it hard to read the worksheet (see a print preview in Figure 7-1), and it wastes paper—I really need it to fit onto a single sheet. How can I manage that?

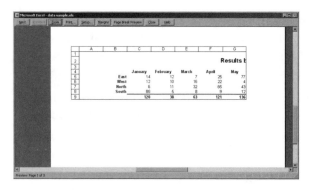

Figure 7-1. Without intervention, critical information will be shunted onto an unwanted second page.

The Fix: To print an entire worksheet on a specified number of pages, choose File → Page Setup, and click the Page tab. Then click the "Fit to" radio button and make sure both fields that follow have 1s in them. This procedure won't affect the way your worksheet looks on-screen, but the results will be highly evident when you choose File → Print, or File → Print Preview (as shown in Figure 7-2).

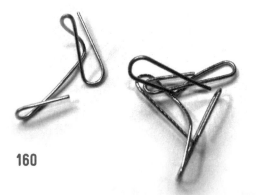

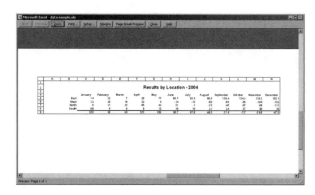

Figure 7-2. By scaling the print job, everything on Sheet1 will print on a single page.

When you scale a worksheet to fit all of its content onto a single sheet of paper, keep in mind that legibility can suffer. If the font size becomes too miniscule, the benefit of cramming everything onto a single page can be lost. Even if you've got the eyes of an eagle, imagine someone with less powerful vision attempting to read your printout, and size it accordingly. Don't forget, of course, to play with the worksheet's margin settings, to print on wider paper (such as 8×14 inches), and other tricks.

PRINT ONLY SELECTED REGIONS

The Annoyance: I have a sales worksheet with the summary at the top and the supporting data in the rows below the summary. My boss is interested in seeing only the summary for now (details confuse him), so I want to print just the summary section. The problem is that when I print the worksheet, I'm getting everything on the active sheet. Is there a way to print just the cells in the summary section?

The Fix: Yes, too much information can be a very bad thing. If you want to restrict your printout to just a smattering of cells—any size range, or even a single cell—select the cells and choose File → Print. In the Print dialog box (see Figure 7-3), click the Selection radio button (it's in the "Print what" section) and you're good to go.

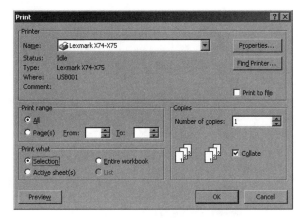

Figure 7-3. Print what? Just the selection, please.

PRINT AN ENTIRE WORKBOOK—OR MULTIPLE SELECTED SHEETS

The Annoyance: I just finished compiling data from 14 colleagues into a workbook that summarizes our company's projects for the first quarter of the year. I'd like to print the entire workbook at once, but Excel's default setting is to print just the active worksheet. Yeah, sure, I could print each sheet in the workbook individually, but I'd save so much time if I could print the whole workbook in one go. Please tell me there's a way!

CREATE FLASH PRESENTATIONS FROM YOUR EXCEL DATA

Have you ever sat through a presentation where the speaker was relying on flashy graphics and animations to mask the lack of content? Or wished that there was less animation on the screen so that you could pay more attention to the underlying information? I've been there, too. After much experimentation, you can discover the right level of splash for a presentation, but the folks at Infommersion have done a pretty good job of hitting the mark with Xcelsius 3.0. Xcelsius enables you to convert your Excel worksheet data into dynamic visual displays such as interactive charts and dashboards (such as the one shown in the following figure) that you can export as Macromedia Flash files and play in PowerPoint or your web browser. The Standard edition runs $195; the Professional edition, which allows real-time database access, costs $495; and the Enterprise edition, which comes with developer software, will set you back $1,995. You can download a trial version of the Standard and Professional editions, or buy the software, at *http://www.infommersion.com/products.html*.

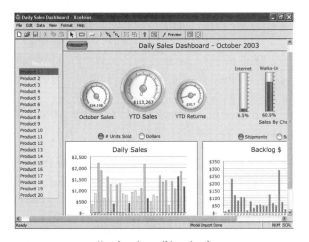

Now here's a striking visual

The Fix: Sure you can print an entire workbook in one go; in fact, you've probably seen the button and never noticed it. To print an entire workbook, choose File → Print and click the "Entire workbook" radio button (it's in the "Print what" section), as shown in Figure 7-4.

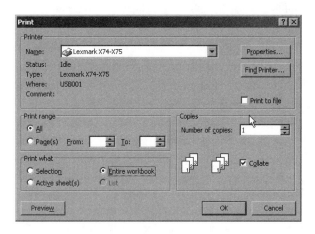

Figure 7-4. Print the whole thing—every sheet—with the Entire Workbook option.

What if you want to print two or three of your workbook's sheets—but not the active sheet and not the entire workbook? Before you choose File → Print, Ctrl-click the tabs of the sheets you want to print. Once the sheets are selected, choose File → Print, and click the "Active sheet(s)" radio button. The selected sheets are considered to be simultaneously active, so they all print when you click OK.

PRINT MULTIPLE WORKBOOKS IN ONE PRINT JOB

The Annoyance: OK, you showed me how to print a whole workbook, but now I need to print *three different* workbooks, and I'm way too busy to open each one individually and use the Print command three times. Why can't I just print all the workbooks I need, all at once?

The Fix: You can, although not with Excel. If you do it through Windows it's quite simple. Assuming all three workbooks are stored in the same folder, go to that folder with the Windows Explorer or via the My Computer window, and then select them all by Ctrl-clicking them with your mouse. Then, right-click one of the files in the

selection and choose Print (as shown in Figure 7-5). The print job will go to the currently selected printer, and each workbook will be printed, in its entirety, with no questions asked. Neat, huh?

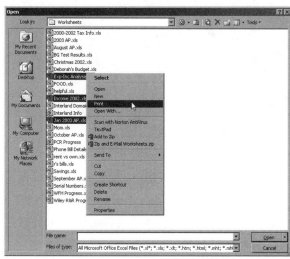

Figure 7-5. Select all the workbooks you want to print and then use Windows to send them all to the printer at once.

To prepare for your multiple-workbook printout, check your workbooks for anything that won't print properly without all of Excel's various printing-control features (scaling, through the Page Setup dialog box, for example, or establishing a new custom Print Area) already set. When you print workbooks via Windows Explorer or My Computer, they're output in their last-saved form. So, for example, if you have a really wide worksheet, be sure to set the orientation to Landscape in anticipation of the quick printing that you'll do through Windows.

PRINT A LIST FROM WITHIN A WORKSHEET

The Annoyance: I like the List functionality in Excel 2003, but I'm having trouble printing just that data. For example, I have a list of records (shown in Figure 7-6) that I built in a worksheet, but I'm not sure how to print just those records. I also want to make sure the field names (column headings) appear in the printout, and that all the records are included even if my list grows significantly before I print it.

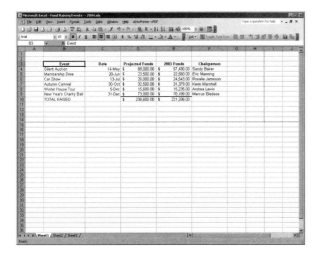

Figure 7-6. New to Excel 2003, formerly ill-defined "datalists" can now be formally identified as Lists, giving you more options for their display and printing.

The Fix: If your list has been made into an actual List (using the Data → List → Create List command that's new to Excel 2003), you can use the Print List button on the List toolbar. To display that toolbar (shown in Figure 7-7), simply right-click any currently displayed toolbar and choose List from the list of available toolbars. Once the List toolbar is displayed, press the Print List button. It prints the list, no questions asked, and no need to select content or do anything else.

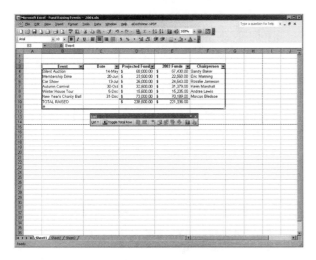

Figure 7-7. The List toolbar gives you tools for editing a designated list of records.

Note that you don't need to have a fully authorized "list" to print it. If your list is simply a series of rows containing data, such as a name and address list, a series of products and prices, or a list of events and dates, you can print those cells using the Page Setup and Print Area tools that I described earlier in this chapter. For more information on Lists in Excel 2003, see Chapter 9.

MAKE PART OF THE WORKSHEET PRINT EVERY TIME

The Annoyance: There's a worksheet I print every day, and I am totally sick and tired of selecting the range to print and then having to remember to use the Selection option in the Print dialog box to make sure I print only that range. I wish there were a way to tell Excel to print just that range every time I use the Print command.

The Fix: Your wish is granted, in the form of Excel's Set Print Area command, found in the File menu. To set an area—any range of cells, including random, noncontiguous cells and ranges—as the print area, select the cells you want to print and choose File → Print Area → Set Print Area. As shown in Figure 7-8, a dashed border appears around the cells you included in the print area. The next time you print the worksheet, all you have to do is leave the Print dialog box's default setting on Active sheet(s) (in the "Print what" section) and just the print area within the active sheet will print.

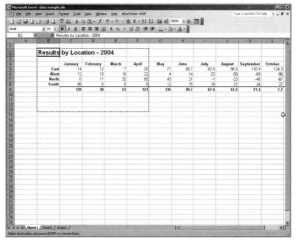

Figure 7-8. Excel surrounds your print area with a dashed border.

To change an established print area in a worksheet, select a new range and repeat the process by choosing File → Print Area → Set Print Area. The new range of cells will replace the previous print area. To clear the print area entirely so that you can print the entire worksheet, choose File → Print Area → Clear Print Area.

If you want just a small part of each worksheet to print when you print an entire workbook, go through each sheet and establish a print area for each one. Next time you print the entire workbook, only the print areas for each worksheet in the workbook will print. Naturally, make sure you use the Clear Print Area command in any sheets that you want to print in their entirety.

PRINT LAYOUT ANNOYANCES

PUT PAGE BREAKS WHERE YOU WANT 'EM

The Annoyance: When I print my multipage worksheet, the content breaks in places where I'd rather it didn't. I'd like to keep certain parts of the worksheet together in the printout, but thanks to the size of the worksheet, the paper I'm printing on, and the formatting of the content, I can't seem to get things to print in the right places.

AUTOMATE REPORT PRINTING WITH REPORT RUNNER

When you work for a large or medium-size company, you often have to print the same workbooks over and over. It's no bother to print out one report every week, but if you have 10 or 12 workbooks you have to print out that often, you need a tool that can automate the process. Enter the Report Runner from OzGrid, which lets you tell Excel to follow a series of steps when it's time to print a batch of workbooks. You don't even need to open the workbooks! Once you tell the program which workbooks you want to print it simply takes over. The main Report Runner dialog box appears in the following figure. Each step has its own built-in instructions, but there are some restrictions and recommendations (print ranges should be named, and so on). I recommend reading the help file so that you know how the Report Runner saves your preferences and sequences, and what your output options are. You can purchase the Report Runner for $29.95 from *http://www.ozgrid.com/Services/ excel-report-runner.htm*. After you download the add-in, you install it by choosing Tools → Add-Ins,

clicking the Browse button, navigating to the directory that contains the add-in, and double-clicking it.

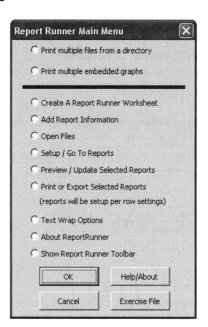

This handy tool helps you create custom printing macros without knowing a lick of code.

The Fix: By default, Excel is a lot like Word when it comes to controlling the flow of content from one page to the next in a printout. When there isn't any more room within the margins on a page, the content simply flows onto the next page. In a text document, this is usually no problem. When it comes to numeric data, however, it can be very confusing when the flow of that data stops abruptly at the bottom or right side of the page—even if it continues on the next page. To establish better control of just which things stay together, or print side by side, or appear as a continuous vertical list, you need to adjust your page breaks. Here's how:

1. Choose View → Page Break Preview. Your workbook will appear in Page Break Preview mode, as shown in Figure 7-9.

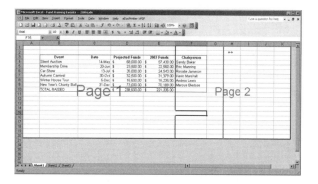

Figure 7-10. Drag your page breaks to allow more content to fit on a page.

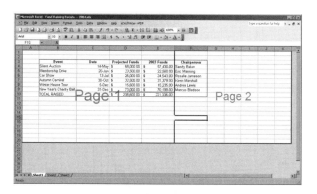

Figure 7-9. Page Break Preview shows you how your printout will lay out.

Scale Happens

When you move page breaks to allow more content to appear on a page, you are also scaling the page at the same time. For example, if you expand the borders of a page to add several rows or columns, the page might end up printing at 90% or less of its original size so that all the content can fit on a single page. You can view the results of your page break adjustments by choosing File → Page Setup and checking the Page tab to see what the Scaling section of the dialog box shows.

2. Using the blue borders—both dashed and solid—drag the side(s) of the worksheet that need to be moved. For example, to allow a few more rows to fit on page 1, drag the bottom blue border down so that all the rows you need to keep together are within the confines of page 1. Figure 7-10 shows such an adjustment in progress. To allow a column or two to remain with content on a page, drag the far right border out so that all the columns are within the blue box that designates a particular page.

3. Once the page numbers (shown in gray behind the worksheet content in Figure 7-11) and borders show you a potential printout that's satisfactory, click View → Normal to return to a normal view. You'll see your page breaks indicated by dashed vertical and horizontal lines (between rows and columns, respectively) as shown in Figure 7-12.

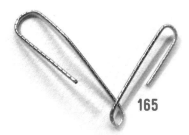

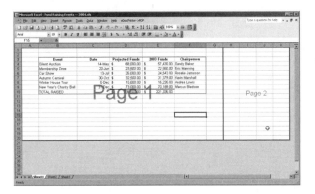

Figure 7-11. Page Break Preview gives you lots of graphical clues as to your worksheet's pagination.

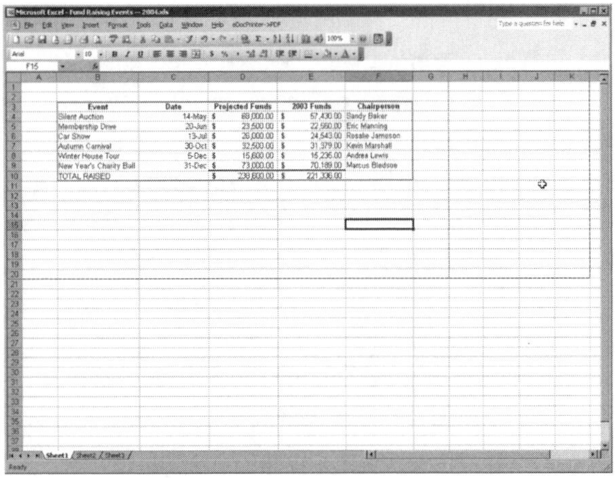

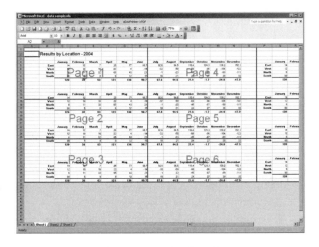

Figure 7-12. Dashed lines remind you where your page breaks will occur when your worksheet is printed.

Just as you drag page break indicators to allow more or less content to fit onto the individual pages of your printout, you also can drag from the corner where two blue borders meet—say, at the top-left or right-bottom corners—and drag outward in a diagonal direction, encompassing more rows and columns. If you drag inward, fewer rows and columns will fit on the page, and the ones that are no longer within the borders will print on subsequent pages.

CHANGE THE ORDER IN WHICH PAGES ARE PRINTED

The Annoyance: My worksheets come out of the printer with the data that's in columns A through G first, followed on subsequent pages by the stuff that's in columns H through M. I want to see the pages come out so that I get the whole width of the worksheet first, columns A through M, and then the rows from further down in the sheet. Is there any way to tell Excel to do this?

The Fix: Just tell Excel to change the order in which your pages print. Here's how:

1. Choose View → Page Break Preview to verify that your page breaks are in the proper places. Figure 7-13 shows the default page order in Page Break Preview, with the worksheet content printing vertically first (pages 1, 2, and 3, as labeled by Excel), then printing the next column (pages 4, 5, and 6), and so on.

Figure 7-13. Is down-then-over not working for you?

2. Choose File → Page Setup and click the Sheet tab to display the Sheet page of the Page Setup dialog box (shown in Figure 7-14). Then select the "Over, then down" radio button, or the "Down, then over" radio button, whichever is appropriate.

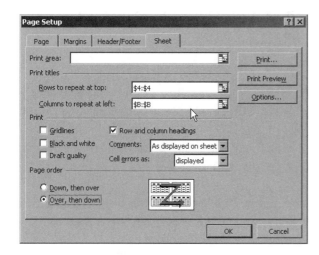

Figure 7-14. Make your page order selection.

3. To verify that your workbook will print properly, choose File → Print Preview. Figure 7-15 shows the print preview and the new print order.

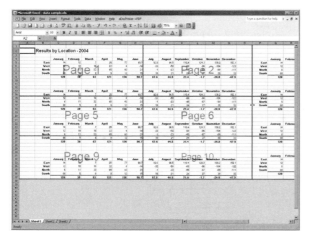

Figure 7-15. Now the pages are in the right order for people to read the printout.

CHANGE WORKBOOK MARGINS

The Annoyance: Everything I want to include on my printed worksheet would fit on one page if I could just reduce the margins a bit—but I don't know how to do that. I don't want to reduce the printed size of the worksheet (if I do, the content will be too small to read);

I just want to increase the area of the paper on which Excel will print. How do I do it?

The Fix: It's just like fitting a Word document on a single sheet of paper—you reduce the top or bottom margin a little until that last sentence sneaks onto the page. In Excel, you do the same thing, in the same way—by dragging the margins around in a WYSIWYG view of the worksheet, or by using a dialog box.

Method one

Choose File → Print Preview, and click the Margins button to make the margins appear. Now grab the horizontal and vertical margin lines and drag them outward to make more room for the worksheet to print, or inward if you want to confine the printable worksheet to a smaller area. (A right margin is being adjusted in Figure 7-16.)

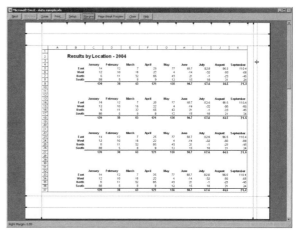

Figure 7-16. Drag your margins to adjust them "by eye."

Method two

Choose File → Page Setup, click the Margins tab (see Figure 7-17), and enter new measurements for any or all of the margins' current settings. Click the Print Preview button on the right side of the dialog box to verify that your change has had the desired effect.

If you opened the Page Setup dialog box from within the Print Preview window, you'll notice that there's no Print Preview button. This button appears only when you open the box by using the File → Page Setup command.

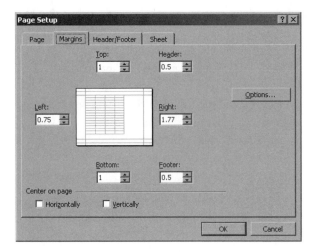

Figure 7-17. Press the Tab key to move between fields in the dialog box, entering new margins for top, bottom, left, and right.

SET PAPER SIZE AND ORIENTATION

The Annoyance: I have a really wide worksheet that I want to print on legal-size paper. How can I tell Excel that I'm printing on bigger paper?

The Fix: Open the Page Setup dialog box (File → Page Setup), click the Page tab, click the down arrow at the right of the "Paper size:" field, and select "Legal 8 1/2×14 in" from the drop-down list. Then click the Landscape radio button and you're ready to rock. (See Figure 7-18.)

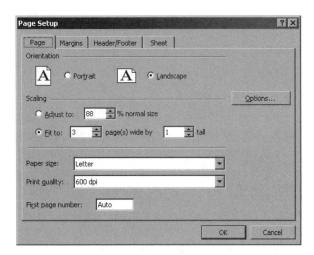

Figure 7-18. Choose from Portrait or Landscape for the worksheet page in question.

ONE PAGE IN LANDSCAPE, ANOTHER IN PORTRAIT

The Annoyance: I have a workbook that contains some worksheets that need to print in landscape mode, while others would be best in portrait. I could print each sheet individually and set its orientation before I print, but that would take forever. Is there some way to print out a workbook with a mix of page orientations?

The Fix: This fix requires some preparatory legwork, but after you've completed the following steps, you will never have to do them again—unless you make major changes to your worksheets that require you to change the orientation of individual pages. You'll also have to repeat the procedure for any new pages—but hey, the process is actually pretty quick:

1. Go to each individual worksheet and choose File → Page Setup, click the Page tab, and choose the appropriate orientation for each active sheet.

2. Save the workbook.

3. To check your work, choose File → Print Preview, and check the orientation of each page.

If you have several worksheets that must be in Landscape orientation (as opposed to Portrait, which is the default) you can save some time by multiselecting the tabs of the Landscape sheets and then performing steps 1 and 2 to make all of them Landscape in one fell swoop. Be sure to ungroup the sheets afterward.

CUSTOM FOLIOS

The Annoyance: When I add page numbers to my printout, they appear simply as 1, 2, and so on. I want to show the total number of pages as well as the individual numbers, as in "Page 1 of 5," so people getting a stapled printout will know right away if a page is missing. Or course, this requires adding the words "Page" and "of" to the header or footer, and I'm not sure how to do that, either. Help!

The Fix: By default, when you add page numbers to your worksheet printout you get just a number. If you want to add more text—such as *Page* before the number, or the total number of pages in the printout—you must type some text into the Header and Footer dialog box, and you must make use of Excel's header/footer customization tool. Here's how:

1. In the worksheet that you want to print (or with all the worksheets you want to print grouped) choose File → Page Setup and click the Header/Footer tab.

2. Click the Custom Header or Custom Footer button, depending on where you want your page numbers to appear—at the top of the pages (header) or at the bottom (footer).

3. In either the Header or the Footer dialog box, click in one of three sections (Left Section, Center Section, or Right Section), depending on how you want your text to align. The box you choose will hold your page numbers and accompanying text.

4. Type Page, followed by a space.

5. Click the Insert Folios button (the small icon with a single # on it, as shown in Figure 7-19). The odd text *&[Page]* will appear in the box; this is an instruction for Excel to insert the correct page number on each page of the printout.

Figure 7-19. The buttons that appear in the Header or Footer dialog box allow you to insert a great deal of information.

6. Click right after the *]* and type [space]of[space] (that's the word *of* surrounded by a space on each side) and click the Insert Total Number of Pages button (that's the button with two plus signs). *&[Pages]*

appears in the dialog box after the word *of*, which tells Excel to insert the total number of pages in the printout. Figure 7-20 shows the entire entry in the Center Section box: *Page &[Page] of &[Pages]*.

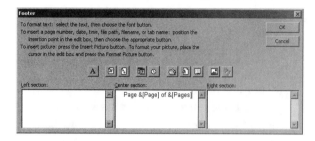

Figure 7-20. You can fit text and page numbers in the center section of the header or footer.

7. If you want to format the text (including the automatically inserted page number data), select the text in the section box and then the Format button (the A button), and use the resulting Font dialog box (see Figure 7-21) to format the header/footer content you selected.

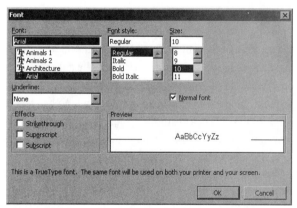

Figure 7-21. Use this Font dialog box to format your header or footer content.

of the screen to display your worksheet's margins, as shown in Figure 7-22. Note that there are two horizontal lines at the top and bottom of the worksheet. The outer lines represent the outer boundary for your header/footer content, and the inner lines represent your text margins. The space between those lines is where your header and footer content will go.

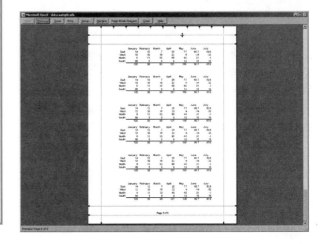

Figure 7-22. There are two sets of margins—inner margins for worksheet content, and outer margins for your header and footer.

MORE ROOM FOR HEADERS AND FOOTERS

The Annoyance: I like my headers (and sometimes my footers) to include the name of the worksheet, the name of the workbook, my name, and a title that's usually quite long. I also have to include the date and time on printouts that contain data that's frequently updated. To make a long story short (or do I mean a long header?) I often run out of places to put things. Is there any way to make more room for my header and footer content?

The Fix: As discussed in a previous annoyance in this chapter, you can adjust margins via the Page Setup dialog box, or in Print Preview mode. But when it comes to the header/footer area, you can adjust the margins only while you're in Print Preview. Keep in mind, though, that it makes sense to enter all the header and footer text *before* you adjust the header and footer margins. To adjust the area designated for header and footer content, follow these steps:

1. Display the sheet you want to print, choose File → Print Preview, and click the Margins button at the top

2. You can use one of two strategies (or a combination) to change the amount of space allocated for either the header or footer. One, drag the text margin line inward to make less room for text and more room for the header or footer—without changing how close to the edge of the paper your printout comes. Or two, drag the header/footer margin line outward to make more space. If you choose this second strategy your printout will come closer to the edges of the paper, and might go beyond the area where your printer is capable of printing. This limit is typically .25 inch from the edge, so be careful not to go beyond that. Figure 7-23 shows the outer margin being moved down to make more room for the footer; the page margin has been left alone.

3. Because you're already in Print Preview, you can observe the effect these changes have on your existing header or footer content.

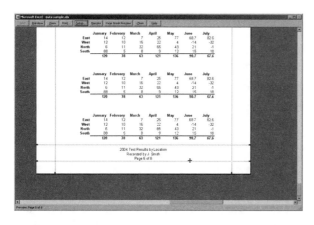

Figure 7-23. Drag the page and/or header and footer margins to make more room for your title, page numbers, and other information.

PRINT CONTENT ANNOYANCES

ADD GRIDLINES TO A PRINTOUT

The Annoyance: My clients find it difficult to read across the rows of my worksheets, especially if there are more than four or five columns (such as in Figure 7-24). Having gridlines would really help them, but my worksheets always print out without the grid. Any ideas?

Figure 7-24. With no gridlines, it's easy to lose your place.

The Fix: Apparently, Excel's designers wanted to make your printouts look more like reports and less like spreadsheets, so they set options such as printing gridlines, column letters, and row numbers off by default. You can easily restore them, though. To add the gridlines, choose File → Page Setup, click the Sheet tab, and check the Gridlines box. This change will apply only to the active sheet (see a preview of a sample sheet in Figure 7-25), but you can add gridlines to multiple worksheets just by Ctrl-clicking the appropriate sheet tabs. You also can record a macro that captures these steps for adding gridlines to the active worksheet. For more information on recording a macro, see Chapter 8.

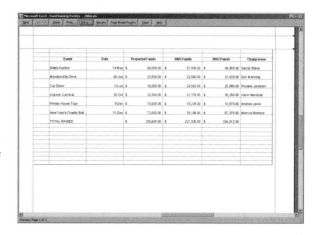

Figure 7-25. With gridlines, it's less likely that someone will lose visual track of the data as they read across the worksheet.

ADD TIME AND DATE TO YOUR PRINTOUT

The Annoyance: You know that worksheet I was complaining about? The one with the big header and footer? Part of the information I need to include in that portion of the printout is the current date and time; that's really important for reports that are printed every day, and sometimes every hour. Currently, I insert the date and time by hand, but this is getting old. Isn't there some way I can get Excel to add the time and date automatically?

The Fix: You bet—and it's not unlike inserting a date or time field in Word. Once it's in place, Excel will update the date and time information every time you print the worksheet or workbook. Here's how:

1. As shown in Figure 7-26, choose File → Page Setup to open the Page Setup dialog box.

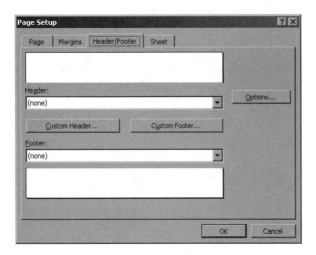

Figure 7-26. The Page Setup dialog box is your savior when it comes to adding features to your printouts.

2. Click the Header/Footer tab, and then click either the Custom Header or Custom Footer button.

3. Click in the Left section, Center section, or Right section and then click the Insert Date button (the little calendar) and/or the Insert Time button (the little clock). The system date and time field codes are inserted (see Figure 7-27), and every time you print the worksheet you'll get the latest date and time.

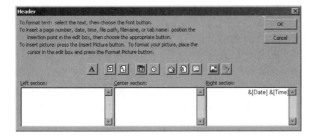

Figure 7-27. I like to put the date and time in the rightmost box at the top of reports, so readers see that information right away.

If you *don't* want a date that changes every time you print your worksheet, you can place a fixed date and/or time into any section of the header or footer. Just type it in like any other text. If you want, you can precede it (or any automatically inserted system information) with `Date:` or similar text.

PRINT COLUMN LETTERS AND ROW NUMBERS

The Annoyance: I often find myself talking on the phone to co-workers—people who work in our branch offices and use the worksheet printouts I send them—and sometimes it's hard to specify exactly which parts of the worksheet I need them to be looking at. If I could say, "Look at cell G19" instead of "See the cell right under March Total Sales for Cleveland?" it would be a big help. Which is a long way of asking, is there a way to print column letters and row numbers on my worksheets?

The Fix: Cell addresses make our lives easier while we're building a worksheet, so why not also have them in a printed report? Again, Excel's designers figured we all wanted a professional-looking report and not the vestiges of the actual worksheet environment. This explains the lack of gridlines, column letters, row numbers, and worksheet names. To make column letters and row numbers appear in your printed worksheets, choose File → Page Setup, click the Sheet tab, and check the "Row and column headings" box (the dialog box appears in Figure 7-28). It's best also to display gridlines if you're going to include your column letters and row numbers, if only so that people can read across or up and down and visually locate the cell you're referring to.

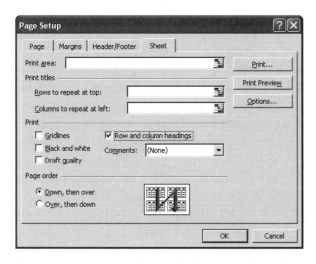

Figure 7-28. Want to point out cell B17? Add column letters and row numbers from this dialog.

PRINT COLUMN HEADINGS AND ROW LABELS ON EVERY PAGE

The Annoyance: When my reports run onto a second page, the column and row headings on page 1 don't appear on the second and subsequent pages (as shown in Figure 7-29). People need to see those headings no matter what page they're on, and when they disappear, it makes it hard to direct people to specific information. There must be some way to make Excel repeat those headings on every page of the report.

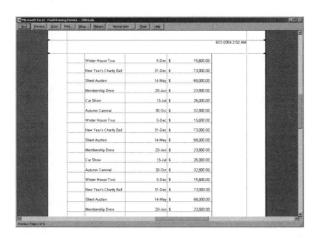

Figure 7-29. Here's page 2 of a long list of events—but without headings, you can't tell what's what in the data rows.

The Fix: By headings, of course, you're referring to the information you type into a worksheet to identify columns and rows of data—not the column letters and row numbers that are part of the Excel workspace. If you know your report will exceed a single page and you want your row and column headings to appear on all the pages, simply tell Excel where the headings/labels can be found. Here's how:

1. Choose File → Page Setup, click the Sheet tab, and click the Collapse Dialog button in the far right of the "Rows to repeat at top" field.

2. Click anywhere in the row that contains the headings you want to see at the top of every page of your printout, and press Enter. Figure 7-30 shows a range of selected cells holding the headings. Figure 7-31 shows the resulting report with column headings appearing on page 4 of an 8-page worksheet.

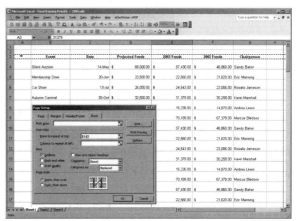

Figure 7-30. "$3:$3" tells Excel to include column headings from row 3 on all pages of the report.

3. Now click the Collapse Dialog button at the far right in the "Columns to repeat at left" field. Click anywhere in the column that contains the headings you want to see at the left of every page of your printout, and press Enter. If you select a cell in column B of the worksheet shown in Figure 7-30, for example, Excel will put column B at the left edge of every page you print out. Click OK and you're good to go.

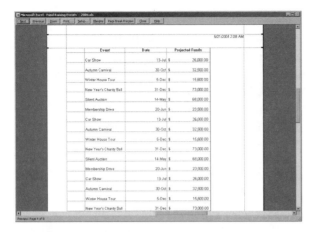

Figure 7-31. On page 4 of 8, you can still see the column headings.

PUT A SPECIAL REPORT TITLE ON EVERY PAGE

The Annoyance: Our company requires that we use very specific file-naming conventions. For instance, a workbook that contains water test results from July of 2004 for region #15 in Las Vegas would be called "JUL04TRLV15." But when it's time to print a report based on that workbook, and I want a title in the header, and I use the appropriate button in the Header dialog box, I get *JUL04TRLV15* when what I really want is something like *Las Vegas Region 15 Test Results—July 2004*. Can I make that title appear on my printed output without changing the name of the worksheet file?

The Fix: Any special text you want to appear on every printed page must be typed into the header or footer, and that's done through Page Setup. If it's a title you're looking to add, it should probably go into the center section of the header to make it print top and center of each page (as in Figure 7-32). The Custom Header dialog box also allows you to format the text big and bold, so it stands out and yells "Important" to all who read your report (see Figure 7-33). To format the text, select it in the

---

ADD CUSTOM FOOTERS TO EXCEL PRINTOUTS

Adding footers to an Excel worksheet is a pain. You have to dig through a bunch of menu levels to find the footer, and then you need to decipher the symbols in the dialog box to create the text you want. The Print Assistant, an Excel add-in from OzGrid, simplifies this task greatly. Not only can you create all the footers that Excel can create, but also you can display a workbook's full directory path (e.g., *C:\Writing\OReilly\ Excel Annoyances\Chapter07\PrintAsstTest97.xls*) in an Excel 97 or 2000 header or footer, which isn't possible in those program versions. Plus you can allow users to enter their own custom footer text, set each page's footer independently, exempt certain pages from the Print Assistant's effects, or turn the Print Assistant off entirely without uninstalling it. (The Print Assistant dialog box appears in the following figure.) After you download the add-in, you install it by choosing Tools → Add-Ins, clicking the Browse button, navigating to the directory that contains the add-in, and double-clicking it. After you install the add-in, a Print Assistant item appears near the bottom of the Tools menu. To purchase the Print Assistant for $29.95, visit *http://www.ozgrid.com/Services/excel-print-add-in.htm*.

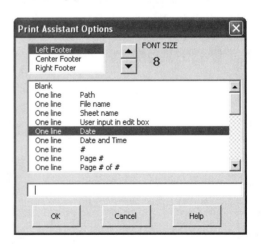

If you're using Excel 97 or 2000, the Print Assistant is an especially valuable tool you can use to improve your printouts.

dialog box and click the A (Format) button to open the Font dialog box. Of course, if you like, you can include the worksheet filename along with your customized title.

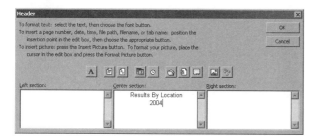

Figure 7-32. Type your title into the Custom Header's center section.

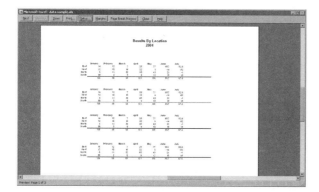

Figure 7-33. This explanatory title will appear on all pages of the report.

PRINT WORKSHEET COMMENTS IN CONTEXT

The Annoyance: Excel has decided (quite incorrectly) that I want my comments to print out as an addendum to my worksheet. What I really want is to see them among the cells they refer to. Tell me how!

The Fix: Actually, by default, comments don't appear at all when you print out a workbook or worksheet, so if you've succeeded in getting them to print at the end, you're ahead of the game. However, if you want them to appear in the body of your worksheet, follow these steps:

1. Choose File → Page Setup, and click the Sheet tab.

2. Open the Comments drop down (see Figure 7-34), choose "As displayed on sheet," and click OK.

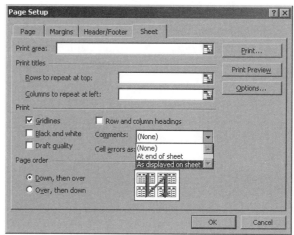

Figure 7-34. Make your choice as to how comments will appear in your report.

3. Choose Tools → Options, click the View tab, and select the Comment & Indicator option in the Comments section (see Figure 7-35). Click OK.

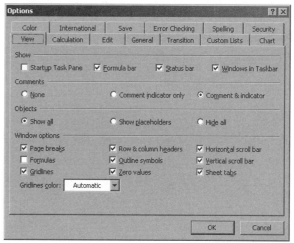

Figure 7-35. Choose how you want comments to appear on-screen—and in print.

4. To see how this printout will look, choose File → Print Preview. As you can see in Figure 7-36, the

comment obscures some data in the column and rows adjacent to the cell tied to the comment. This might be a problem for your report, depending on its audience and purpose. You might consider printing it twice: first this way (to show people where comments are) and then without the comments (so that all the data is visible). If the Comment & Indicator option is selected (meaning comments are displayed continuously) you can move a comment out of the way of important information by clicking the comment to activate it, grabbing the comment's border, and dragging it to the desired location.

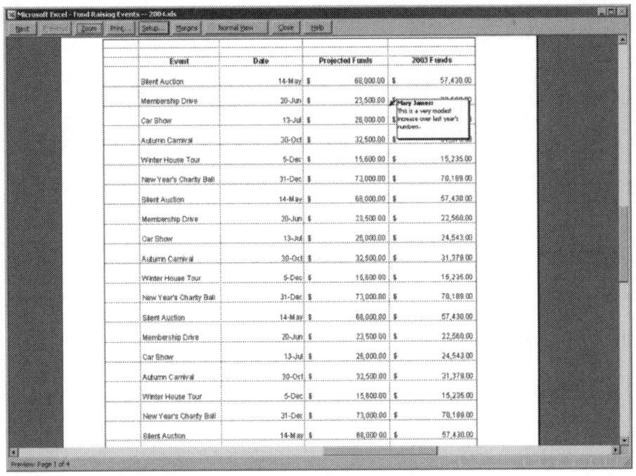

Figure 7-37. Comments at the end of the report are quite useful.

![Figure 7-36 screenshot]

Figure 7-36. Does it matter if the comment covers up other data in the report? If the answer is yes, print the report both with and without the comments in context.

If you're wondering how the comments will look when they're placed at the end of the worksheet printout, see Figure 7-37. This option is probably the most effective way to print comments; you get the cell addresses the comments pertain to, you get the comments themselves, and all the data in the worksheet is visible.

To print a version of a worksheet that indicates which cells contain comments but that *doesn't* display the comments in the body of the worksheet or at the end of the printout, choose Tools → Options, click the View tab, and select the "Comment indicator only" option in the Comments section (see Figure 7-35).

PRINT PIVOTTABLES, NOT THE REST OF THE WORKSHEET

The Annoyance: Is it possible to print just the PivotTable and not the data and other stuff that's on the same sheet? I need to show people various views of the PivotTable data, but printing out the rest of the data on the sheet would just confuse them. How do I print the PivotTable, the whole PivotTable, and nothing but the PivotTable?

The Fix: Just like any other portion of a worksheet you want to see printed on its own, the PivotTable can be selected. To print just the PivotTable, click any cell in the PivotTable, press Ctrl-*, choose File → Print, and then choose Selection.

BLOCK PRINTOUT OF ERROR MESSAGES

The Annoyance: Some of my worksheets contain error messages because cells that contribute to the formulas contain text; it's there as a sort of placeholder until the numeric data is gathered and verified. In the meantime, I don't want the #VALUE! error to appear in my printouts. Why can't I suppress this somehow?

The Fix: If you don't want error messages to appear on your printout, just say so! Choose File → Page Setup, click the Sheet tab, open the "Cell errors as" drop down, and select either blank, two dashes (--), or #N/A from the list (see Figure 7-38). The #N/A choice still looks like an error, and might arouse questions you don't want to answer, so you might opt for the two dashes; that way you won't forget that a formula lives in that cell (as a blank might allow you to do). Better yet, no one but you will know that your formulas aren't working. Note: this works only in Excel 2002 and later versions.

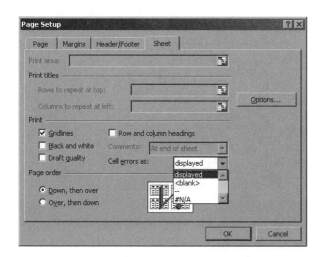

Figure 7-38. With error messages replaced with the innocuous "--" no one is the wiser that your formulas aren't working.

PRINTER MANAGEMENT ANNOYANCES

SET A DEFAULT PRINTER

The Annoyance: I use a lot of color in my worksheets, but all my work ends up going to a black-and-white laser printer in the office next door. I wish I could send my worksheets to the color inkjet on my co-worker's desk, but I don't know how to make that happen.

The Fix: You can choose your printer for each print job through the Print dialog box. To select a default printer, choose File → Print, click the down arrow at the right of

the Name field, and select the printer from the Name drop-down list. As shown in Figure 7-39, you can see all the printers your computer has access to, whether directly (via a parallel or USB cable) or indirectly (over a network). Click the one you want, view its status (just so that you're not surprised to find out someone's currently using it for a 100-page report), and then go about your printing.

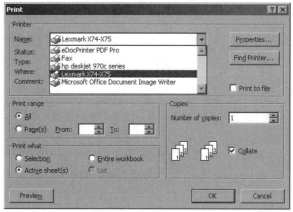

Figure 7-39. Pick a printer for the current print job. It will remain the default until you choose a new one.

To set a printer as your default (that's the one Excel always goes to without your needing to select it), go to Windows' Printers window (Start → Settings → Printers, or Start → Settings → Printers and Faxes, depending on your version of Windows). Right-click the desired printer, and choose Set as Default Printer from the pop-up menu (see Figure 7-40).

Once you set a printer as your Windows default, it will be the default for *all* your applications. This can be a nasty surprise if you want to output your fancy graphics work in Photoshop and your default printer is a lousy, beat-up LaserJet. Make any changes to any defaults with care. (Of course you can always choose a different printer for each and every print job, regardless of which printer is your default, but it's an extra step.)

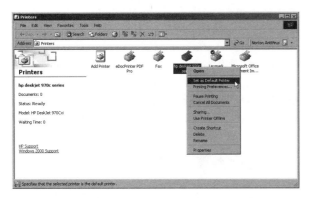

Figure 7-40. Making a particular printer Excel's default will make it every application's default, too.

PRINT A WORKSHEET IN GLORIOUS BLACK AND WHITE

The Annoyance: Printing in color is a waste of time for me because I end up faxing all my worksheets to a remote salesperson, and many of the colors, especially blue, don't show up well on the faxes. I need to print worksheets in black and white—but I can't delete the colors or change them in the actual worksheets themselves because the colors are integral to other departments using the worksheets.

The Fix: Well, you could always email the worksheets to your remote salesperson and let him open and print them, in color, at his location—but you'll probably tell me all he has is an ancient black-and-white dot matrix printer. Oh well. If your remote sales rep has only a traditional fax machine, you need to print your color worksheet in black and white before you fax it.

To print your worksheet in black and white, choose File → Page Setup, click the Sheet tab, and check the "Black and white" box. This setting affects only how Excel prints the active worksheet, not how it's formatted or displayed.

If your worksheet contains charts, you can have Excel render your colors as black-and-white patterns that are more readable on a fax. To do so, select the chart, choose File → Print Preview, click the Setup button, click the Chart tab, and check the "Print in black and white" box.

SET OPTIMUM PRINT QUALITY

The Annoyance: One of our managers comes from a graphics and marketing background, and if we send a report to a client that's not perfectly crisp and clear, with exquisite color density in the charts and pictures, he gets really upset. I need to print my worksheets at the highest possible quality, and don't know how to get the printer to do that.

The Fix: You can adjust print quality through the Print dialog box. When you're ready to print, simply choose File → Print, and click the Properties button. A dialog box opens with an interface provided by your printer's manufacturer. Not all of these dialog boxes are created equal, but usually there's a way you can adjust print quality. In the dialog box shown in Figure 7-41, the choices are Quick Print, Normal, Better, and Best. Your printer's Properties dialog box might offer choices such as Good, Better, or Best. No matter what the terminology, you should be able to easily adjust the printer's setting for this print job, increasing its quality to meet the needs of a particular boss or client.

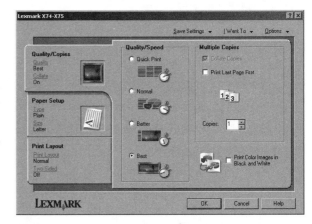

Figure 7-41. Your printer's Properties box might be different—but it probably will offer many of the same options as you see here.

While you're messing around with printer properties, you also might want to let the printer know what kind of paper you're using. For example, your printer will behave differently if it's printing on regular laser or copier paper, as opposed to glossy photo paper. Most printers adjust themselves for the paper, so you'll get the best results when your paper and the printer's paper setting match.

CHECK THE STATUS OF YOUR PRINT JOB

The Annoyance: I spend half my life standing at the printer in the copy room, waiting for my worksheets to come out. After a while, someone else's worksheet comes out, and I realize I was waiting around for nothing. Eventually my worksheets appear, but it would be great if I could find out how many print jobs are ahead of mine so that I can stop wasting so much time!

The Fix: Once you've sent your print job to the printer, it typically goes into a printer queue—a waiting line—where it sits until the printer is done printing all the jobs that got there first. If it's your own desktop printer, to which you have exclusive (or virtually exclusive) access, the printer usually begins the job after only a few seconds. If many people use the same printer, you might have to wait quite a while.

To find out what's ahead of you in the queue, double-click the small printer icon in the Windows System Tray (at the bottom right of the screen) and check out the status box that appears (see Figure 7-42). You'll see a list of all the print jobs in the queue, including the "owner's" name, the time/date the job was sent to the printer, its size, and its status. If you see that the job is paused, or it's a small print job and it's just not coming out, you might want to call the person who sent the job and ask him to check on it. The printer might be out of paper, there could be an error in his communication with the printer, or he might have tried to cancel the print job but it didn't work.

Figure 7-42. Waiting in line is no fun. See how many people are ahead of you before you start kicking the printer.

SEND A WORKSHEET AS A FAX

The Annoyance: Some of our remote sales reps don't have laptops, so they receive worksheet printouts via fax. I would prefer to avoid making printouts and then putting them into the fax machine. Can I fax them directly from Excel?

The Fix: Absolutely! Of course, your computer has to have a fax modem in it and the requisite software, or you must be on a network which has a fax server and software installed—but assuming those ducks are in a row, you can easily fax from within Excel. To do so, choose File → Send to and choose either Recipient Using Fax Modem or Recipient Using Internet Fax Service (see Figure 7-43). The latter option appears if you have subscribed to or installed a fax service. If you have another fax program on your computer, such as SmartFax 2004 from RingCentral (you can buy the program for $79.99 from *http://www.ringcentral.com/*), you can use it to send your document.

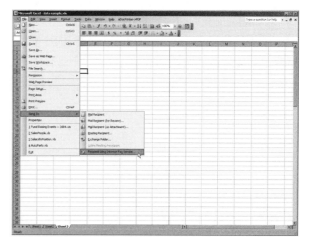

Figure 7-43. Forget the fax machine—you can fax your worksheets directly from Excel.

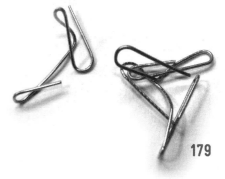

CRYSTAL REPORTS: A PREMIUM REPORTING TOOL

If you work as a programmer for a large corporation, you've probably written way too much code to automate business processes that off-the-shelf software doesn't quite address. Some software vendors recognize your plight and let you call their programs (or at least some of their programs' functions) from within your custom application. Business Objects, the company behind Crystal Reports, is one such vendor. Crystal Reports is a report- and chart-generating tool that can connect to (and output) all kinds of data sources, including Excel; consumer databases such as Access and FoxPro; enterprise-level databases such as SQL Server, Oracle, IBM DB2, and Sybase; and other data stores such as online analytical processing (OLAP) or Extensible Markup Language (XML) collections. You can see a sample Crystal Reports document in the following image. Some of the many features that Crystal Reports offers—that Excel notably lacks—include the ability to design a report visually, to let users set parameters limiting the data they want in their report without affecting the original data, and to highlight information that meets criteria you define.

which you launch by choosing Tools → Crystal Reports Wizard 10 (or whatever your version number is). You also receive a series of modules that let you add Crystal Reports capabilities to programs written in Java, .NET, and the Component Object Model (COM). Even if you're not up for doing a lot of fancy programming to integrate Crystal Reports into your custom applications (or if you don't have any custom applications to integrate), you can use the Crystal Reports add-ins to generate reports in Excel or Access. After you select the data you want to report on, you can change the report's grouping and sorting options to emphasize specific aspects of your data. (The Crystal Reports wizard appears in the following image.)

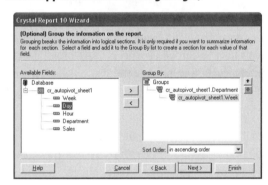

Crystal Reports lets you organize and format your reports for maximum readability.

Customizing reports brings your data into sharper focus.

When you install Crystal Reports, the setup program includes the Crystal Reports Wizard as an Excel add-in,

Crystal Reports is good, but it ain't cheap. You'll have to pay $495 for the Professional edition, which lets you create custom reports and connect to OLAP and XML data sources, or $788 for the Developer edition, which lets you create custom solutions. Neither price is onerous for a business that needs to streamline its reporting, considering what you get in terms of the base program and the developer tools that come with the Developer edition. Business Objects offers a 30-day trial version, which you can download (after filling out a form) from *http://www.businessobjects.com/products/reporting/crystalreports/eval10/eval_download.asp*.

OLD SCHOOL

If you love classic arcade games, you'll be pleased to discover that you can actually play *Space Invaders* in Excel. The programmer, No-buya Chikada, uses individual cells as pixels by cranking the zoom level to 10% and making the cells as small as possible. Try changing the zoom level to 25% while the game's running to see what's going on! You can download this game for free from *http://www.xl-logic.com/xl_files/ games/cellvader_e.zip*. To play, just unzip the file and run the Excel workbook. The left and right arrow keys move your ship, and pressing the Z key fires your gun.

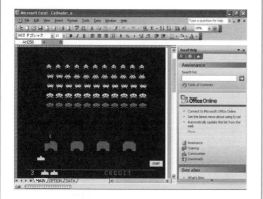

Once again, I must apologize for the imminent drop in business productivity.

Customization, Macro, and VBA
ANNOYANCES

The Excel interface can sometimes drive you a little nutty. There's the "adaptive" menu system in Excel 2002 (thankfully turned off by default in Excel 2003) that guesses (usually incorrectly) what menu options you want; silly limits in the filesystem; and dialog boxes that have so many tabs, checkboxes, and fields that some third-party developers make good money creating substitutes.

Ironing out these wrinkles—putting a toolbar button where you want it, or keeping snoops out of your files—is easy once you know a few insider moves. In this chapter, you'll learn how to customize the interface, secure your data, undo changes you made in the distant past, and create macros to automate those mind- and finger-numbing repetitive tasks. You'll also write a little Visual Basic for Applications (VBA) code to really rework and expand Excel's capabilities.

INTERFACE CUSTOMIZATION ANNOYANCES

EXPAND THE RECENTLY USED FILE LIST

The Annoyance: I work with many workbooks every day, and I hate having to dig through my drives to find the files I need. The recently opened file list at the bottom of the File menu shows only the last four files I opened. How do I make it show more files?

The Fix: Simple. Choose Tools → Options, click the General tab, and in the "Recently used file list" field set the value to 9 (the maximum number allowed). If you don't want Excel to list recently used files at all, uncheck the "Recently used file list" box.

ALWAYS SHOW FULL MENUS

The Annoyance: I use Excel 2002, and I hate those stupid "adaptive" menus! Sure, it's sort of cool that they change based on the features I've used recently, and sometimes that's handy, but most of the time they hide the choices I want and make it nearly impossible for me to follow directions from a book—or teach my co-workers how to use the program. How do I get those nice, long, stable menus back?

The Fix: To force Excel 2002 and 2003 to always show full menus, choose Tools → Customize, click the Options tab, and put a check in the "Always show full menus" checkbox. In Excel 2000, uncheck the "Menus show recently used commands first" box.

PROTECT YOUR WORKBOOK

The Annoyance: Most of the folks in my office use my Excel workbooks, but only for data entry. Some of them understand about not making changes in the workbook structure, but others accidentally delete worksheets, resize sheets, and so on. I don't mind them experimenting

on a blank workbook, but I've got to prevent them from mucking with *my* workbooks. How do I limit what a user can do?

The Fix: To prevent worksheet users from changing the structure of a workbook, follow these steps:

1. Hide any toolbars and menus you don't want your users to see. See "Hide or Display a Built-In Toolbar" later in this chapter.

2. Then choose Tools → Protection → Protect Workbook to display the Protect Workbook dialog box (shown in Figure 8-1).

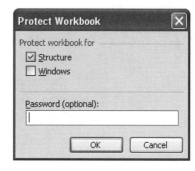

Figure 8-1. If someone doesn't know the password, they can't change your workbook.

3. Check the Structure box to prevent users from adding or deleting worksheets, and check the Windows box to prevent users from resizing Excel windows. Add a password if you like, and click OK.

4. To remove workbook protection, choose Tools → Protection → Unprotect Workbook. If you assigned a password, you will have to type it in.

PROTECT YOUR DATA

The Annoyance: Protecting the structure of a workbook is fine, but my users can still change my data and overwrite my formulas. How do I protect the *contents* of a worksheet?

The Fix: To start with, you must unprotect the worksheet (if it's protected in the first place). Choose Tools → Protection (shown in Figure 8-2) and make sure your sheet is unprotected. Type in the password if necessary to complete unprotection. Once you make the following changes you will reprotect the sheet. Here's how:

Figure 8-2. Users can do lots of things to your worksheets, if you let them.

LOCKED CELLS VERSUS PROTECTED WORKSHEETS

You can set cells as locked or unlocked by choosing Format → Cells and clicking the Protection tab. The default is locked. However, the "lock" doesn't actually do anything (it's only a *potential* lock) until the entire sheet is protected. And vice versa: when you protect your worksheet, that protection applies only to locked cells. Once cells are locked and worksheet protection is enabled, users won't be able to make any changes to locked cells—but for you to change cells from locked to unlocked and back again, the sheet must be unprotected. Everybody clear? All right...

---

1. Select the cells that users will be allowed to change— that is, the cells in which they will enter data.

2. Choose Format → Cells, click the Protection tab, and uncheck the Locked box. Click OK. Repeat until all cells for data entry are unlocked.

3. Click Tools → Protection → Protect Sheet.

4. For Excel 97 and 2000, add a password if you like and click OK.

5. Excel 2002 and 2003 have checkboxes representing tasks that everyone, including users who don't know the password, are allowed to perform. The "Select locked cells" and "Select unlocked cells" boxes are checked by default. Uncheck them if you want to prevent users from copying values from these types of cells. Otherwise, leave them checked. Make sure the "Protect worksheet and contents of locked cells" box is checked, add a password if you like, and click OK.

If you make that last set of changes (in Excel 2002 or 2003), Excel will prevent changes in locked cells but allow data entry in unlocked cells.

In Excel 2002 and later, you also can selectively protect ranges of cells by user. This lets some users, but not others, edit selected cells. To protect ranges by user, take the following steps *before* protecting the worksheet:

1. Select the range of cells you want to protect.

2. Choose Tools → Protection → Allow Users to Edit Ranges. Excel displays the Allow Users to Edit Ranges dialog box.

3. Click the New button. Excel displays the New Range dialog box with the range of the selected cells listed in the "Refers to cells" field.

4. Click the Permissions button to display the Permissions dialog box, and click the Add button. Excel displays the Select Users or Groups dialog box.

5. Type in the names of users you're allowing to edit the range. Usernames take the form *<machinename>\ <username>* for workgroup-based networks, or *<domainname>\<username>* for domain-based networks. You also can simply type the username and

click Check Names to look up a user's machine or domain name if you don't know it. To list multiple names, separate them with a semicolon. Click OK when you're done. Excel adds the names to the list in the Permissions dialog box.

6. If you want to require the user to enter a password before editing the range, select the username and check the Deny box. Click OK when done. Excel returns you to the New Range dialog box.

7. Enter a password for the range, if you like, and click OK. Excel prompts you to confirm the password and then returns you to the worksheet.

8. Finally, protect the worksheet by selecting Tools → Protection → Protect Sheet. Excel does not enforce range-level protection until the worksheet is protected.

Still Not Secure?

Even password-protected and -encrypted workbooks are susceptible to guessing attacks launched by VBA programs. To make those attacks harder, use passwords which are at least eight characters long and include both numbers and symbols.

REQUIRE A PASSWORD TO OPEN OR MODIFY A WORKBOOK

The Annoyance: I have a workbook that contains sensitive data. For now, I'd prefer that only the partners in my company be able to see it. However, I don't want anybody but me (not even my working partners) to be able to change it. Can I password-protect my workbook on those two levels?

The Fix: If you use Excel 97, sorry, there's no fix. For users of 2000 and later, however, just follow these steps:

1. Choose File → Save As, and in the dialog box click the Tools menu at the top right. Then select General Options to display the Save Options dialog box (shown in Figure 8-3).

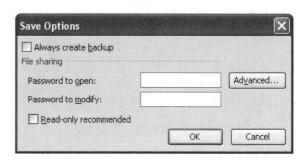

Figure 8-3. You can require users to know two different passwords to get at your data.

2. To require users to enter a password to open and/or modify the workbook, type the passwords in the appropriate fields and click OK.

3. Reenter the passwords when prompted, to verify you typed them correctly.

To remove a workbook's password protection, open the workbook, choose File → Save As → Tools → General Options, and delete the passwords from the "Password to open" and "Password to modify" fields.

If you really want to secure a workbook, you need more than passwords. Read the next annoyance and fix to find out why.

OPEN A PROTECTED WORKBOOK

The Annoyance: Remember that workbook I protected? I, um...can't remember the password. Is there any way to crack Excel's password protection?

The Fix: There are a lot of third-party services and tools to find Excel passwords. I did a quick search on Google using the string *+excel+password+recovery*. Here are the URLs for companies and products that appeared on the first two results pages:

- *http://www.ozgrid.com/Services/excel-password-recover.htm*
- *http://www.lostpassword.com*
- *http://www.lastbit.com*
- *http://www.passwordrecoverytools.com/en/excel.shtml*
- *http://www.straxx.com/excel/password.html*
- *http://www.elcomsoft.com/ae2000pr.html*
- *http://www.softpicks.net/software/Accent-Excel-Password-Recovery-2208.htm*
- *http://www.intertek.org.uk*
- *http://www.password-crackers.com/crack/guaexcel.html*

Does that list make you feel, um, insecure? The average advertised time for these companies to crack a password runs as low as two days—if *they* do it. If you prefer to run the products on your own computer, the average advertised solution time is around 14–18 days. I have no personal experience with any of these companies or products—except for Ozgrid.com, the company run by David and Raina Hawley (the authors of *Excel Hacks* from O'Reilly). Do your homework before choosing a service or product, and insist on a money-back guarantee.

CODE-BUSTING TECHNOLOGY

Most password recovery programs don't actually guess passwords. When you type a password into Excel, it uses a complex algorithm to create a mathematical summary, or *hash*, of your password. The next time you type in your password to open or modify a file or worksheet, Excel checks your password's hash against your input's hash value. If they're the same, Excel opens the file. Most password recovery tools can test all possible hashes (there are 2^{40} of 'em) in about 25 days on a computer with a 1.6MHz Pentium 4, or in as little as one day on a dedicated computer cluster.

FORGET PASSWORDS! USE ENCRYPTION

The Annoyance: Let me get this straight: you're telling me that the average time for a dedicated service to open my protected workbook is two days? That is seriously uncool. Isn't there a more effective way to protect my workbooks from prying eyes?

The Fix: For Excel 2000 and earlier, you don't have a good alternative within Excel itself. Your only options are to set effective user permissions in Windows XP Professional or 2000, and use third-party security tools. For instance, you could compress your Excel file as a zip file and use WinZIP's built-in 250-bit AES encryption. (Of course you'd need to unzip it before you could use it, but any encryption algorithm is going to slow you down.) You can find a list of freeware encryption tools at *http://www.all-internet-security.com/file_encryption_tools_freeware.html*, but if you're a company or an individual who works with sensitive personal data (such as Social Security numbers) you should strongly consider acquiring a top-notch third-party tool. A Google search for *+windows+file+encryption+tools* returned literally thousands of hits, but I recommend using one of the following tools:

- Cryptainer LE, which you can download for free from *http://www.cypherix.com/cryptainerle/tech_specs.htm*, lets you set up encrypted 5MB containers on your hard drive that you can use to store files securely. Cryptainer LE uses the Blowfish algorithm, which was one of the finalists in the Advanced Encryption Standard competition. More powerful Cryptainer versions let you create larger encrypted file containers. The ME version (offering up to 500MB containers) costs $29.95, and the PE version (5GB containers) costs $45. A companion product, SecureIT, lets you encrypt individual files. SecureIT costs $29.95 for a single-user license.

- Cryptomathic File2File is another free file-level encryption tool; *Information Week* columnist Fred Langa recommends it highly. You can download File2File from *http://www.cryptomathic.com/file2file/index.html*.

For Excel 2002 and later, follow these steps to protect your workbook using strong encryption:

1. Choose File → Save As → Tools → General Options to display the General Options dialog box.

2. Type passwords into the appropriate fields, and click the Advanced button.

3. Select the advanced encryption option (any but the first two). The scheme's key length appears in the dialog box (shown in Figure 8-4).

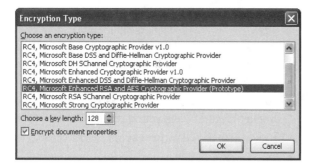

Figure 8-4. Some of these schemes are stronger than others.

4. Which one is best? The U.S. federal government recently held a contest to find the best encryption algorithm to use as its Advanced Encryption Standard (AES). If you consider winning a U.S. government contest to be a positive endorsement, you should choose the scheme named RC4, Microsoft Enhanced RSA and AES Cryptographic Protocol (Prototype).

5. Reenter the passwords when prompted to verify you typed them correctly.

When you use any encryption tool, you face the possibility of not being able to open your files if you forget their passwords. Please, please, please follow one or more of the following steps to ensure you don't lose your data:

- Store written passwords in a secure offsite location, such as a bank safe deposit box.

- Store written passwords, in pieces, in two or three (or more) safes around your office.

- Store each password in a strongly encrypted document file on a computer that is not connected to any network, especially not the Internet.

- As George Smiley would say, "Use Moscow rules."

USE EXCEL 2003 WORKBOOK PERMISSIONS

The Annoyance: OK, you've seriously scared me. Isn't there *any* way to be sure my workbook data doesn't leak out? I mean, I've got J.Lo's phone number in there.

The Fix: If you have Excel 2003, you can use permissions to protect your workbook from prying eyes. Rather than using passwords, which can be guessed, cracked, or stolen, protection uses *identities* to determine who can and can't read or edit a workbook. Identities are somewhat safer than passwords because they are based on the account you use to sign on to your computer or network. If someone tries to guess your account password, they usually get locked out after a couple of bungled attempts.

You also can use permissions to control whether a user can distribute, print, or copy sections of the workbook. The downside of permissions is that your network must have a Rights Management Server installed, and you'll need a Microsoft Passport account to prove your identity.

To set permissions for a workbook in Excel 2003 for the first time:

1. Choose File → Permission → Do Not Distribute. Excel starts the Windows Rights Management Wizard which first checks to make sure you've installed the client and, if you haven't, encourages you to download the latest version.

2. Then the Wizard walks you through creating Rights Management credentials and downloading them to your computer. When you are done, Excel displays the Permission dialog box as shown in Figure 8-5.

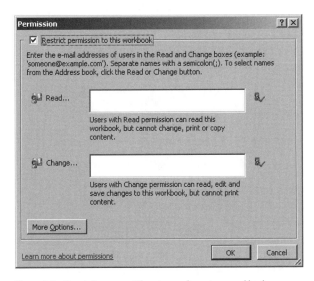

Figure 8-5. Permissions are a different way of securing a workbook.

3. Check the "Restrict permission to this workbook" box to set permissions. Excel activates the dialog box so that you can add users.

4. Enter a list of the users allowed to Read and/or Change the workbook. Users are identified by email addresses. Separate multiple addresses with semicolons.

5. Set additional permissions by selecting the user and then changing the permission settings in the Permission dialog box (Figure 8-6). Click OK when done.

Figure 8-6. Set the permissions for users.

Now, when users try to open the workbook one of several things will happen:

- If they are included in the workbook's user list, and they have Excel 2003 installed, the workbook opens.

- If they are not included in the workbook's user list, and they have Excel 2003 installed, they see a description of where to send email to get permission to use the workbook (Figure 8-7).

Figure 8-7. If you don't have permission to read a workbook, you're told how to get it.

- If they don't have Excel 2003, they will see a description of how to get the Information Rights Management add-in for Internet Explorer. Once they install the add-in they can view (but not edit) the workbook—if they have permission.

There are two obvious downsides to permissions: one, you and everyone else need Excel 2003, along with a Passport account. Two, it's a relatively new approach, so not everyone will be familiar with it, and it might require some education before you roll it out in your company.

INCREASE THE NUMBER OF UNDO LEVELS

The Annoyance: On a good day, you might get from six to eight levels of undo from Excel. Sometimes you get lucky and get 16. Even so, that's not nearly enough undo levels for me. I make a lot of changes when I work in Excel, and I don't want to be caught in a situation where I made a change 18 steps ago that I can't undo because I've done other things since. Surely there must be some way to increase the number of undo levels?

The Fix: In Excel 2000 and later, you can change the number of undo levels, but you'll need to edit the Registry. First, back up your Registry! For instructions, see the sidebar titled "Always Back Up Your Registry" following this fix.

Now, to edit the Registry itself, follow these steps:

1. Choose Start → Run and type **Regedit** in the Run dialog box, then press Enter to start the Registry Editor (shown in Figure 8-8).

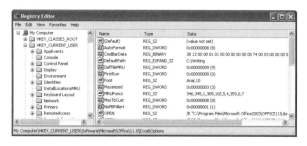

Figure 8-8. The Registry is Windows' Grand Central Station, tracking your apps and their settings. Be careful what you change or you could end up with a train wreck.

2. Navigate down the tree until you have displayed HKEY_CURRENT_USER\Software\Microsoft\Office*version*\Excel\Options (where *version* is the Excel version you want to change—for Excel 2000, it's 9; for Excel 2002, it's 10; and for Excel 2003, it's 11).

3. Right-click the Options key and select New → DWORD Value.

4. Replace the default name NewValue #1, which has appeared at the bottom of the righthand window, with the name **UndoHistory**.

5. Now double-click the new UndoHistory entry to display the Edit DWORD Value dialog box (shown in Figure 8-9).

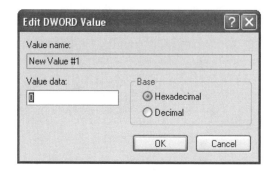

Figure 8-9. Here's where you tell Excel how many steps it should be able to undo.

6. Select the Decimal option, type **100** in the "Value data" field and click OK.

7. Close the Registry Editor and restart Excel.

ALWAYS BACK UP YOUR REGISTRY

The Registry is where Windows keeps track of your programs and their settings. A bad change can make your system unusable, so you should always back up your Registry settings before you make any changes. Make sure you print out these instructions!

☒ To back up and restore your registry in Windows 95, 98, and Me, follow the instructions at *http://support.microsoft.com/default.aspx?scid=kb;en-us;322754*.

☒ To back up and restore your registry in Windows NT 4, follow the instructions at *http://support.microsoft.com/default.aspx?scid=kb;en-us;323170*.

☒ To back up and restore your registry in Windows 2000, follow the instructions at *http://support.microsoft.com/default.aspx?scid=kb;en-us;322755*.

☒ To back up and restore your registry in Windows XP and Server 2003, follow the instructions at *http://support.microsoft.com/default.aspx?scid=kb;en-us;322756*.

TOOLBAR AND MENU BAR ANNOYANCES

SHOW ALL YOUR BUTTONS

The Annoyance: For the next few weeks I'm stuck working on a computer with a monitor that offers only 800x600 resolution. That means my Excel window (which is designed for my regular 1024x768 display) takes up a lot more room, and half the buttons on my Standard and Formatting toolbars slide off the screen (as shown in Figure 8-10). Is there any way to give those toolbars more room to breathe? And how can I find the buttons that have slid off-screen?

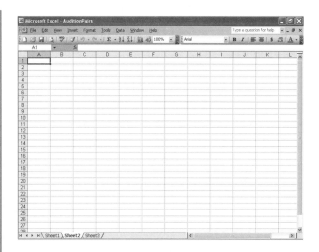

Figure 8-10. These toolbars are a bit cramped, but the buttons are still there.

The Fix: To display toolbar buttons that aren't shown on the toolbar due to space, click the Toolbar Options button at the far right edge of the toolbar. It looks a bit like a face without a nose: two larger-than symbols over a down-pointing triangle.

You also can try displaying the Standard and Formatting toolbars on separate rows—if they aren't that way already. In Excel 97, just hover the mouse pointer over the vertical bars that separate the icons, and drag the Formatting toolbar below the Standard toolbar.

In Excel 2000, choose Tools → Customize, click the Options tab, and uncheck the "Standard and Formatting toolbars share one row" box.

In Excel 2002 and 2003, choose Tools → Customize, click the Options tab, and check the "Show Standard and Formatting toolbars on two rows" box.

ADD STANDARD BUTTONS TO YOUR TOOLBAR

The Annoyance: I recently visited one of our suppliers' offices, and noticed that he had some very hip Excel toolbar buttons I'd never seen before. He said his technical guy had found them in some dialog box or another, but he couldn't remember where. How did he do it, and what buttons are available?

The Fix: To add a toolbar button to a toolbar, choose Tools → Customize, and click the Commands tab (shown in Figure 8-11).

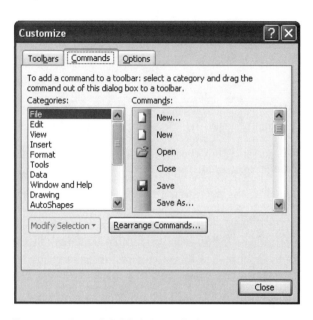

Figure 8-11. You can find all the built-in toolbar buttons, even those not displayed on any toolbar by default, in the Commands tab of the Customize dialog box.

In the Categories pane on the left, select the category of buttons you want (such as Tools). Then scroll down the Commands pane on the right until you see the button you'd like to add to your toolbar, and drag the button from the Commands pane to a blank spot on the target toolbar. When you grab the button, a little gray rectangle and a small *x* will appear. When the button is at a valid location, the *x* turns into a plus sign. To remove a button from a toolbar, return to the Commands tab, drag the button from the toolbar, and drop it anywhere in the Commands tab. (P.S.: this also works if you want to remove an entire menu from Excel's menu bar.)

Table 8-1 lists a number of useful toolbar buttons and the category where they're stored.

Table 8-1. Useful toolbar buttons available on the Commands tab of the Customize dialog box, by name and category.

Command	What it does	Suggested uses
Publish As Web Page (File)	Displays the Publish dialog box accessed from the Save As Web Page dialog box.	Displays the Publish dialog box accessed from the Save As Web Page dialog box.
Select Visible Cells (Edit)	Selects only those cells not hidden by a filter.	Add button to a toolbar to avoid selecting hidden cells.
Paste Values (Edit)	Pastes the values copied (not cut) from one or more cells.	Add button to the Standard toolbar to avoid opening the Paste Special dialog box every time you want to replace formulas with their current values.
Current Region (Edit)	Selects all cells in the current region.	Add button to the Standard toolbar so that you don't have to remember the Ctrl-Shift-8 keyboard shortcut.
Custom Views (View)	Displays a list of custom views available for the active worksheet.	Add list box to a custom toolbar for use in a presentation.
Cycle Font Color (Format)	Changes cell text to the next color in the Font Color palette.	Add to the Formatting toolbar.
Scenario (Tools)	Displays a list of scenarios available for the active worksheet.	Add listbox to a custom toolbar for use in presentations.
Refresh Status (Data)	Reports on the progress and success of data refresh operations.	Add button to a custom toolbar attached to workbooks with external data queries.
Lighting (Drawing)	Changes the lighting sources and characteristics for objects on a worksheet.	Add button to the Drawing toolbar.

Command	What it does	Suggested uses
Reset Picture (Drawing)	Returns an edited picture to its original state.	Add button to the Drawing toolbar.
Chart Objects (Charting)	Lists the editable objects in the selected chart.	Add listbox to the Chart toolbar.

ADD A NEW BUTTON TO A TOOLBAR

The Annoyance: I recorded a macro that I'd like to run by clicking a toolbar button, not by digging through a series of menu options. Is there any way to run a macro from a toolbar button?

The Fix: To assign a macro to a new toolbar button, choose Tools → Customize, click the Commands tab, select Macros from the Categories list on the left, and drag the smiley-face Custom Button from the pane on the right to any toolbar. Right-click the button, choose Assign Macro, and select the desired macro from the list in the Assign Macro dialog box (shown in Figure 8-12).

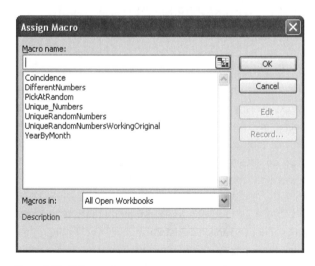

Figure 8-12. Pick a macro, any macro.

CHANGE THE APPEARANCE OF A TOOLBAR BUTTON

The Annoyance: The smiley-face button that Excel uses as the default for custom toolbar buttons was cute in the 1970s, but now, it's truly annoying. Can't I replace it with another button? As a matter of fact, is there any way to see all the buttons that are available in Excel? And can I create my own toolbar buttons?

The Fix: Yes, yes, and yes. To change the appearance of a toolbar button, choose Tools → Customize. With the Customize dialog open, go back up to any Excel toolbar, right-click any button, choose Change Button Image, and select the image from the palette that appears. There are 42 images in the palette, but if none of them catches your fancy you can create a custom button image with the Button Editor. To display the Button Editor (shown in Figure 8-13), choose Tools → Customize, right-click any button on any toolbar, and choose Edit Button Image.

Figure 8-13. The Button Editor looks silly, but you can use it to create, or at least edit, art.

To change a pixel in the button's image, click the color you want the pixel to be and then click the corresponding square in the button's image. You can drag the mouse pointer to fill in multiple squares in one pass, or use the eraser to clear all color from a square.

You can find a list of all the buttons available in Excel by downloading the *FaceID.xls* workbook from *http://msdn. microsoft.com/library/default.asp?url=/library/en-us/ dno97ta/html/faceid.asp* (yes, it's an Excel 97 article, but the macros in the workbook apply to every version of Excel from 97 to 2003). When you open it, a form asks you for a range of FaceIDs you'd like to display. A FaceID is Excel's internal record of a button's image, or *face*. If you ask to see FaceIDs 1–200, the workbook displays the toolbar shown in Figure 8-14.

Figure 8-14. Here are the first 200 of many toolbar button faces in Excel.

If you want to use any displayed toolbar buttons as the face for your custom toolbar button, right-click the desired button image, choose Copy Button Image, right-click the custom toolbar button, and choose Paste Button Image.

You also can give your button a text string as a "face." Choose Tools → Customize, right-click the button, and type a new value in the Name field that appears in the shortcut menu. After you've typed in the new name, right-click the button again and choose Text Only (Always).

Later in this chapter, you'll find out how to create entire toolbars and menus in VBA.

HIDE OR DISPLAY A BUILT-IN TOOLBAR

The Annoyance: I created a PivotTable and used some of the buttons on the PivotTable toolbar to manipulate the table, but somehow I managed to hide the toolbar. How do I bring it back?

The Fix: To display a hidden toolbar, right-click any toolbar you *can* see and click the name of the toolbar you *want* to see. If the desired toolbar doesn't appear in the list, choose Tools → Customize, click the Toolbars tab, and check the box next to the toolbar you want to see. You can, of course, use these steps to hide a toolbar, as well.

CREATE A CUSTOM TOOLBAR

The Annoyance: I'm building a workbook that uses a number of custom macros, and I'd like to create a custom toolbar to hold the buttons that launch those macros. I mean, there's no more room on either the Standard or Formatting toolbar. Can I create a custom toolbar?

The Fix: Choose Tools → Customize, click the Toolbars tab, and then click the New button. Type a name in the Toolbar name field and click OK. Your new toolbar, with space for one button, will appear in the Excel window. As soon as you add a button, the toolbar will expand to accommodate another.

RESET A TOOLBAR OR MENU TO ITS DEFAULT SETTINGS

The Annoyance: I've made a lot of changes to the toolbars in my copy of Excel, but I'm leaving for two weeks and my assistant will need to use my computer to access my files. She's used to the default toolbar settings on her computer, so I'd like to reset my toolbars for her. How do I reset the toolbars I've changed? And how do I restore my versions when I return?

The Fix: To reset a toolbar or menu to its default settings, choose Tools → Customize, click the Toolbars tab, click the name of the toolbar you want to restore to its original state, and click Reset. If you want to reapply your changes when you get back, you'll need to create a new toolbar and copy any custom toolbar buttons or menu items you created to it. When you return, you'll have to copy the custom buttons and menu items back to the original toolbar. You also will need to remove any standard toolbar buttons that clicking Reset brought back.

ADD A BUILT-IN MENU TO A TOOLBAR

The Annoyance: I use the Protection menu a lot to set passwords for my workbooks and worksheet, and it's kind of a pain that it's buried under the Tools menu. Is there a way to put the Protection menu at the top level of a menu bar?

The Fix: To add a built-in menu to a toolbar, choose Tools → Customize, click the Commands tab, and in the Categories pane on the left, select Built-In Menus. Find the menu you want in the Commands pane on the right, and drag it to the target toolbar.

CREATE AND POPULATE A CUSTOM MENU

The Annoyance: I'm one of those folks who prefer to use menus instead of buttons. Instead of packing the Excel toolbar with buttons, why can't I put *menus* on the thing? And specifically, menus which run my macros?

The Fix: To Excel, a menu bar and a toolbar are exactly the same thing, so you can create a menu toolbar using the same procedure detailed in the "Create a Custom Toolbar" annoyance. To add a menu to a toolbar, follow these steps:

1. Choose Tools → Customize, click the Commands tab, scroll down the Categories pane on the left and select New Menu, then click the New Menu item in the Commands pane on the right and drag it to the target toolbar.

2. Right-click the New Menu item, and in the Name field type a new name for the menu. Now let's create a menu option placeholder.

3. In the Categories pane of the Commands tab, click Macros.

4. In the Commands pane to the right, drag Custom Menu Item to the new menu item you just created. When you hover the Custom Menu Item over the new menu, a small blank menu will appear below the

menu name (as shown in Figure 8-15). Drop the Custom Menu Item on that blank menu.

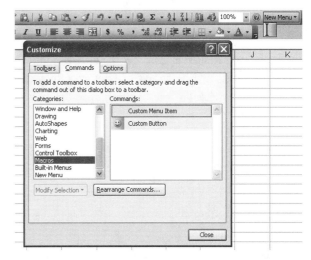

Figure 8-15. You have to wait for a second in the right spot to add a menu item.

Now that you have the placeholder Custom Menu Item in place, you can assign a macro to it by following the steps in the "Place Your Macro on a Toolbar or Menu" fix later in this chapter.

To create a submenu on a menu, drag a New Menu Item to that existing menu.

It's All the Same to Excel

You've probably noticed that the toolbar and menu systems duplicate each other to some extent. Actually, forget "to some extent"; they *do* duplicate each other. The Excel programmers keep both systems around because toolbar buttons, which are great for the quick stuff, take up interface room and it's hard to remember what dozens of them do. Menus take up less space and are easier to read, but they can bury frequently used items several levels down.

MACRO ANNOYANCES

RECORD A MACRO

The Annoyance: I can't believe how much of my day I spend doing the same few things over and over again. I could save myself a lot of time by automating those processes. How do I record my steps and play them back at a later time?

The Fix: To record a series of actions as a macro, follow these steps:

1. Choose Tools → Macro → Record New Macro.

2. Type a name for the new macro in the "Macro name" field and click OK.

3. Perform all the steps you want to record, and when you're done click the Stop Recording button on the Stop Recording toolbar (shown in Figure 8-16).

Figure 8-16. The Stop Recording button looks like the Stop button on a remote control.

RUN A MACRO

The Annoyance: I recorded a formatting sequence just as you outlined, but no matter what I try I can't get Excel to replay it! This is very annoying!

The Fix: To run a macro, choose Tools → Macro → Macros, highlight the macro you want to run, and click the Run button. Or you can put the macro on a button. To learn how, see "Place Your Macro on a Toolbar or Menu," later in this chapter.

RECORD A MACRO WITH RELATIVE REFERENCES

The Annoyance: I use Excel to track the results of the games in my city's soccer leagues. We use a system of promotion and relegation, which means that teams in one league can be promoted to a higher league,

or relegated to a lower one, based on their performance. Here's what's going on: I selected the first two cells in my list, started recording a macro, changed the formatting of those first two cells to bold (representing automatic promotion), the next four cells to italic (representing teams in a playoff for promotion), and the last three cells in the list to red (representing teams that will be relegated). So far, so good—but when I run the macro on other team lists in different columns in the same worksheet, it changes the top two teams correctly, but then goes back and executes the rest of the changes to the cells in the *original* list I started with! How do I make the macro work just on the cells in the current column?

The Fix: What happened is that Excel recorded the absolute addresses of the cells you selected while you went through your procedure. Here's a look at the code you created:

```
Selection.Font.Bold = True
Range("B4:B7").Select
Selection.Font.Italic = True
Range("B19:B21").Select
Selection.Font.ColorIndex = 3
```

The first line of code changes the selected cells' formatting to bold, but the second and fourth lines change the ranges B4:B7 and B19:B21, respectively. To have Excel record your macro using *relative* cell references instead of absolute references, you need to click the Relative Reference button on the Stop Recording toolbar (the icon to the right, shown in Figure 8-16). When you click the Relative Reference button and go through the same procedure discussed earlier, Excel creates *this* code:

```
Selection.Font.Bold = True
ActiveCell.Offset(2, 0).Range("A1:A4").Select
Selection.Font.Italic = True
ActiveCell.Offset(15, 0).Range("A1:A3").Select
Selection.Font.ColorIndex = 3
```

Don't be thrown off by the appearance of the cell ranges A1:A4 and A1:A3 in the code. Here's what's happening:

- Excel changes the two selected cells' formatting to bold.

- Excel selects the four cells below the currently selected range. If you had selected the range C2:C3 before running the macro, Excel would now select cells C4:C7. The `Offset` method (more on that later) tells Excel to affect cells starting two rows below the current selection. It then refers to the first four cells in that range as cells A1:A4.

- Similarly, the fourth line of code tells Excel to move 15 rows below the currently selected range and affect the next three cells.

PLACE YOUR MACRO ON A TOOLBAR OR MENU

The Annoyance: I created my macro and it's working correctly, but it's a lot of work to dig through the Tools menu every time I want to run it. Is there any way I can create a toolbar button that runs the macro?

The Fix: To run a macro by clicking a toolbar button or menu item, follow these steps:

1. Choose Tools → Customize and click the Commands tab.

2. In the Categories list, click Macros.

3. Drag the Custom Button or Custom Menu Item to the desired spot on a toolbar.

4. Right-click the button or menu item and choose Assign Macro, select the macro you want, and click OK and then Close. Now when you click the button or menu item, Excel will run the macro you assigned.

STEP THROUGH A MACRO

The Annoyance: There's something wrong with my macro, but I can't tell what it is. When my mom taught me how to cook, we'd go step by step to make sure I had everything right before moving on to the next step. Can I do the same thing with a macro?

The Fix: Well, if you really want Excel to act like your mother and move through a macro one step at a time, follow these steps:

1. Choose Tools → Macro → Macros, highlight the macro you want to check, and click the Step Into button to display the macro in the Visual Basic Editor (shown in Figure 8-17).

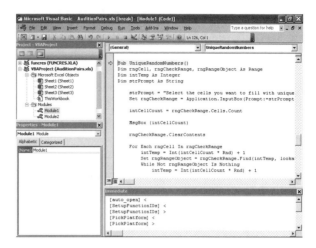

Figure 8-17. The Visual Basic Editor is your home for custom coding.

2. Use the following key sequences to manage the stepping process:

- Press F8 to run the highlighted step and move to the next step.

- Press Shift-F8 to skip the highlighted step and move to the next step.

- Press Ctrl-Shift-F8 to end the stepping process.

- Place the pointer in a line of code and press Ctrl-F8 to execute the macro code starting from this point.

EDIT A MACRO

The Annoyance: I use templates to save time when I create new workbooks, but I just changed several of my templates—and as a result some data is now in new cells. The macros I created as part of those templates are pretty long, so rather than rerecord them I'd like to just change the cell references. How do I edit a macro?

The Fix: To edit a macro, choose Tools → Macro → Macros, highlight the name of the macro you want to edit, and click the Edit button to open the macro in the Visual Basic Editor. When you're done editing the macro, click the Save toolbar button and then choose File → Close to return to Microsoft Excel.

RUN A MACRO STORED IN ANOTHER WORKBOOK

The Annoyance: I create a lot of macros, and I can't always remember where I stored them. Can I run a macro that's stored in another open workbook?

The Fix: To run a macro in another open workbook, choose Tools → Macro → Macros, and in the "Macros in" drop down, select All Open Workbooks, highlight the macro you want to run in the box above, and click the Run button.

MACRO SECURITY ANNOYANCES

AVOID MACRO VIRUSES

The Annoyance: VBA is a powerful language, but it can get you into trouble if you're not paying attention. Macro viruses, which I never heard of five years ago, have become the bane of my existence! How can I make sure my people only run macros I know are safe?

The Fix: First, purchase and use antivirus, antiworm, and anti-Trojan software. This is particularly important in Excel 97 because this version has no macro security setting. If you're running Excel 97 and you absolutely can't upgrade to a more recent version, make darn sure that your antivirus software is up-to-date and it's set to actively scan all incoming files. If you have a computer you use as a gateway to the Internet, you should strongly consider putting one antivirus program on the gateway and a package from a different provider on your users' machines; if a virus or worm slips by one of them, the other will probably swat it.

Second, if you're running Excel 2000 or later, make sure your users have their macro security level set to High or Very High.

Third, you should strongly consider purchasing a digital certificate from a certificate authority and using it to sign the macros you want your users to be able to run. Then you can prevent your users from running macros that aren't signed by setting Excel's macro security level to High.

Once your antivirus software is in place, make sure that every user's computer has Excel's macro security level set to High (at least). To do that, choose Tools → Macro → Security, select the Security Level tab, and click the High radio button. The High macro security setting won't let your users run a macro unless it's from a trusted source. (See the next annoyance for details on trusted sources.) The Very High macro security setting, available only in Excel 2003, also requires that the macro be in a workbook that is stored in one of two trusted locations:

- *\Documents and Settings\<username>\Application Data\Microsoft\Excel\XLSTART*
- *\Program Files\Microsoft Office\Office11\XLSTART*

If you want to disable macros entirely in Excel 2003, follow these steps:

1. Choose Tools → Macro → Security and click the Very High radio button.

2. Click the Trusted Publisher tab.

3. Uncheck the "Trust all installed add-ins and templates" checkbox.

This procedure also disables all COM add-ins and dynamic link library (DLL) files, so be sure you aren't using any programmed extensions to Excel before setting your security level to Very High.

In Microsoft Office 2003 or later, Excel checks all XML (Extensible Markup Language) files that have references to XSL (Extensible Stylesheet Language) files that contain executable scripts. When macro security is set to High or Very High, Excel won't run the script. When macro security is set to Medium, you will be asked if you want to run the script. If you have macro security set to Low, Excel will run the script without asking—one good reason you should *never* set macro security to Low.

ADD A PUBLISHER TO YOUR TRUSTED PUBLISHERS LIST

The Annoyance: I set my macro security level to High, so I am able to run macros from only trusted publishers. There's just one problem: how do I create a list of trusted publishers?

The Fix: To add a publisher to your list of trusted publishers, that publisher must send you a workbook with a macro they signed with their digital certificate. When you open the workbook, you'll see a dialog box like the one shown in Figure 8-18.

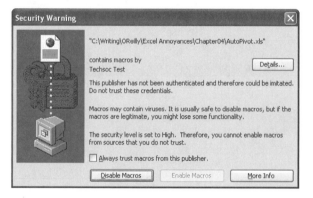

Figure 8-18. Excel evaluates the certificate your sender used to sign the workbook.

This dialog box suggests that you shouldn't trust the certificate because Excel doesn't recognize the entity that created the certificate, which is reasonable considering the fact that I signed the workbook myself and, hey, what do you know about me? If Excel does recognize the certificate source, and everything about the certificate checks out (it hasn't expired, the "valid from" date isn't in the future, the certificate hasn't been revoked, etc.), you'll see a version of the dialog box telling you everything is OK.

Once you decide to trust the publisher, check the "Always trust macros from this publisher" box to add the publisher to your trusted publishers list. To view your trusted publishers list, choose Tools → Macro → Security and click the Trusted Publishers tab. (For details on certification authorities, see the upcoming "Acquire a Digital Certificate" annoyance.)

REMOVE A PUBLISHER FROM YOUR TRUSTED PUBLISHERS LIST

The Annoyance: I'm no longer doing business with a publisher who was on my trusted publishers list. All their products seem to crash. How can I remove them from my list?

The Fix: To delete a trusted publisher from your list, choose Tools → Macro → Security, click the Trusted Publishers tab, highlight the name you wish to remove, and click Remove.

Attention System Administrators

Microsoft provides a handy tool for managing your users' certificates across a network. Check out the Microsoft Management Console Certificates snap-in (*CertMgr.msc*). You can download *CertMgr.exe* and a collection of other free management programs from *http:// www.microsoft.com/downloads/details. aspx?familyid=2B742795-D0F0-4A66-B27F-22A95FCD3425&displaylang=en.*

ACQUIRE A DIGITAL CERTIFICATE

The Annoyance: I'm a software developer, and some of my customers refuse to run my macros because I don't add digital signatures to my workbooks—which means they can't add me as a trusted publisher. I'd like to purchase a digital certificate so that I can sign the workbooks I create with custom VBA solutions. Where can I buy one?

The Fix: One company, VeriSign, Inc., has pretty much cornered the market by buying up all its competitors. You can buy an annual license for a digital certificate from *http://www.verisign.com* or *http://www.thawte.com*. VeriSign, Inc. owns both sites.

Many organizations now provide their own certificates for in-house use by configuring the Microsoft Certificate Authority Service on a Windows 2000 or 2003 server within their network. To create certificates in Windows 2003 Server, you use the Certificate Services package that comes with the operating system. You can find more information online at *http://support.microsoft.com/default. aspx?scid=kb;en-us;838427*. To manage certificates in Windows 2000, visit the Microsoft information site at *http://www.microsoft.com/technet/prodtechnol/ windows2000serv/deploy/depopt/2000cert.mspx*. Find out if your company already provides its own certificates before purchasing one.

When you receive your digital certificate, the provider will give you instructions on how to install it on your computer.

DIGITALLY SIGN A WORKBOOK

The Annoyance: I acquired a digital certificate, but I can't figure out how to use it to sign my workbook. What gives?

The Fix: There are actually two ways to sign a workbook with a digital signature—but only if you're using Excel 2002 or later. You can sign the workbook itself, or you can sign the VBA code itself. Just follow these steps:

1. Choose Tools → Options.
2. Click the Security tab and then click the Digital Signatures button to display the Digital Signature dialog box.

3. Click Add to display the Select Certificate dialog box, select the digital certificate you want to use, and then click OK three times to close the three dialog boxes.

To sign your workbook's VBA code, follow these steps:

1. Press Alt-F11 to open the Visual Basic Editor.
2. In the Visual Basic Editor, choose Tools → Digital Signature, and click the Choose button to display a list of available certificates (shown in Figure 8-19).
3. Highlight the certificate you want to use, and click OK twice.

Figure 8-19. Every digital certificate you've acquired appears in the dialog box.

Multiple Certificates Are Better than One

If you can afford to do so, be sure to purchase certificates from more than one certificate authority. Each authority checks your company's documentation against public records, so owning multiple valid certificates is like having several people provide positive references for you.

VBA ANNOYANCES

MEET OBJECT-ORIENTED PROGRAMMING

The Annoyance: I read somewhere that Visual Basic for Applications (VBA), the macro programming language that underlies Office programs such as Excel, uses an object-oriented programming model. What the heck is that?

The Fix: Object-oriented programming is a metaphor that helps you organize the things in your programming environment. Five basic elements form the basis of object-oriented programming:

- *Objects*, which represent things (such as worksheets, workbooks, cell ranges, and so on)

- *Properties*, which describe objects (such as a worksheet's name, or a cell's value)

- *Methods*, which refers to which procedures an object knows how to do (such as save a workbook or activate a worksheet)

- *Events*, which are what an object knows how to respond to (such as activating a cell or saving a workbook)

- *Collections*, which are sets of objects (such as all the worksheets in a workbook or all the cells in a range)

You concatenate an object's properties and methods using dot notation: when you name the object, follow it with a period and then type the property or method you want to call. Here are two examples:

```
Worksheet("Sheet1").Name = "January"
Range("A1").Calculate
```

The first statement sets the name of the worksheet called *Sheet 1* to *January*, while the second statement uses the Calculate method to make Excel recalculate the result of the formula in cell A1.

Programming in VBA is just like programming in any other language: there's a learning curve. For many of the annoyances and fixes in the remainder of this section, I'm going to assume you know something about programming. If the going gets too geeky for you, turn to one of the many books or online tutorials for basic training. But I'll keep the first few easy...

COLLECT PREWRITTEN VBA ROUTINES

If you don't have a lot of experience programming Excel with Visual Basic for Applications, OzGrid is prepared to sell you a collection of macros and programming resources. You get two separate books as part of the package. The first book is an overview of programming in Excel, and the second is a collection of 1,200 macros sorted by category. Example categories include looping, setting cell values, manipulating PivotTables, and manipulating toolbars and menus. You can buy the two e-books together for $44.95 from *http://www.ozgrid.com/Services/ VBAExampleList.htm*.

CREATE A NEW CODE MODULE

The Annoyance: I'm a clueless, first-time VBA programmer. How, where, and when do I type in the VBA macros I see listed in this book—or elsewhere?

The Fix: Open the Visual Basic Editor by pressing Alt-F11, or choose Tools → Macro → Visual Basic Editor. To begin creating a code module, choose Insert → Module. The code module appears in the Visual Basic Editor (the result is shown in Figure 8-20). Start typing.

There is one potential snare if you paste in code from another source. Allow me to introduce the bane of my editor's existence: Smart Quotes. I write some of my code in Microsoft Word and paste it into the Visual Basic Editor. The problem is that my copy of Word is set to replace straight quotes, which look like this (") with Smart Quotes, which look like this ("). The Visual Basic Editor doesn't *like* Smart Quotes; in fact, the Visual Basic Editor generates a syntax error when it finds one. To fix this problem, copy a Smart Quote from your Word document, press Alt-F11 in Excel to run the Visual Basic Editor, choose Edit → Replace to open the Replace dialog box, paste the Smart Quote in the "Find what" field, and type a quote mark in the "Replace with" field. (You might discover that the paste function doesn't work in the "Find what" or "Replace with" fields. Thank you, Microsoft. You still can perform a paste function by pressing Ctrl-v.)

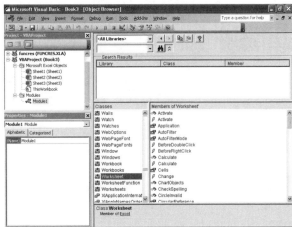

Figure 8-21. When you select an object, such as a worksheet, the Object Browser displays its properties, methods, and events.

CREATE A SUBPROCEDURE

The Annoyance: I'm fine with the built-in functions and formulas in Excel, but I want to do some things in Excel, such as displaying reminder message boxes, that I can't do with formulas. I think I need...procedures? Am I right? And if so, how do I create procedures?

The Fix: Right you are! To create a procedure that can affect Excel objects, create a Sub() procedure. To do that, create a new code module and type Sub name (), where *name* is the name of your procedure. Excel will add a corresponding End Sub() line to your module. The name of the procedure has to start with a letter, and it can't use any of VBA's reserved words, such as *Name*, *And*, *Function*, and so on.

FUN WITH VARIABLES

The Annoyance: The Excel VBA help file says I don't need to declare a variable before I use it. In other words, I can say Result=Value1/Value2 and Excel will create a new variable named Result right then and there. However, one of my programmer friends said that using variables in this way forces Excel to use the Variant datatype, which takes up a lot of memory. Is it better to

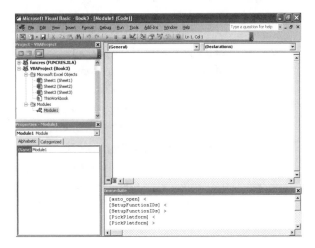

Figure 8-20. Start typing! Here's where VBA code goes.

VIEW THE OBJECT MODEL

The Annoyance: I've typed in a few macros from books and online sources, but now I'd like to create some on my own. To do that, I need to see a list of objects and their properties, methods, and events I can use. Can I display all this stuff?

The Fix: To display the Excel object model in the Visual Basic Editor, choose View → Object Browser. Figure 8-21 shows the Object Browser with the Worksheet object selected.

Click anything in the Members of Worksheet pane to display the required syntax at the bottom of the pane. You can click the objects in that topic to get Help on a particular object. You also can get a graphical view of the Excel object model by looking at the Excel Object Model topic in the Visual Basic Editor's help system.

tell Excel what type of data to expect for each variable I create?

The Fix: Your friend is partly right. Variants do take more memory than some other datatypes, but the real problem is that they don't allow *type checking*, which can let subtle errors get through. It's easy enough to define a variable's datatype with a `Dim` statement, such as the following:

```
Dim Result As Integer
```

If you like, you can define multiple variables of the same type on the same line of code, as in the following example:

```
Dim datStartDate, datEndDate As Date
```

Table 8-2 lists the scalar datatypes (basically, numbers, characters, and strings) and their characteristics.

Table 8-2. VBA datatypes.

Datatype	Value range
Byte	0 to 255
Boolean	True or False
Integer	-32,768 to 32,767
Long	-2,147,483,648 to 2,147,483,647
Double	-1.79769313486231E308 to -4.94065645841247E-324 for negative values; 4.94065645841247E-324 to 1.79769313486232E308 for positive values
Currency	-922,337,203,685,477.5808 to 922,337,203,685,477.5807
Decimal	+/-79,228,162,514,264,337,593,543,9 50,335 with no decimal point; +/-7.92 28162514264337593543950335 with 28 places to the right of the decimal; smallest non-zero number is +/-0.00000 0000000000000000000001
Date	January 1, 100 to December 31, 9999
String (variable-length)	0 to approximately 2 billion
String (fixed-length)	1 to 65,526
Variant (with numbers)	Any numeric value up to the range of a Double
Variant (with characters)	Same range as for variable-length String

To assign a value to a variable, use the equals sign, as in this line of code:

```
curSales = Range("B14").Value
```

The advantage of using a specific datatype over variants is that if you assign the wrong kind of data to a variable an error will occur. That helps you detect mistakes in your code sooner rather than later. If you need to change data from one type to another, you can always use the VBA conversion functions. For example, the following code gets a number from a user:

```
Dim num As Double, var As Variant
On Error Resume Next
var = InputBox("Enter a number.")
num = CDbl(var)
If Err Then MsgBox "You didn't enter a number."
```

DECLARE VARIABLES BEFORE USING THEM

The Annoyance: One of my most frequent programming errors is when I forget a variable name (or type it incorrectly) which causes a divide by zero error, or an empty string in my code output. I could have found and fixed the problem a lot faster if I had declared the variable in the first place, but I hate going back to the top of the procedure when I'm in mid-flow. Is there a way I can force myself to declare variables before using them?

The Fix: You bet! Display the code module you want to affect, open the Procedure drop down in the upper-right corner, and select (Declarations), which will position the cursor above the first procedure in the code module. With the cursor in that position, type in this code:

```
Option Explicit
```

Now if you attempt to use an undefined variable in any procedure in the module, Excel will display a "Variable not defined" error box and halt execution.

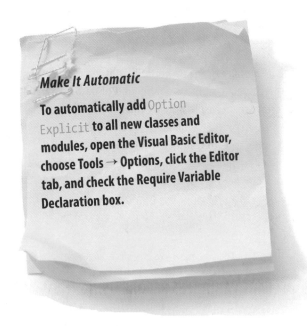

Make It Automatic

To automatically add Option Explicit to all new classes and modules, open the Visual Basic Editor, choose Tools → Options, click the Editor tab, and check the **Require Variable Declaration** box.

ADD COMMENTS TO VBA CODE

The Annoyance: I work for a local hamburger chain, and in my spare time I'm teaching myself to do simple coding in VBA. As a practice project I put together a couple of Excel workbooks to track sales, inventory, employee hours, and so on, which my bosses like so much I might get promoted away from the patty-flipping station. The only trouble is they want me to add comments to my code, but every time I try the code quits running. How do I add a comment to my VBA code?

The Fix: To add a comment to your VBA code, precede the line(s) with a single quote, as in the following example:

```
'This subroutine calculates a rep's commission.
```

CONTINUE A LINE OF CODE ON A SECOND LINE

The Annoyance: I'm concatenating some pretty long strings to create formulas for the cells in my workbook. In fact, some of the code lines are so long they go beyond the right edge of the code window. Is there some way I can let Excel know that a line of code is actually a continuation of the code on the previous line?

The Fix: To continue a line of code onto the line in the code window, type a space followed by an underscore after the last character on the line to be continued, as in this example:

```
strTargetFormula = "=" & _
ActiveCell.Offset(0,-2).Address & _
" + " & ActiveCell.Offset(0, -4).Address
```

CREATE VARIABLES THAT REFER TO OBJECTS

The Annoyance: I've had no trouble creating variables that use values from worksheet cells, but when I try to use variables to refer to worksheets themselves I keep getting errors. Here's the code I'm using...what am I doing wrong?

```
Dim shtMySheet As Worksheet
shtMySheet = ActiveWindow.ActiveSheet
```

The Fix: The problem is that you're trying to assign a worksheet (an Excel object) to a variable that's expecting a value of another sort. In other words, the Dim shtMySheet As Worksheet line, by itself, isn't enough to let Excel assign a worksheet object to the variable. To assign an Excel object to a variable, you need to use the Set keyword, as in this example:

```
Dim shtMySheet As Worksheet
Set shtMySheet = ActiveWindow.ActiveSheet
```

The Set keyword assigns a reference to the worksheet object. If you want to get rid of that reference, set the object variable to Nothing, as in the following line of code:

```
shtMySheet = Nothing
```

Setting an object variable to Nothing means that variable no longer refers to an object. That happens automatically when a procedure ends if the variable was declared within that procedure. But if the variable was declared at the module level (that is, outside of a procedure) or declared as Static, that reference stays around and can be used as long as the workbook is open.

Sometimes that's what you want—module-level variables are available across procedures, and they can be a useful way to share global settings. But in other cases, you might want to explicitly set an object variable to Nothing so that it is no longer available. An example of this occurs when you are using objects from other applications as shown by the following code:

```
Dim m_word As Object

Sub StartWord()
 ' Starts Microsoft Word invisibly.
 Set m_word = CreateObject("Word.Application")
End Sub

Sub CloseWord()
 ' Closes Microsoft Word if it is not visible.
 Set m_word = Nothing
End Sub
```

The StartWord procedure launches Microsoft Word in the background from Excel. After you run that procedure you can use Word's objects to perform word processing tasks from within Excel. When you are done, CloseWord destroys the m_word variable's reference to Word, which causes that instance of Word to quit, and recovers the considerable memory used by Word.

However, if Word has been made visible in code (m_word.Visible = True), Word won't quit when m_word is set to Nothing. That's usually what you want to do in this situation because it's good practice to let users close visible applications manually, instead of doing it automatically from code.

CREATE A FUNCTION PROCEDURE

The Annoyance: I created a procedure that calculates a sales representative's commission based on her length of service with my company, and I'd like to be able to call the procedure as if it were a standard Excel function. How do I create a procedure that I can call as a function in a worksheet cell?

The Fix: The trick is to create a function procedure. The following sample procedure shows the structure you need to follow:

```
Function Divide(Value1,Value2)As Single
 Divide = Value1/Value2
End Function
```

The first line of this procedure indicates the procedure is a function (that is, it returns a value to a worksheet), that the function's name is Divide, that it expects two inputs (Value1 and Value2), and that it returns its result as a single-precision decimal number. The second line calculates the value and returns the result, and the third line indicates the end of the procedure.

FORCE A MACRO TO AFFECT THE ACTIVE WORKBOOK

The Annoyance: I wrote a macro and linked it to a custom toolbar button I added to the Standard toolbar—which means the button appears in Excel even when that workbook (the one that contains the macro code) isn't open. Now, whenever I try to run the macro on another workbook it affects the original workbook where the code is saved, not the active workbook. What's up with that?

The Fix: You probably used ThisWorkbook instead of ActiveWorkbook as the object from which you drew the address of the currently selected cells. Excel's default behavior is to remember the last active selection on each worksheet, and to reactivate that selection when you display the worksheet. The following macro records the address of the currently selected cell range and makes that range the selection on the next worksheet in the active workbook, regardless of the last active selection on the next worksheet:

```
Sub NextSheetSameCell()
 Dim strCellAddress As String
 ' Get address of selected range.
 strCellAddress = _
 ActiveWorkbook.Selection.Address
 ' Check if this is the last sheet in workbook.
 If Worksheets.count > ActiveSheet.Index Then
 ' Not the last sheet, so activate the next one.
 ActiveSheet.Next.Activate
 Else
 ' Is the last sheet, so activate the first sheet.
 Worksheets(1).Activate
 End If
 ' Select the range.
 Range(strCellAddress).Activate
End Sub
```

PREVENT A PROCEDURE FROM BEING CALLED FROM ANOTHER WORKBOOK

The Annoyance: I created a macro to calculate my sales representatives' commissions, but I don't want anyone else on my network to be able to call the procedure from another workbook and figure out how much someone else is making. How do I do this?

The Fix: To hide a macro from other Excel users on your network, and to keep it out of the available macros list in other workbooks on your *own* computer, use the Private keyword before your procedure call, as in the following line of code:

```
Private Sub CalculateCommission()
```

Making the Sub private means you can't call it from your own Run Macro dialog box. You can, however, make it visible from your workbook, but not elsewhere, by creating the Sub in the workbook or worksheet class and declaring it as Friend:

```
' Use Friend in a class module.
Friend Sub CalculateCommission()
```

BEGONE DULL SCREEN FLICKER

The Annoyance: I created a procedure to update the cells in my workbook, but when I run it the screen flickers enough to send...viewers...into...a...trance. Is there a way to stop the flicker?

The Fix: To stop the screen from flickering as your macro runs, you need to turn off screen updating. Just add this line of code below your variable declarations:

```
Application.ScreenUpdating = False
```

Also add this line of code just above the End Sub line to turn screen updating back on:

```
Application.ScreenUpdating = True
```

SAMPLE MACROS ON THE MSDN WEB SITE

Frank Rice, an Office programming expert from Microsoft, wrote an August 2004 article on the Microsoft Developer Network (MSDN) with several macros that you can use to extend Excel's capabilities. The available macros are:

- ☒ **Export a Text File with Comma and Quote Delimiters**
- ☒ **Use Saved Property to Determine If Workbook Has Changed**
- ☒ **Concatenate Columns of Data**
- ☒ **Use Saved Property to Determine If Workbook Has Changed**
- ☒ **Total Rows and Columns in an Array**

To view the article, visit *http://msdn.microsoft.com/office/default.aspx?pull=/library/en-us/odc_xl2003_ta/html/odc_XL_Samples.asp*.

MACROS MAKE MY COMPUTER SLUGGISH

The Annoyance: I run a lot of macros, and after a while my system starts slowing down—I see a lot of excessive disk activity, too. Eventually, my computer becomes so unusable I have to reboot it. What's going on?

The Fix: It's possible that you're creating external objects, and not freeing up the memory they use when you're done. For example, you might use this line of code to start a new instance of Excel invisibly:

```
Dim m_excel As Excel.Application

Sub StartExcel()
  Set m_excel = New Excel.Application
End Sub
```

Because Excel starts invisibly, it's easy to forget it's there—but it is, and it takes up a lot of memory. To close

---

the new instance of Excel and recover the memory it uses, set m_excel to Nothing using this code:

```
Sub CloseExcel()
 Set m_excel = Nothing
End Sub
```

Incidentally, Excel and Word follow different rules when you set their object references to Nothing. Word closes only if it's not visible. Excel closes whether or not it's visible.

There are three other simple techniques you can use to make your macros run more quickly. The first line of code turns off screen updates (see previous annoyance); the second prevents Excel from recalculating page breaks when a worksheet changes (that eats up a lot of time); and the third prevents Excel from recalculating a worksheet whenever a cell is changed (that can eat up a lot of time, too):

```
Application.ScreenUpdating = False
Activesheet.DisplayPageBreaks = False
Application.Calculation = xlManual
```

USE AN IF...THEN CRITERION STATEMENT

The Annoyance: I use a table to track the hours worked by the ushers who volunteer for shows at the theater I manage. I'd like to find the rows in the table which correspond to shows during a particular month. Is there a way to find rows that correspond to performances with dates that start with the number 3, as in 3/15/2005?

The Fix: Create an If...Then criterion that finds data that fits a pattern using the Like operator, as in the following code snippet. This finds the cells that contain values which start with the number 3, records the first cell's address as first, and then updates last until there are no more occurrences:

```
Sub SelectMarch()
Dim first As Range, last As Range
' Find the first and last cells for March.
FindLike "3*",first,last
' Select the range.
Range(first,last).Select
End Sub
```

```
Sub FindLike(str As String, first As Range, _
 last As Range)
Dim cel As Range, i As Integer
For Each cel In ActiveSheet.UsedRange
If (cel.Value Like str) Then
i=i+1
If i=1 Then Set first=cel
Set last=cel
End If
Next
End Sub
```

These procedures assume that the values starting with 3 are in a list sorted by date, so all the March shows are in contiguous table rows. Table 8-3 lists the wildcard characters you can use with the Like comparison operator.

Table 8-3. Wildcard characters you can use with Like.

Wildcard	Matches
?	Any single character (e.g., bi? matches bin and bid, but not binary)
*	Zero or more characters (e.g., 2* matches 2, 20, and 200, but not 3)
#	Any single digit (e.g., 200# matches 2003, 2004, and 2005, but not 20035)
[charlist]	Any single character in charlist (e.g., bi[d, g, t] matches bid, big, and bit, but not bin)
[!charlist]	Any single character not in charlist (e.g., bi[!d, g, t] matches bin, but not bid, big, or bit)

CREATE A STRING FROM VALUES IN MORE THAN ONE CELL

The Annoyance: I want to display the address of a cell range in a message box to help me debug a procedure I'm writing. I know I'll have to add a colon in the middle to make it look like A1:A4 or whatever. How do I use VBA to create a single string from the variables in the procedure, and how do I add the colon to make the string into a valid range address?

The Fix: To combine strings, use the concatenation operator &, as in the following code:

```
strAllShows = strFirstAddress & ":" &
strLastAddress
```

This code takes the text that is stored in the variable strFirstAddress, appends a colon, and then adds the text stored in the variable strLastAddress to create a string. For example, if the text in strFirstAddress were A1 and the text stored in strLastAddress were G45, strAllShows would contain the text A1:G45.

You can use & as many times as you like to create quite long strings in VBA. Often, you'll see them continued on separate lines using the line-continuation character:

```
msg = "This is a really long message " & _
  "that I want to display in a dialog box " & _
  "but I also want to fit in the code window."
MsgBox msg
```

As I've mentioned before, a space followed by an underline (_) lets you break the code onto multiple lines, but it doesn't add line breaks to the string. To do that, add a vbCrLf constant:

```
msg = "This is a long message that I want " _
& vbCrLf & "to display in a dialog box " _
& vbCrLf & "with line breaks."
MsgBox msg
```

AFFECT EVERY MEMBER OF A COLLECTION

The Annoyance: I've got so many workbooks that half the time I don't remember how many worksheets each one has, especially if some of them are hidden. Is there a construct I can use to affect every worksheet in the workbook, regardless of how many there are? For example, could I create a procedure to make all the worksheets in a workbook visible?

The Fix: Sure. Some things, such as worksheets in a workbook or cells in a range, are part of a *collection*. To affect every member of a collection, such as each individual worksheet in the Worksheets collection, use a For Each...Next loop, as in the following procedure:

```
Sub UnhideAllSheets()
 Dim wksMySheet As Worksheet
 For Each wksMySheet In Worksheets
 wksMySheet.Visible=True
 Next wksMySheet
End Sub
```

To view a list of all collections in Excel 2003, press Alt-F11 to display the Visual Basic Editor, press F1 to display the Visual Basic help system, click the Microsoft Excel Visual Basic Reference item in the Visual Basic Help task pane, and then click Collections. Click any letter to see the collections that begin with that letter.

For previous versions of Excel, you'll need to search the help system using the term *collection* and whatever you're searching for. For example, if you want to search for the collection that contains all open Excel workbooks, you would search using the keywords *collection* and *workbook*.

RUN A MACRO WHEN AN EVENT HAPPENS

The Annoyance: I'm in the middle of creating a custom VBA solution for a client, and I'd like to run a macro that displays a message box indicating what's planned for each worksheet in the workbook whenever my customer views a worksheet. Can I do this?

The Fix: To run a macro when a specific event occurs, you must put the macro code in the body of an event procedure. Excel has a number of events defined for objects such as a workbook, a worksheet, and so on. To run a macro when a user views a worksheet, follow these steps in the Visual Basic Editor:

1. In the Project Window at the upper-left corner of the Visual Basic Editor (shown in Figure 8-22), double-click the object you want to affect. In this case, double-click Sheet 1 to display a new code window.

2. Open the Object drop down at the top left of the code window, and choose Worksheet.

3. Open the Procedure drop down at the top right, and choose Activate to have Excel create an Activate event procedure.

4. Type MsgBox ("This worksheet summarizes project A3802 expenses for Q4.") between the Sub and End Sub lines.

5. Close the Visual Basic Editor and activate Sheet 1 to view the effect of your event procedure.

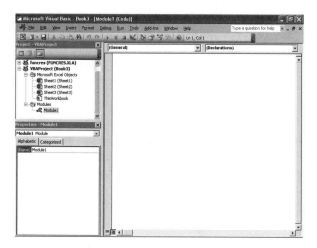

Figure 8-22. This code window is associated with the worksheet, not the workbook as a whole.

REQUIRE A PASSWORD TO VIEW VBA CODE

The Annoyance: I don't want just anyone to be able to take a look at my code. How do I password-protect a VBA code module?

The Fix: To password-protect the VBA code in a workbook, follow these steps:

1. From inside the Visual Basic Editor, Choose Tools → VBAProject Properties, click the Protection tab, and check the "Lock project for viewing" box.

2. Type a password in the Password field and again in the Confirm password field.

3. Save and close your workbook.

ABBREVIATE OBJECT REFERENCES IN VBA CODE

The Annoyance: I can create conditional formats with up to three conditions by choosing Format → Conditional Formatting, but I want to create five conditional formats for my data. I can do that easily enough in VBA with commands such as:

```
If cel.Value > 10000 Then
Worksheets("January").Range("A1").Font.Bold _
= True
```

```
Worksheets("January").Range("A1").Font.Italic _
= True
Worksheets("January").Range("A1").Font. _
ColorIndex = 30
End If
```

What irks me is having to type `Worksheets("January"). Range("A1").Font` every time. That text appears in each command in the `If...Then` statement. Is there any way to save my fingers from all that typing?

The Fix: You can abbreviate your code with a `With... End With` statement, as in the following example:

```
If cel.Value > 10000 Then
  With Worksheets("January").Range("A1").Font
      .Bold = True
      .Italic = True
      .ColorIndex = 30
  End With
End If
```

Be sure to preface each property and method with a period!

When you use `With`, you lose VBA's nifty autocomplete feature. Autocomplete is handy when you're learning VBA because it gives you a list of all the possible methods and properties when you type the period after the object name. To keep that feature, create an object reference as a shorthand instead of using `With`:

```
Dim rng As Range
Set rng = Worksheets("January").Range("A1")
rng.Font.Bold = True
rng.Font.Italic = True
rng.FontSize = 12
```

EXCEL OPENS A WORKBOOK IN REPAIR MODE

The Annoyance: I just started using a new version of Excel that IT installed on my computer this morning, and when I tried to open one of my workbooks that contains macros I saw this error message:

Errors were detected in AutoPivot.xls, but Microsoft Excel was able to open the file by making the repairs listed below. Save the file to make the repairs permanent.
Lost Visual Basic project.
Lost ActiveX controls.

Does this have something to do with Visual Basic for Applications? Excel did ask if I wanted to install Visual Basic for Applications, but I clicked No because it was already installed. I didn't save my file without the Visual Basic project (that would have erased my code), but should I have let Excel try to install VBA again?

The Fix: Actually, the Office Setup program doesn't always include VBA when it installs Office on your computer. Some network administrators have a policy of not installing it unless a manager tells them that particular users need VBA for their jobs. Not being able to run macros at all cuts down on the risk of macro viruses, for sure, but it also can get in your way.

In this case, clicking No when Excel asked if you wanted to install VBA ultimately resulted in the error message you saw. If you have access to an Office installation disk, start Excel, choose Tools → Macro → Visual Basic Editor, and click Yes to install VBA.

CAN'T SAVE FILE WITHOUT NETWORK CONNECTION

The Annoyance: One of my co-workers just ran by my office yelling that the network was going down, and I should save my work immediately. I was messing with a PivotTable in a workbook that was actually stored on another computer on the network, and I tried to save it on the remote drive by clicking the Save button as quickly as I could. I wasn't fast enough, I guess, because I saw this error message:

> *Microsoft Excel cannot access the file \\Sebastopol\ NetShare\AutoPivot.xls. You may receive this error message for the following reasons:*
> *The file name or path does not exist.*
> *The file that you are trying to open is being used by another program. Close the document in the other program, and try again.*
> *The name of the workbook that you are trying to save is the same as the name of another document that is read-only. Try saving the workbook with a different name.*

Still, I could see the worksheet on my computer screen, so I tried to save it on *my* hard disk, and I got a *Document not saved* error message. Why couldn't I save the file on my own computer, which had it in memory?

The Fix: You've encountered one of the many quirks in Excel 2000 and later. If you try to save a remote file to your own computer *after your network connection goes down*, and that file contains a PivotTable, VBA code, or embedded objects such as clip art or other Office documents, Excel can't get all the information it needs for the save. If your workbook contains none of those elements, you can save it to your own computer.

When you work with a file over a network in Excel 97, all you can do to head off this problem is save your changes frequently. In Excel 2000 and later, you can have Excel store your working copy of the remote file locally by adding two keys to your Registry: *NetworkResiliency* and *PivotTableNetworkResiliency*. Any changes you make will be written to your computer's memory; when you save the workbook, Excel writes all changes to the file on the remote computer.

To begin with, back up your Registry! For instructions, see the sidebar titled "Always Back Up Your Registry" earlier in this chapter. Then, to add the keys, follow these steps:

1. Start Regedit (Start → Run → Regedit) and navigate to the *HKEY_CURRENT_USER\Software\Microsoft\ Office\version\Excel\Options* key, where *version* is the Excel version you're using. For Excel 2000, it's 9; for Excel 2002, it's 10; and for Excel 2003, it's 11.

2. Right-click the Options subfolder in the left pane and choose New → DWORD Value.

3. Replace the default NewValue #1 name in the right-hand pane with the name `NetworkResiliency`.

4. Double-click the new NetworkResiliency entry and type `1` in the Value data field. If you're using Excel 2000, you can now close the Registry Editor and restart Excel. If you're using any later version of Excel, continue on to step 5.

5. In Excel 2002 and later, right-click the Options subfolder in the left pane and choose New → DWORD Value.

6. Replace the new NewValue #2 name in the righthand pane with the name **PivotTableNetworkResiliency**.

7. Double-click the new PivotTableNetworkResiliency entry and type **1** in the Value data field.

8. Close the Registry Editor and restart Excel.

These two keys tell Excel to create a full copy of the workbook in your local computer's temporary file directory. (Note: your files will take longer to open and save.) You'll still see the long error message shown previously if you lose your network connection and you attempt to save a workbook that contains a PivotTable, a VBA code module, or an embedded object. But because Excel has written a full copy of the workbook to your computer, not just a list of the changes between the original file and the edited version, you will be able to save the file to your local computer even though you've lost contact with the original file.

RUNTIME RUNAROUND

The Annoyance: I like to use the `MROUND()` function, which lets you round a value up to the nearest *x*. For example, the formula `=MROUND(A8, 4)` rounds the value in A8 to the closest multiple of 4. If the value in A8 were 6, the function would return 8. I also like the `MROUND()` function because I can use it in my VBA code without having to use the `Application.WorksheetFunctions` notation I usually have to write to call a workbook function. So, instead of typing `ActiveCell.Value = Application.WorksheetFunctions.Mround(A8, 4)` I can just write `ActiveCell.Value = Mround(A8, 4)` in my code modules. That saves me time and typing, which is very cool.

However, when I tried to run a workbook that uses the `MROUND()` function on a co-worker's computer I was rewarded with this error message:

Run-time error '1004': 'ATPVBAEN.XLA' could not be found. Check the spelling of the file name, and verify that the file location is correct.

What's going on? Why can't I use my function?

The Fix: The problem is that your macro is calling the `MROUND()` function from the Analysis ToolPak add-in—and although your co-worker might have the Analysis ToolPak installed, if the Analysis ToolPak VBA add-in *isn't* installed, you're out of luck. To install the Analysis Tool-Pak VBA add-in, choose Tools → Add-Ins, check the Analysis ToolPak-VBA box, and click OK. You don't even have to restart Excel to be able to run your macro!

The following VBA procedure shows how to test if an add-in is installed:

```
Private Sub Workbook_Open()
 If CheckAddin("ATPVBAEN.XLA") = False Then _
 MsgBox "Please install Analysis ToolPak adding " & _
 "before using macros in this workbook."
End Sub

Function CheckAddin(addname As String) As
Boolean
 Dim ad As AddIn, res As Boolean
 res = False
 ' Check for the addin in the Addins collection.
 For Each ad In AddIns
 ' If found, return true.
 If ad.Name = addname Then res = True
 Next
 CheckAddin = res
End Function
```

Excel VBA for Engineers and Scientists

Most of Excel's resources are geared toward the business community, but Gilberto E. Urroz of Utah State University has put together a great free resource for students in his Numerical Methods in Engineering I class. It includes solutions for linear equation solutions, numerical integration, and trigonometric equations. Download it from *http://www.engineering.usu.edu/cee/faculty/gurro/Software_Calculators/ExcelVBA/ExcelVBAExamples.htm*.

RANGE.CALCULATE ERROR

The Annoyance: I'm trying to run a macro in a workbook that uses a lot of VLOOKUP() formulas. I don't want Excel to have to recalculate all the formulas in the workbook, so I use the Range.Calculate method to specify the cells I want to recalculate. For example, the statement Range("A4:A5").Calculate would recalculate the formulas in cells A4 and A5. The only problem is that when I try to run my macro on my colleague's computer, I see this error message:

> Run-time error '1004'
> Calculate method of Range class failed

What's going on? The macro runs perfectly well on my computer.

The Fix: The problem is that you're trying to use the Range.Calculate method on a workbook that has the Manual calculation option selected and the Iteration checkbox checked. These workbook settings prevent the Range.Calculate method from working properly, resulting in the error you encountered. To get rid of the problem, choose Tools → Options, click the Calculation tab, and select the Automatic option, or uncheck the Iteration box. Or both.

If you'd rather automate the process, you can check the calculation method in code before calling the Calculate method as shown here:

```
Dim rng As Range
Set rng = Selection
If Application.Calculation = _
  xlCalculationManual Then
    Application.Calculation =_
      xlCalculationAutomatic
    rng.Calculate
 Application.Calculation = xlCalculationManual
Else
rng.Calculate
End If
```

HANDY VBA PROCEDURES

CREATE A WORKBOOK WITH A WORKSHEET FOR EACH MONTH

The Annoyance: I have a group of administrative users who occasionally need to create a workbook with a worksheet for each month of the year. I could do it using a template, but I'd rather automate the process and let them create the workbook by clicking a toolbar button. Is there a VBA procedure I can run that can do this?

The Fix: The following procedure will do the job. It even names the worksheets with the abbreviated month name and puts the sheets in chronological order!

```
Sub YearByMonth()
Dim intSheetCount As Integer
Workbooks.Add
Worksheets.Add Count:=12 - _
ActiveWorkbook.Worksheets.Count
For intSheetCount = 1 To 12
Worksheets(intSheetCount).Name = _
Format(DateSerial(1, intSheetCount, 1), "mmm")
Next intSheetCount
End Sub
```

PICK RANDOM ENTRIES FROM A LIST

The Annoyance: I'm setting up auditions for a play and I want to pair the male actors I've invited to the second round of auditions with the female actors I've called back. The names of the men are stored in cells A2:A8; the names of the women are stored in cells B2:B8. How can I pick entries from two equal-length lists at random, and without repeats?

The Fix: Well, actually, you need to pick only one set of values at random. If one list changes order, the other one doesn't have to. You can use this code to solve the problem:

```
Sub PickAtRandom()
Dim i As Integer, intRank As Integer
```

```
Randomize
Range("B2").Select

For i = 8 To 14
  ActiveCell.Offset(i, 0).Value = _
  ActiveCell.Offset(i - 8, 0).Value
  ActiveCell.Offset(i - 8, 2).Value = Rnd
Next i

For i = 8 To 14
intRank = Application.WorksheetFunction.Rank _
(ActiveCell.Offset(i - 8, 2).Value, _
Range("D2:D8"))
ActiveCell.Offset(i, 1).Value = _
ActiveCell.Offset(intRank - 1, 1).Value
Next i

End Sub
```

GENERATE NONREPEATING RANDOM VALUES

The Annoyance: I'm a teacher, and I try to call
on each of my 20 students during a class period. But instead of going in alphabetical order, or desk by desk, I
prefer to do it at random. It would be great if I could use
Excel to create a list of random values tied to the students' names. Unfortunately, although I have only 30 students in my class, when I use Excel's random number generator it generates repeat numbers and I have to go
through a couple of pages of random numbers before I get
through even the first 20 students. I'm sufficiently over-
whelmed already without adding to my class workload.
Can I generate a list of unique random values so that I
need only 30 numbers to call on all 30 students?

The Fix: To create a list of random values in a given
cell range, copy this into a code module and run it:

```
Sub UniqueRandomNumbers()
Dim rngCell As Range, rngCheckRange As Range
Dim rngRangeObject As Range
Dim intTemp As Integer, intCellCount As Integer
Dim strPrompt As String

strPrompt = "Select the cells you want to " & _
  "fill with unique random values."
```

```
Set rngCheckRange = _
  Application.InputBox(Prompt:=strPrompt, _
  Type:=8)

intCellCount = rngCheckRange.Cells.Count
MsgBox (intCellCount)

rngCheckRange.ClearContents

For Each rngCell In rngCheckRange
intTemp = Int(intCellCount * Rnd) + 1
Set rngRangeObject = _
  rngCheckRange.Find(intTemp, lookat:=xlWhole)
While Not rngRangeObject Is Nothing
intTemp = Int(intCellCount * Rnd) + 1
Set rngRangeObject = _
  rngCheckRange.Find(intTemp, lookat:=xlWhole)
Wend
rngCell.Value = intTemp
Next rngCell

End Sub
```

ANOTHER ARCADE CLASSIC

In my continuing quest to destroy office productivity, I now bring you *Unbreakable*, a free
version of the arcade classic *Arkanoid*. As with his
Pac-Man and *Space Invaders* clones, programmer
Kouichi Tani uses each cell in a worksheet as a
pixel in his games. You can download *Unbreakable* from *http://www.xl-logic.com/xl_files/
games/unbreakable.zip*. Just unzip the file and
start playing…the directions are all there.

Excel 2003
ANNOYANCES

Excel's basic functions haven't changed in years. Of course, Microsoft has to add new stuff to give you a reason to upgrade to the latest version. In Excel 2003, that reason was support for the Extensible Markup Language (XML). XML lets you transfer data between applications without worrying about whether your programs know how to open some other program's files. And although Microsoft didn't invent XML, it did come up ways that make the XML/Office 2003 combination appealing for business folks. XML is seriously cool, but it does require some explaining. (You can get Microsoft's take on using XML with Office and other applications at *http://msdn.microsoft.com/xml/*. For O'Reilly's detailed take, check out *Office 2003 XML*, which focuses on using XML with Word, Excel, Access, and Infopath.)

Unfortunately, Excel 2003 also includes some new and interesting ways to break down. For example, the random number generator, which is supposed to generate a decimal value between 0 and 1, sometimes generates negative numbers. And there's also a bug which causes the chart tool to come up with a sum of squares that's a *negative* number—quite impossible unless you're working with imaginary numbers.

Oh, yes…I almost forgot: Excel can crash if you try to run it with another graphics-intensive program. Microsoft has designed Office 2003 to compete for the same video resources that games and other full-screen programs need, and sometimes your computer just gives up. You might be able to minimize this problem by turning off your video card's hardware acceleration; instructions and more follow.

EXCEL 2003 LIST ANNOYANCES

CREATE A LIST

The Annoyance: I've used data lists since my first days with Excel back in the early 1990s. They let me create PivotTables, sort and filter my data, and transfer data to and from databases easily.

I was pleased to see that 2003's Data menu now has a List submenu. When I clicked Data → List → Create List, I saw a dialog box that seemed to want me to select a range of cells, but I chickened out and backed away. Are the lists in Excel 2003 much different from the data lists I use to create PivotTables and filters and such? What the heck are these new lists, and should I convert my old lists to the new type?

The Fix: In Excel 2003, lists are a formalization of the loosely defined data lists you've used in previous versions. For example, in Excel 2002 and earlier versions, when you created PivotTables from a data list the cells in the list were just regular worksheet cells—data columns with headers and no blank lines. (See "What's a Data List?" in Chapter 4 for a fuller definition.) A list in Excel 2003 doesn't look very different, as you can see in Figure 9-1, but there's a bit more going on under the hood.

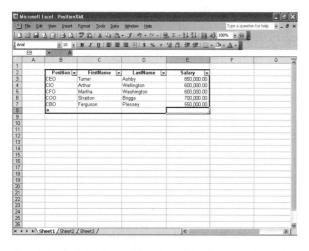

Figure 9-1. Excel 2003 lists combine filters and data forms to make your data entry life easier.

The lists in Excel 2003 combine the best features of filters and data forms—now there's a data entry row at the bottom of a list. Now you can add a total row to the bottom of the list by selecting any cell in the list and choosing Data → List → Total Row. And now you can move around in a list as if it were an Access table. In fact, if you use Access, the bottom row of an Excel 2003 data list should be quite familiar because it's the same data entry row you'll find at the bottom of Access tables displayed in datasheet view. To enter data into the list, press the Tab key to move to the next field, or Shift-Tab to move to the previous field. When you press Tab after filling in the last cell in the row, Excel creates a new row for you and moves the total row (if you added one) down as well. The upshot of moving the total row is that you don't need to create a SUBTOTAL() formula and add a new row whenever you want to add data to a list. The filter arrows at the right edge of each column label let you limit the data displayed in the list.

If you're wondering whether you should change your existing lists into the new Excel 2003 type of list, the answer is that you probably don't need to if you don't expect the list to grow, you don't need to filter it, or you will never need to summarize the data in the list without creating a PivotTable. Of course, if your answer to any of those questions is yes...

To turn an existing list into an official Excel 2003 data list, follow these steps:

1. Select the list and choose Data → List → Create List to display the Create List dialog box (shown in Figure 9-2).

Figure 9-2. Here's where you make the transition from an unstructured data list to a structured data list.

2. Make sure the "Where is the data for your list?" field shows the correct range of cells. If it doesn't, click the Collapse Dialog button to the right of the field, select the cells in the worksheet that hold your data list, and press Enter.

3. If your data list has headers, check the "My list has headers" box and click OK.

To create a new data list, select a row of blank cells that span the desired width of your list, choose Data → List → Create List, and click OK.

XML EDITING AND MORE

The world of XML grows increasingly complex every day. Where there were only simple XML development tools available a few years ago, you can now use XML with databases, to represent styles in addition to data structures, or to translate HTML tables into XML data. One powerful package you should try is the Stylus Studio XML program suite from Sonic Software. You can download a 10-day trial version of the package from *http://www.stylusstudio.com/xml_download.html* (extended to 30 days if you register); be prepared for a powerful tool with a lot of options. In addition to three XML editors (one of which is shown in the following figure), the suite includes tools to generate XML maps, to create extensible style sheets that conform to the XSLT standard, to create database queries using the XQUERY standard, and to generate statements that mix SQL and XML. Stylus Studio includes built-in support for SQL Server, Informix, IBM DB/2, Oracle, and Sybase, but there is also a facility to link to other databases such as Microsoft Access.

Stylus Studio costs $395 for a single user, though Sonic Software offers price breaks if you purchase a multiuser license.

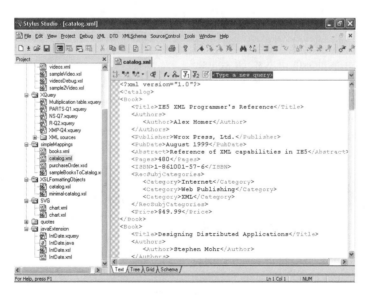

Stylus Studio is a powerful and versatile tool for working with XML.

REMOVE LIST BORDERS

The Annoyance: I guess the Excel programming team must be pretty proud of their new list feature because they go out of their way to make sure the lists stand out on your worksheet. While I'm entering data into a list, Excel surrounds the list with a blue border—which is fine. The problem is that Excel leaves that blue border around *every* list, whether I'm editing it or not, and it's distracting. My worksheets are complicated enough already. Can I hide the borders?

The Fix: To hide the borders, choose Data → List → Hide border of inactive lists.

EXCEL 2003 XML ANNOYANCES

GET A GRIP ON XML

The Annoyance: A big company just acquired my company, so we need to change all our business processes to match theirs. One of the changes we'll have to make is to convert our data into Extensible Markup Language (XML) formats so that we can move the data among applications with a minimum of fuss. Of course, the "minimum of fuss" kicks in only after we get all our data into XML in the first place. I've done some reading, but I don't have a firm handle on how the standard works, or how to implement it in Excel. How can I find out what I need to know?

The Fix: Think of XML as a language that lets you store information *about* your data right along with the data itself; something city slickers call *metadata*. In contrast to the Hypertext Markup Language (HTML), which only specifies how data will be displayed in a web browser, XML records whether a piece of data is a name, a position title, a product category, or whatever. Here's what it looks like. (The following bit of XML defines a structure you could use to store information about a company's officers.)

```
<element name="Officer" maxOccurs="unbounded">
<complexType>
<sequence>
<element name="Title" type="string" />
<element name="FirstName" type="string" />
<element name="LastName" type="string" />
<element name="Salary" type="decimal" />
</sequence>
</complexType>
</element>
```

When you look past the procedural information in the declarations, you can see that you're creating a data structure named `Officer` that stores an individual's title, first name, last name, and salary. There are nuances, of course, but the basic premise remains the same: you use XML to define a structure, or schema, which is both computer-readable and (more or less) human-readable.

Once you've established the schema, you can populate a datafile with your XML data. The following code listing shows what a datafile with information on two corporate officers would look like:

```
<?xml version="1.0" encoding="UTF-8" ?>
<Root xmlns:xsi="http://www.w3.org/2001/
XMLSchema-instance" xsi:noNamespaceSchemaLocation
="Officers.xsd">
<Officer>
 <Title>CEO</Title>
 <FirstName>Turner</FirstName>
 <LastName>Ashby</LastName >
 <Salary>850000</Salary>
</Officer>
<Officer>
 <Title>CIO</Title>
 <FirstName>Arthur</FirstName>
 <LastName>Wellington</LastName >
 <Salary>600000</Salary>
</Officer>
</Root>
```

If you're new to XML, the first thing you should do is visit the World Wide Web Consortium's overview site at *http://www.w3schools.com/xml/*, where you can find lots of information about XML and its syntax, as well as links to tools that can help you create and use XML documents. You also should look back at the "And Now...a Quick Overview of Database Technology" sidebar in Chapter 6.

INFER A SCHEMA FROM XML DATA

The Annoyance: My boss just emailed me an XML datafile that I need to get into Excel. I've looked over examples of XML schemas and visited various tutorial sites, but I absolutely do not have the time to create a schema on my own to match my boss's datafile. Isn't the whole idea of XML to make it easier to exchange data? The way I figure, that *ought* to mean I can import the data into Excel without using up too much of my valuable time. Right? Right??

The Fix: If the file you want to import contains valid XML data, but doesn't contain a reference to a schema (a file with a *.xsd* extension which Excel—or any other XML-enabled application—uses to create the data structures into which it will import the data) Excel can infer the schema from the data. To import the data and have Excel infer the schema, click the cell you want to be the top-left corner in the new list in your Excel worksheet, and choose Data → XML → Import. Navigate to the file and double-click it. At this point, Excel displays a dialog box indicating that it can't find a valid schema and that it will attempt to infer one from the data in the file. Click OK twice to bring the data into Excel. To view the schema Excel created, choose Data → XML → XML Source to display the XML Source task pane, which contains the schema.

TROUBLESHOOT IMPORTING SCHEMAS

The Annoyance: Some days I just can't win. I imported the data my boss sent me with no trouble, but now one of our egghead IT guys sent me *another* XML datafile. He claims that it works perfectly well for him in Access, but Excel choked on it and told me it couldn't import the data because it contained unsupported elements. What the...? Does Excel know how to do XML or not?

The Fix: The straight answer is that Excel knows how to do *some* XML, but not *all* XML. When you get a bunch of computer nerds together, they are capable of creating some complex techniques that work perfectly well for anyone initiated into the fraternity, but are quite confusing for the rest of us. I've included a list of unsupported XML schema constructs here. I recommend opening your IT guy's XML datafile in Notepad and searching for the following tags—none of which Excel supports. I can't tell you how to fix your XML datafile without destroying important data, but even if you don't find one of these tags in the file, you have a lot of things to tell your IT guy to look for:

- `<any>` is a wildcard tag that lets you include elements not declared in the schema.

- `<anyAttribute>` is a wildcard tag that lets you include attributes not declared in the schema

- `<substitutionGroup>` is a tag that lets you substitute any tag in the group for another tag in the group.

- Excel does not support recursive structures that are more than one level deep, such as using a `<person>` element inside another `<person>` element to describe family relations.

- Excel does not support abstract elements, which are used to create expandable element collections. For example, the schema statement:

      <xsd:element name="Publication"
      abstract="true" type="PublicationType"/>

  lets you define elements in your XML code as you go, as with a statement such as:

      <xsd:element name="Book" substitutionGroup=
      "Publication" type="BookType"/>

  which creates a new element named Book that takes on the characteristics defined for the abstract element Publication. Basically, if your schema contains the text string abstract="true", it won't work in Excel.

- Excel doesn't allow you to have any other types of tags, such as HTML tags, in your XML document. If you do, Excel will die a horrible death.

STEP THROUGH AN XML SCHEMA

The Annoyance: I understand that I need to create a schema to define my XML data structures. The problem is that I don't have a clear idea of what such a schema looks like, or how I can go about creating one in Excel 2003. Are there tools I can use to create a schema without worrying about the fine details?

The Fix: The rules for creating a schema go beyond the scope of this book, but you can find out more about them by visiting that XML site I mentioned earlier, *http://www.w3schools.com/xml/*. Having said that, I'll try to give you a quick example of what an XML schema looks like. The following XML code listing represents the XML schema for the data in Figure 9-3. This process is very much the same as defining the fields in a database table—you assign a name, their position in the document, and the type of data they can hold.

```
<?xml version="1.0" encoding="utf-8" ?>
<schema xmlns="http://www.w3.org/2001/XMLSchema">
<element name="Root">
<complexType>
<sequence>

<element name="Officer" maxOccurs="unbounded">
<complexType>
<sequence>
<element name="Title" type="string" />
<element name="FirstName" type="string" />
<element name="LastName" type="string" />
<element name="Salary" type="decimal" />
</sequence>
</complexType>
</element>
</sequence>
</complexType>
</element>
</schema>
```

It's usually a good idea to match the XML element names to the column labels in your worksheets—consistency reduces confusion. In this case, the Title, FirstName, LastName, and Salary elements in the schema map directly to the column labels in *PositionXML.xls* as shown in Figure 9-3.

So, how do you go about creating a schema? If you're an experienced XML coder, or a masochist (or both) you can do it in Notepad, the Windows text editor program. But if you value your time and sanity, use a dedicated XML editor. The instructors at the World Wide Web Consortium's XML school recommend XMLSpy from Altova. You can download a free copy of XMLSpy Home Edition from *http://www.altova.com/download_spy_home.html*. The folks at PerfectXML, an XML consultancy, recommend Syntext Serna. It will set you back $299, but you can download a free trial from *http://www.syntext.com/*.

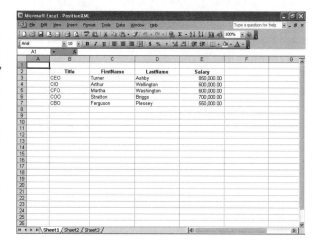

Figure 9-3. The structure described in the schema matches the structure of the data in this worksheet.

After you create your schema you must save it as a *.xsd* file. In Notepad, choose File → Save As, click in the File name field, and enter a filename with a *.xsd* extension. Be sure to use quotes around the filename, or Notepad will add a *.txt* extension, which you don't want. For instance, you might type in "sales.xsd"—including the quote marks. Then press Enter. It's important to save your file with a *.xsd* extension, so other applications will recognize the text file as an XML schema document.

To determine whether your schema is well-formed, use the online schema validator at *http://apps.gotdotnet.com/xmltools/xsdvalidator/*.

If you have two supposedly similar XML files that produce different results when you import the data into Excel, you can highlight the differences between them by running the XML Diff demo on *http://apps.gotdotnet.com/xmltools/xmldiff/*. Click the Download link on the left to save the XML Diff program to your PC.

CREATE A DATA MAP

The Annoyance: OK, I took the time to create an XML schema that I can use with Excel, Access, Word, and whatever other XML-enabled programs there are out there. I'd love to start entering data into an Excel worksheet so that I'll actually have some data to export to those other programs, but I can't figure out how to assign the schema to my worksheet so that Excel knows the data goes with the schema. Please tell me I didn't learn all that stuff for nothing.

The Fix: Actually, you assign an XML schema to a worksheet by defining a correspondence between schema elements and worksheet columns. This correspondence, called an *XML map*, is the key to using custom XML constructions in Excel.

To create a data map in a blank worksheet, follow these steps:

1. Choose Data → XML → XML Source to display the XML Source task pane.
2. Click the XML Maps button to open the XML Maps dialog box. Click the Add button, navigate to your *.xsd* file, click Open, and then click OK to add your schema to the list of available data maps in the XML Source task pane (shown in Figure 9-4).

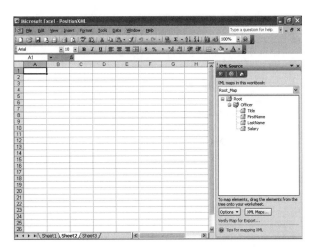

Figure 9-4. Use your schema to structure the data you enter into your worksheet.

3. Drag the first element below the root (in this case, the Officer element) to the cell where you want the first column to start. The result appears in Figure 9-5.

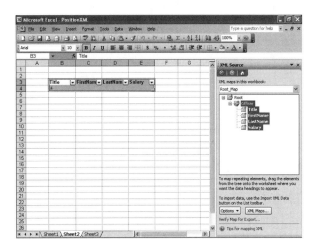

Figure 9-5. When you drag an element with subelements to your worksheet, Excel creates a list based on your schema.

To remove an element from a data map, right-click the element name in the XML Source task pane and choose Remove Element.

POPULATE AN XML-MAPPED WORKBOOK

The Annoyance: I was so successful creating a schema for my customer contact information that my boss asked me to modify that schema a bit so that he could save *his* contact info in Excel as well. It was no problem adding a few extra elements, such as customer birthdays, anniversaries, and so on, in an Excel file. The schema corresponds perfectly to his data, but there's no obvious way to import the data from his XML customer contact datafile to his worksheet. Where's the command hiding?

The Fix: To import data into a mapped worksheet, you need to use the XML submenu. To import your data, choose Data → XML → Import, browse to the datafile, and click the Import button.

EXPORT DATA FROM AN XML-MAPPED WORKBOOK

The Annoyance: I created a schema, mapped it to my worksheet, and brought in my data. Fine. But now I can't export my data from Excel! I tried choosing File → Save As and selecting the XML Spreadsheet file type, but I didn't get the data! Excel just created a new workbook saved as an XML file. When I opened the resulting XML file in Notepad I saw thousands of what I assume were spreadsheet-related XML codes that absolutely don't match the minimalist schema I created for my data. I'm starting to lose it. What did I do wrong?

The Fix: If you want to export the data from your list to a separate XML file, click any cell in the list and choose Data → XML → XML Source. Then, in the XML Source task pane, click the Verify Map for Export link at the bottom. You need to verify your schema for export because there are a number of schema types that Excel can't export. The first limitation is that you can't export data from a list that contains a sublist. For example, if you created a list of orders and created a sublist enumerating the parts ordered, you wouldn't be able to export the orders list. You also can't export XML data that contains an element that's supposed to occur only once (in XML-speak, where the maxoccurs attribute is set to 1). When Excel attempts to export the data, it creates multiple instances of the element.

After you verify that the map is OK to export, choose Data → XML → Export, type a filename, and click Export. When you open that file in Notepad, you'll see your data in all its minimalist glory.

EXCEL 2003 MENU AND FUNCTION ANNOYANCES

CLOSE BUTTON IS UNAVAILABLE

The Annoyance: I use Excel 2003 at work, where we also have the Novell GroupWise office collaboration package installed on our network. We installed GroupWise after Office, and as soon as we did, the Close button at the top-right corner of the Excel window went gray and quit responding. I can still choose File → Exit to quit Excel, but I prefer to use the Close box. Why is it unavailable?

ANOTHER GAME TO WHILE AWAY YOUR...UH...PERSONAL TIME

Remember the kid's game of Connect 4? An Excel version is available from *http://www.xl-logic.com/xl_files/games/connect4.zip* (and shown in the following figure). Just download *connect4.zip*, unzip the file (it contains a single workbook), and start playing. You can play against another human or against a built-in neural network-based program that creator Guy Cartwright wrote for the game. Yes, there is a pattern you can follow to win every time when you have red and move first, but I challenge you to go beyond the pattern and test your wits against the program! I should note that the program code doesn't find the winning sequence for red, even though it gets the first two moves right and the next move forcing victory is obvious to a human player.

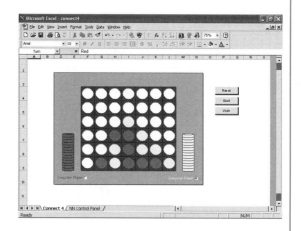

This game is fun, but the code behind it is also interesting.

The Fix: The problem, as I'm sure you figured out already, is a nasty interaction between Excel and Group-Wise. GroupWise versions 5.1, 5.2, and 5.5 (at least) store a number of add-ins in the Excel startup folder, and other places, that they use to control how certain Excel functions are executed.

If you can live with your Close box being unavailable, or if your network administrator doesn't want you to disable the GroupWise functionality, don't get rid of the add-ins. However, if you do want to use the Close box and removing the GroupWise add-ins won't mess up how you interact with your network, you can remove all instances of the add-in file *Gwxlus.xla* (for GroupWise 5.1) or *Gwxl97.xla* (for GroupWise 5.2 or later) and restore the Close box. To restore your Close box, follow these steps:

1. Quit Excel, right-click My Computer, and select Explore. Then delete the appropriate GroupWise file from the C:\Program Files\Microsoft Office\Office11\ Xlstart folder.

2. Back in Excel, click Tools → Options, click the General tab, and examine the field titled "At startup, open all files in:". If a folder is listed in that field, return to Windows Explorer, open that folder, and delete the *Gwxl97.xla* or *Gwxlus.xla* file.

3. Run Excel and choose View → Toolbars → Customize, click the Toolbars tab, check the Worksheet Menu Bar box, and click the Reset button. Click OK when Excel asks you if you're sure you want to reset the changes made to the Standard toolbar. Click the Close button.

CHART TOOL GENERATES WRONG R-SQUARED VALUE

The Annoyance: As part of my statistical demonstrations, I like to create a chart with a trend line to show how the data progresses. I generally have Excel calculate and display an R-squared value, which indicates how well the trend line fits the data. Excel's statistical problems have been well documented, but the statistics suite built into Excel 2003 is better (though still not perfect). The problem is that the R-squared value the Excel

2003 chart tool calculates is different from the value that the LINEST() worksheet function generates for the same data set. I encountered the same problem in earlier versions of Excel: the R-squared values were never right when I checked the Set Intercept = 0 box. What's going on, and how do I fix it?

What the Heck Is an R-Squared Value?

An R-squared value is a measure of how well a linear regression line approximates a data series. If every plotted point on the linear regression line fits the data set (meaning both lines have the same slope and cross the vertical axis at the same point), the R-squared value is 1.

The Fix: The problem is that the Excel chart tool has its own linear regression routine which isn't always accurate. It doesn't call the LINEST() function, which was upgraded in Excel 2003 (and which provides the correct answer). To calculate the correct R-squared value in Excel 2003, follow these steps:

1. If necessary, choose Tools → Add-Ins, check both the Analysis ToolPak and Analysis ToolPak-VBA boxes, and click OK to install the Analysis ToolPak add-in.

2. Then choose Tools → Data Analysis → Regression to display the Regression dialog box (shown in Figure 9-6).

3. Check the Constant is Zero box and click OK to generate a new worksheet with your data (shown in Figure 9-7, reformatted slightly).

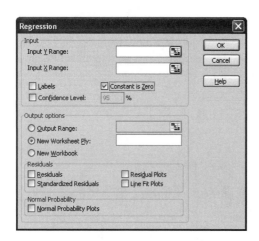

Figure 9-6. Use the Regression dialog box to perform a detailed statistical analysis of your data.

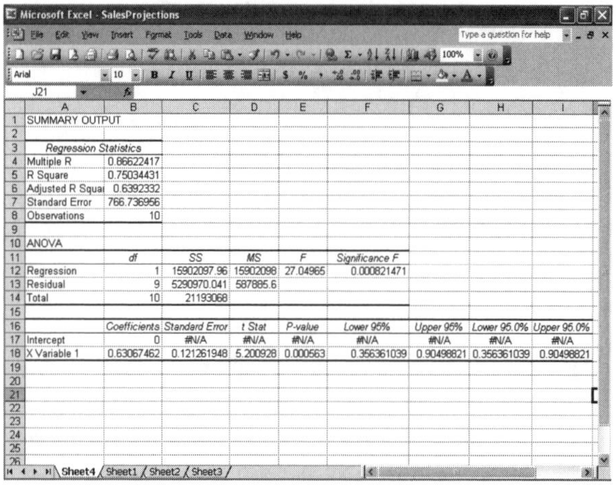

Figure 9-7. These statistics tell you how closely your projections match your empirical data.

EXCEL RANDOM NUMBER GENERATOR GENERATES NEGATIVE NUMBERS

The Annoyance: I teach statistics at a large university, and I have to come up with demonstrations that can hold the attention of the 500 students sitting in my lecture hall. I have a system that projects my laptop's display onto a screen, and one of my regular lectures uses the RAND() function in Excel to show how little statistical measures such as average and standard deviation change when applied to large random data collections. I just upgraded to Excel 2003, and to my horror, when I tried using the RAND() function at a recent lecture, after a few recalculations I saw negative numbers in my worksheet! RAND() never generated negative numbers before, and it's not supposed to do so now! What's going on?

> **Big Fun with RAND()**
>
> If you want to impress your friends and students, you can make it appear that Excel is going through a huge number of calculations before coming up with an answer. Just fill every cell displayed on your screen with the formula =RAND() and hold down the F9 key. With a little formatting and a wacky font, you can make it look like a screen from *The Matrix*. Wasn't that exciting? OK, go back to work.

The Fix: There's a bug in Excel 2003's random number generator. The good news is that the problem shows up only after a large number of recalculations. The bad news is that, at least until Microsoft releases Office 2003 Service Pack 1, you'll have to beg Microsoft for the patch. The company's explanation for making you contact them is that the rep needs to decide whether you really need the hotfix. Because the hotfix isn't as fully tested as a Service Pack, Microsoft is reluctant to distribute it to anyone who doesn't really need it. If you don't feel it's worth the trouble to contact them, (they figure) you don't need it.

You can find out lots more about the hotfix, and how to request it, at *http://support.microsoft.com/default. aspx?kbid=833855*. The hotfix also solves some other problems, such as Excel quitting after you delete cells and recalculate a worksheet.

EXCEL 2003 PROGRAM INTERACTION ANNOYANCES

CAN'T EXPORT A WEB PAGE TO AN EXCEL WORKBOOK

The Annoyance: My company uses an intranet to make documents available to our workers in satellite offices, and one of my colleagues publishes her workbooks to a web page. In the past, all I've had to do to save one of her web worksheets to my hard drive is to right-click the sheet in my web browser and choose Export to Microsoft Excel from the shortcut menu. Everything worked fine until I reinstalled Office in a new directory. Now, when I click Export to Microsoft Excel, nothing happens. I don't see any error messages or get any sort of warning, and I still can use both Internet Explorer and Excel, but the web workbook doesn't open in Excel as it's supposed to. What's going on?

The Fix: The problem is that when you changed the location of Excel on your computer, Internet Explorer lost track of the Excel executable and can no longer launch it when you try to export the web file. You can either reinstall Office 2003 to its original directory, or you can follow these steps to edit your Registry so that Internet Explorer knows where to find Excel. (Note: editing your Registry is an advanced exercise. If you're not comfortable doing this, get someone to help you—or just reinstall.)

1. Choose Start → Run, type `Regedit`, and press Enter.
2. Choose File → Export → All, type a name for the exported backup copy of the Registry, and press Enter.
3. Navigate to HKEY_CURRENT_USER\Software\Microsoft\Internet Explorer\MenuExt\Export to Microsoft Excel.
4. Right-click Export to Microsoft Excel and choose Delete
5. Right-click the MenuExt folder and choose New → Key.

6. Rename the key `Export to Microsoft Excel`.
7. In the right pane, double-click (Default).
8. In the Edit String field, type `res:// drive \ path \EXCEL.EXE/3000`, where *drive* is the letter of the drive where Excel is installed, and *path* is the full path to the *Excel.exe* file.
9. Exit Regedit and restart your computer.

EXCEL CRASHES WHEN I RUN LIVEMEETING

The Annoyance: I'm the Excel guy at my company, so I end up doing a lot of training. While I was trying to show folks the new XML capabilities in Excel 2003, Excel crashed. Just before it did, I received the following, highly informative message:

Microsoft Excel has encountered a problem and needs to close. We are sorry for the inconvenience.

What happened? Nothing like this ever happened when I did my training with Excel 2000.

The Fix: All the Office 2003 programs, Excel included, compete with other programs for direct access to your display. These programs all try to write their changes to the display memory buffer through the Display Control Interface (DCI) or GDI+ (the .NET class for two-dimensional graphics, imaging, and typography that's used in Office 2003). Some possible factors leading to the crash are:

- DCI times out due to heavy system resource usage.
- Another program locks the DCI.
- The DCI resigns under pressure from the White House (sorry, flashing back to my work in the defense industry in D.C.).
- Another program changes the Windows display mode.
- A program claims the full screen through a DirectX call.
- You reposition a window (oh, *that's* great...).

The most likely time for such a crash to occur is when you're running LiveMeeting or a game that claims an entire window.

You can avoid this problem by not running games, or other graphics-intensive programs, while Excel is open, but if that's not an option, go ahead and turn off your video card's hardware acceleration routine. Here's how you do it in Windows XP:

1. Choose Start → Settings → Control Panel, double-click Display, click the Settings tab, click the Advanced button, and click the Troubleshoot tab (the resulting page appears in Figure 9-8).

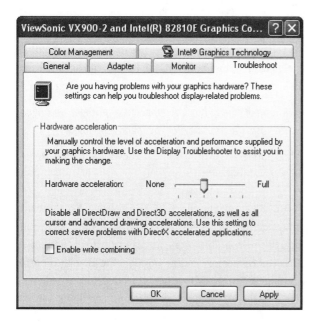

Figure 9-8. Go here to prevent Excel from crashing when you run other graphics-heavy programs.

2. Slide the Hardware acceleration control to the third tick from the left. The specific message you'll see depends on your graphics controller; on my system it says *Use this setting to correct severe problems with DirectX accelerated applications* as the description. Click OK.

Here's what you do in Windows 2000:

1. Choose Start → Settings → Control Panel, double-click Display, select the Settings tab, click the Advanced button, and select the Troubleshoot tab.

2. Slide the Hardware acceleration control to the third tick from the left. The specific message you'll see depends on your graphics controller; on my system it says *Disable all DirectDraw and Direct 3D accelerations, as well as all cursor and advanced drawing accelerations. Use this setting to correct severe problems with DirectX accelerated applications* as the description. Click OK.

A TOOL TO HELP YOU DECIDE WHEN YOU JUST CAN'T DECIDE

Every business has its metrics, measures, and meetings to help executives decide what to do. But when you can't decide what to do, you always can fall back on the magic 8-ball (shown in the following figure). And you don't even need to leave Excel to use it! Just download the *dss.zip* ("dss" is short for "decision support system") file from *http://www.xl-logic.com/xl_files/games/dss.zip* and have at it. The program code is available for editing, so you can create your own custom messages. If the code window with the responses isn't visible when you open the Visual Basic Editor, just choose Tools → Macro → Visual Basic Editor, expand the Forms item in the Project window, right-click the EightBall form, and click View Code to get where you need to be.

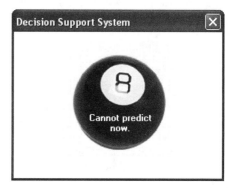

Don't laugh—lots of folks use this tool to make tough decisions.

Index

Symbols

(number signs), data appears as in PivotTables, 99
#VALUE! error, 59
3D charts, 128
   changing colors in, 129
   floor turns black, 130
   pie explosions in, 130

A

A1 notation versus R1C1 notation, 50
Abacus, 59
absolute references
   toggling between relative and, 48
   versus relative references, 48
Accent Excel Password Recovery, 187
Access
   linking data to Excel worksheet, 147
   moving data between Excel and, 145
   tables
      copying data from Excel and pasting into, 145
      identifying, 133
      truncated data in, 147
Advanced Filter command, 79
aggregate functions, 144
alternative data sets, 88
Analyse-it, 55
apostrophes, 153
Arkanoid, 213
array formulas, 58
ASAP Utilities, 10
AutoCorrect feature, 8
   using to advantage, 9

autocounter (database tables), 136
AutoFilter command, 78, 81
AutoFit command, 16
AutoFit Selection command, 16
Autoformat, applying in PivotTables, 98
autonumber record number field (database tables), 136
AVERAGE, 50

B

bioinformatics research, 3
blackjack game for Excel 2000 and later versions, 114
blank cells in range, counting, 73
blank rows, removing, 10
buttons, toolbar (see toolbar buttons)

C

calculated fields, using in PivotTables, 100–105
Calculated Field command, 101
Calculated Item command, 101
calculations (see formulas, recalculating)
Calculation tab, 60
carriage returns, 7
cells
   carraige returns, adding, 7
   counting blank cells in range, 73
   counting nonblank cells in range, 72
   displaying dependent, 57
   displaying formulas, 52
   formatting (see formatting cells)
   highlighting as they change, 55
   inserting or deleting multiple, 13

inserting or deleting single, 13
locked versus protected worksheets, 185
marking those containing formulas, 52
pasted, changing formats, 12
performing same operation on group of, 53
referencing in PivotTables, 50
referring to on another worksheet, 49
remembering last active, 15
renaming in named ranges, 69
visible (see visible cells)
Cell Color Assistant, 34
   downloading, 35
Certificate Services package, 200
CertMgr.exe, 199
Character Map command, 8
CHARTrunner, 129
charts
   2D and 3D graphics packages, 129
   3D (see 3D charts)
   add-ins, 127, 129
   adding text to axis, 115
   changing vertical axis data, 114
   CHARTrunner, 129
   Chart Wizard (see Chart Wizard)
   copying as pictures, 118
   copying from Excel to Word, 124
      chart image chopped, 127
   creating quickly, 108
   decision modeling software, 129
   disappearing axis labels, 126
   disappearing scatter plot point on web page, 122
Drawing toolbar, 117

finding first or last match in arrays, 87

problems mixing text and numbers in lookup table, 85

speeding up multiple lookups, 87

W

"what-if" analysis, 88–92

creating scenarios, 88

finding values that generate specific results, 89

Solver, using to solve multivariate problems, 90–92

Walkenbach, John, 127

Watch Window, 54

web addresses, keeping as plain text, 9

web publishing

controlling worksheets, 150

Excel 2003, 225

Excel data, 149

interactive documents, 150

PivotTables work in Excel but not on Web, 155

WEEKNUM function, 65

weeks, finding number of, 65

Wilson, Berry, 55

WinSTAT, 55

Word tables, copying into Excel 97, 9

workbooks

calculations (see recalculating formulas)

copying another workbook's color palette, 33

creating template, 30

creating worksheets for each month, 212

digitally sign, 200

embedding other program files, 148

Excel 2003 permissions, 188–190

exporting data from XML-mapped, 222

hiding macros from other workbooks, 206

linking other program files, 148

opening in repair mode, 209

opening protected, 186

populating XML-mapped, 221

protection, 184

Protect Workbook command, 39

requiring passwords to open or modify, 186

Unprotect Workbook command, 39

formatting (see formatting workbooks)

worksheets

changing tab colors, 28

creating named ranges from multiple, 68

creating templates, 31

dividing into multiple scrollable areas, 18

filtering data, 77

hide/unhide, 39

moving charts to own, 118

multiple, entering data into, 6

printing (see printing)

protected versus locked cells, 185

referring to cells on another, 49

remembering last active cell, 15

searching portion of, 17

split, 18

splitting database records across multiple, 136

wrapping text, 28

X

Xatellitesheet, 125

Xcelsius, 161

XLStat, 55

XLSTAT-3DPlot, 128

XLSTAT-Pivot, 102

XLSTAT-Pro, 128

XMLSpy, 220

XML Diff, 220

XML in Excel 2003, 218–222

data maps, 221

exporting data from XML-mapped workbook, 222

inferring schema from XML data, 219

populating XML-mapped workbook, 221

schemas overview, 220

troubleshooting importing schemas, 219

XY (Scatter) plot chart, 119, 120, 122

XY Scatter graph, 118

Y

Yahtzee, 144

Z

zeros, retaining leading, 2

Zip Codes, 44

Zoom field, 16

Colophon

Our look is the result of reader comments, our own experimentation, and feedback from distribution channels. Distinctive covers complement our distinctive approach to technical topics, breathing personality and life into potentially dry subjects.

Genevieve d'Entremont was the production editor and proofreader for *Excel Annoyances.* Audrey Doyle was the copyeditor. Genevieve d'Entremont did the typesetting and page makeup. Emily Quill and Claire Cloutier provided quality control. Julie Hawks wrote the index.

Volume Design, Inc. designed the cover of this book using Adobe Illustrator and produced the cover layout with Adobe InDesign CS using Lineto Gravur and Adobe Sabon fonts.

Patti Capaldi designed the interior layout using Adobe InDesign CS. The text and heading fonts are Rotis Sans Serif, Lineto Gravur Condensed, and Myriad Pro; the code font is TheSans Mono Condensed. Julie Hawks converted the text to Adobe InDesign CS. The screenshots and technical illustrations that appear in the book were produced by Robert Romano and Jessamyn Read using Macromedia FreeHand MX and Adobe Photoshop 7. The cartoon illustrations used on the cover and in the interior of this book are copyright © 2004 Hal Mayforth.